THE
AMERICAN COUNCIL
ON MARTIAL ARTS
Instructor
Certification
Manual

FIRST EDITION

BY JOHN CORCORAN
AND JOHN GRADEN

DEDICATION
To the white belts in all martial arts schools for their trust in us and the courage to try.
—*John Graden*

For my late, great mentor, Academy Award-winning screenwriter Stirling Silliphant (1918-1996), who's gone but never forgotten.
—*John Corcoran*

ACKNOWLEDGEMENTS
The following experts and professionals offered invaluable advice and recommendations in the compilation of this book.

SPECIAL RECOGNITION
Rob Colasanti, St. Petersburg, FL; Michael DeMarco, Publisher, "Journal of Asian Martial Arts," Erie, PA; Jim Graden, Seminole, FL; Charles Hodges, St. Petersburg, FL; Lynette Houston, Largo, FL; Scott Kelby, Dunedin, FL; Joe Lewis, Wilmington, NC; Jim Patterson, Largo, FL; Keith D. Yates, Garland, TX.

ACADEMIA
Jerry Beasley, Ed.D., Radford University, Radford, VA; Crista R. Cabe, Mary Baldwin College, Office of College Relations, Staunton, VA; Rainer Martens, Ph.D., Founder, American Sport Education Program, Champaign, IL; Margaret Oglesby, Professor of Chemistry, Retired, St. Petersburg Junior College, Ocala, FL; Ida Lee Wootten, Senior News Officer, University of Virginia News Office, Charlottesville, VA.

MARTIAL ARTS
Andrew Breen, Somerville, MA; David Dise, Richmond, VA; Mike Johnson, American Black Belt Academy, Arlington, TX; Master Sang H. Kim, Wethersfield, CT; Andre Tippett, Boston, MA.

Published in the United States by Graden Media Group.

Manufactured in the United States of America.

IBSN 0-9655539-3-0

FIRST EDITION

Others Book By The Authors
By John Corcoran:
The Original Martial Arts Encyclopedia
The Martial Arts Sourcebook
The Martial Arts Companion
How To Become a Martial Arts Star in Your Town
The Overlook Martial Arts Dictionary
The Complete Martial Arts Catalogue

By John Graden:
Black Belt Management: A Guide to Success without Selling Out
How to Open and Operate a Successful Martial Arts School
The Only Martial Arts Book You'll Ever Need (work-in-progress)

Graden Communications Inc. Periodical:
Martial Arts Professional (monthly magazine)

If you decide to open a martial arts school you must expect to invest a lot of time and energy. Every effort has been made to make this manual as complete and as accurate as possible. However, there may be mistakes both typographical and in content. Therefore, this text should be used only as a general reference and not as the ultimate source of martial arts school instruction management. Furthermore, this manual contains information and systems only up to the printing date.

The author and publisher shall have neither liability nor responsibility to any person or entity with respect to any loss or damage caused, or alleged to be caused, directly or indirectly by the information contained in this book. All information in this book is simply the opinion of the author and has been compiled through years of personal experience and research. The author has gathered this information over the past twenty years and will continue to gather information and ideas for years to come. Where possible, original sources of some ideas shared in this book are recognized in the acknowledgments with great appreciation.

TABLE OF CONTENTS

TABLE OF CONTENTS

About the Contributors

B. ANN BOYCE, Ph.D.
University of Virginia
Charlottesville, VA

B. Ann Boyce is an Associate Professor of Pedagogy at the University of Virginia. She earned a Ph.D. in Teacher Preparation/Pedagogy with a specialization in Instructional Design from Florida State University in 1982. She currently coordinates the five-year teacher education program in physical education as well as the master and doctoral level programs.

Dr. Boyce has co-written two books in areas related to instructional strategies and teacher effectiveness, including *Case Studies in Sport Psychology* (Jones & Bartlett Publishing Company, Boston, MA). Among her 40-plus published articles are "Inappropriate Student Behavior: A Problem for Student Teachers" for the "Journal of Physical Education, Recreation and Dance," and "The Effect of Self-Efficacy and Goal-Setting on Bowling Performance" for the *Journal of Teaching in Physical Education.*

Dr. Boyce's research and consulting roles include the Army Research Institute, Federal Bureau of Investigation and USA Shooting (United States Olympic Committee).

A black belt in Tae Kwon Do, Ann has been studying martial arts for 20 years. She has studied at both traditional as well as non-traditional schools and has a special interest in self-defense.

SARAH CHUNG, M.A.
University of Ottawa, Ontario
Canada

Sarah Chung is currently a Ph.D. student in Psychopedagogy at the University of Ottawa, Ontario, specializing in Curriculum Design and Educational Psychology, by virtue of a four-year Sabah State Government Academic Scholarship for Doctorate Studies. She writes and speaks six languages fluently and has a basic knowledge in two others.

Ms. Chung earned her Master of Arts in Human Kinetics, with a specialization in Sport Psychology - Performance Enhancement, in 1995 at the University of Ottawa, Ontario, and earned her Bachelor of Education in Physical Education at the University of Agriculture of Malaysia, where she was on the Dean's List.

Ms. Chung has been a research assistant in a number of projects for the Faculty of Education at her current university in Ottawa. Since 1994, she has lectured on such topics as "Mental Strategies of International-Level Taekwondo Athletes" to "Introduction to Sport Psychology" to "Goal-Setting in Sports" and "Elements of Excellence." Among her many leadership awards is an Ahli Mangku Negara ("Special Royal Member for the Country"), the youngest woman ever to be so honored, presented to her by His Majesty King of Malaysia in 1992.

Ms. Chung is a 5th-degree black belt in Taekwondo and has been a world-class competitor since 1987. She was a quarterfinalist at the 1992 Barcelona Olympics in Spain, and her final bout was broadcast on international television. She has won five separate gold medals at the Southeast Asian Games from 1987-95, a gold in the 1992 Asian Championships, and was a quarterfinalist in the 1993 World Taekwondo Championships in New York City. She is also certified by the World Taekwondo Federation as an International Judge/Referee, and since 1997 sits on the Board of Advisors for the Coaching Certification Program for the Malaysia Taekwondo Association.

SCOT CONWAY, Esq.
San Diego, California

Scot Conway is an attorney at law in California and the founder of Guardian Kempo Christian Martial Arts in San Diego, CA, a unique kempo system with a dual emphasis on complete martial arts training and effective self-defense/defense of others.

As an attorney, Mr. Conway focuses on business issues, evaluation of business opportunities, protecting businesses from liability and theft, and consulting. Unlike many attorneys who only consider the legal issues, he is a businessman first, who tries to find effective techniques to deal with legal issues without interfering with the normal operation of business. He prefers to consult with business people on defensive law, avoiding problems before they arise, rather than helping with litigation already underway.

Mr. Conway holds black belts in a variety of systems. He believes that founders are responsible for creating arts that are effective for what they claims the art does. He set out to create a system that would be effective against criminals on the street, and to date, 17 violent criminals have been defeated by students using skills Mr. Conway teaches, even when two men attacked one woman.

Several years ago, Mr. Conway recognized that earning a black belt did not necessarily mean that a martial artist was ready to teach. There were many skills that teachers and leaders needed that not all students learned in the ordinary course of training. To solve that problem, he established the Guardian Kempo Instructor Program. All Guardian Kempo Certified Instructors have graduated from a two-year program in addition to their normal rank training, followed by a substantial apprenticeship period. Now, as a member of the American Council on Martial Arts, he is helping to bring similar skills to martial arts instructors everywhere.

Mr. Conway also teaches a wide variety of seminars on such subjects as: Ki, Gun Defense, Defense of Others, Functional Anatomy (using the body properly), Health and Healing, Relationships, Academic Achievement, Goal-Setting Matrix Planning (an advanced goals-setting system), and more.

JOHN J. DONOHUE, PH.D.
Medaille College
Buffalo, NY

John J. Donohue holds a doctorate in anthropology with a research concentration in the cultural aspects of Japanese martial arts. A professional educator, he has worked as a teacher and administrator at a variety of institutions of higher education. His experience spans the range of educational environments from two- to four-year colleges, public and private institutions, teaching colleges and universities. An academic specialist in the design of programs for non-traditional students and the underprepared, he is currently chief academic officer at Buffalo's Medaille College, where he holds the rank of Professor of Social Science.

His 1987 doctoral dissertation, "The Forge of the Spirit: Structure, Motion, and Meaning in the Japanese Martial Tradition," was subsequently published in 1991. A continuing interest in the systems of meaning embedded in martial arts practice led to the publication of his 1994 work, "Warrior Dreams: The Martial Arts and the American Imagination." The recently published "Herding the Ox: The Martial Arts as Moral Metaphor" explores this area further. An active researcher and writer, Dr. Donohue has published a number of articles on anthropology and the martial arts, many of which have appeared in the "Journal of Asian Martial Arts." He serves as an associate editor for that publication.

He is currently at work on a number of projects: completing a manual on kendo scheduled for publication in 1999; a manuscript on martial arts pedagogy and its implications for broader educational venues; and a cycle of short stories that deal with coming-of-age issues and the martial arts, entitled " Soft Science."

Dr. Donohue has been involved in teaching the martial arts for the last seven years. He currently teaches karate-do at Medaille College and actively trains in kendo. In addition to these arts, he has studied aikido, judo, iaido and taijiquan.

DON KORZEKWA, Ph.D.
Carrollton, Texas

Don Korzekwa is a Licensed Psychologist in Texas who brings years of clinical, management and consulting experience to organizations who are striving to continually improve their internal systems, and the services which they provide to their customers.

Dr. Korzekwa received a Master's Degree in 1985 from the University of Texas at Austin in Educational Psychology with an emphasis in Program Evaluation. He went on to receive a Ph.D. in Educational Psychology from the Counseling Psychology program at that same university, completing his internship at Austin State Hospital in 1989. Both the Counseling Psychology program and the internship program have the distinction of accreditation by the American Psychological Association.

Dr. Korzekwa's clinical expertise includes work with children ages three years and up, adolescents and adults. He has provided psychological testing, as well as individual, group and family therapy to assist these persons in dealing with trauma and difficult issues in their lives. He has also served as a consultant to a children's home facilitating foster care placement. As a Staff Psychologist at Dallas Child Guidance Clinic, Dr. Korzekwa provided clinical supervision for psychology staff and interns who were working toward their Ph.D.s in Psychology.

Dr. Korzekwa assumed the responsibilities of Director of Collin County Child Guidance Clinic when it was brought under the umbrella of Dallas Child Guidance. His experience as a manager also includes having been director of a geriatric psychiatric inpatient unit, Texas clinical manager for one of the nation's largest behavioral health managed care organizations, and operations director for a psychiatric physicians' group.

He has applied his knowledge of educational psychology and program evaluation to the development, implementation and evaluation of a number of training programs and quality assurance activities. These include training programs for nursing facilities which exceed the certification standards established by the Texas Department of Health, as well as supervisory and management training programs. He served as Director of Psychology Training at Dallas Child Guidance Clinic, an internship program approved by the American Psychological Association for Ph.D. candidates. He has also developed Quality Assurance programs in behavioral health for various clinical settings and managed care organizations.

Dr. Korzekwa and his wife Christi live in Carrollton, TX, just north of Dallas. Both he and Christi train in Tae Kwon Do at Carrollton Martial Arts Academy, and hold the rank of black belt.

MICHAEL MALISZEWSKI, PH.D.
Harvard Medical School
Boston, MA

Michael Maliszewski received his Ph.D. in psychology from the University of Chicago. He has held a number of academic positions in a variety of different areas at the University of Chicago, including Asian studies, history of religions, psychiatry and the National Opinion Research Center.

Also while in Chicago, he created and directed the largest behavioral medicine program in the world at a medical setting which treated over 20,000 patients annually from all over the United States, Europe and the Middle East.

Dr. Maliszewski has served on the editorial board of some six journals including two dealing with the martial arts. He has published books and articles on diverse topics ranging from medicine to religious studies. He is currently in the Department of Psychiatry at Harvard Medical School.

In the area of martial arts, Dr. Maliszewski has travelled around the world interviewing hundreds of teachers and masters of different styles, exploring the physical, healing and spiritual components of their teachings. Some of the results of his work have appeared in the "Journal of Asian Martial Arts" (where he serves on the editorial board) and in his book, "Spiritual Dimensions of the Martial Arts" (Tuttle, 1996).

He has studied many different types of martial arts and holds instructor/black belt-level rankings in wing chun, tedo and escrima.

Dr. Maliszewski is currently working on the formulation of martial teaching strategies which aim to accelerate outcome results in areas of physical training, internal capabilities and psychological changes of practitioners.

TIM NIILER, M.S.
University of Delaware Sports Science Lab
Newark, DE

In 1993, Timothy A. Niiler left his career in space physics for the burgeoning field of sport biomechanics. Having graduated from the University of Delaware with a B.S. in Physics in 1991, and an M.A. in Astronomy from Boston University, he returned to the University of Delaware to enroll in the Biomechanics and Movement Sciences Program and has since earned his M.S. in Biomechanics.

His master's thesis involved the study of the landing mechanics in wushu jump kicks and was titled, "Landing Impact, loading and injury risk to the lower extremities in Chinese Wushu." Mr. Niiler is now working at the University of Delaware Sports Science Lab towards his doctorate in biomechanics.

Mr. Niiler has been involved with a number of research projects in addition to his aforementioned thesis. Other martial arts projects include a computer code to model the impact of a punch as a function of glove weight, and a study of side kick mechanics.

However, he has also been involved with orthopedic biomechanics. Work in this area includes a study published in Gait and Posture entitled, "Reliability of Kinematics During Clinical Gait Analysis: A Comparison Between Normal and Children with Cerebral Palsy," and his current work utilizing neural networks to predict the outcomes of rectus tranfer surgery. His greatest effort has gone into writing a comprehensive package for analyzing the motion of subjects involved in any dynamic activity.

Mr. Niiler has been involved in the Chinese martial arts for 15 years and practices traditional Shaolinquan as well as contemporary Changquan. He is a 2nd degree black sash under Sifu Anthony Goh, who is president of the USA Wushu Kungfu Federation (USAWKF). Mr. Niiler's previous instructors include Sifu Xu Yuru, a former coach of both the Chinese and U.S. Wushu Teams; Sifu Wang Yang, a former member of the Szechuan Wushu Team; and Sifu Anh Nguyen, his first instructor.

In addition to his background in kung-fu, Mr. Niiler also holds a 2nd-degree black belt from the World Taekwondo Federation, which he obtained under instructor Celie Hanauer. He has been involved in teaching the martial arts for the past nine years at such places as the University of Delaware and Boston University, and currently teaches at the Delaware Wushu-Kungfu Club.

Mr. Niiler is also an avid competitor and judge. He placed second in the 1995 USA Wushu Kungfu Federation's (USAWKF) national tournament in Changquan, Broadsword and Staff and has medaled in numerous other USAWKF tournaments. More recently, he has been involved in running several USAWKF tournaments in the Mid-Atlantic Region and has hosted two Delaware State Wushu-Kungfu tournaments. Mr. Niiler is currently chair of the USAWKF's Delaware State Association.

WILLY PIETER, PH.D.
School of Health and Sports Science
University of North London
London, United Kingdom

Dr. Willy Pieter did his doctoral work in sociology of non-western societies at the University of Leiden, The Netherlands, and his Ph.D. in physical education at the University of in Eugene, Oregon. After having been a visiting assistant professor at the University of Oregon, he worked as an Adjunct Professor of martial arts in the Department of Eastern Forms of Physical Culture, Lesgaft Institute of Physical Culture, St. Petersburg, Russia; a visiting Associate Professor in physical education at the University of the Philippines, Diliman, QC, Philippines; and is now an Associate Professor in sports science in the School of Health and Sports Science, University of North London, London, United Kingdom, as well as a consultant for the Institute of Sports Science, University of Asia and the Pacific, Metro Manila, Philippines.

Before leaving for the USA, Dr. Pieter set up the certification program for taekwondo instructors in The Netherlands in 1980, which received governmental recognition. Although his initial research on martial arts was in the area of Oriental philosophy, he later initiated the multi-disciplinary Oregon Taekwondo Research Project (OTRP) while at the University of Oregon, which is believed to be the largest scientific research project on taekwondo to date. His research was based on testing the American national and Olympic taekwondo teams at the US Olympic Training Center in Colorado Springs, CO. The injury data for the OTRP were collected at various US national championships.

In 1991, Dr. Pieter started the International Combative Sports Project (ICSP). The ICSP aims to study martial arts at the recreational and competitive levels from various sports scientific disciplines, including kinanthropometry, sport physiology, sport psychology, sport pedagogy, sport biomechanics, epidemiology of martial arts injuries, growth and development, and nutrition. So far, data for the ICSP have been collected in Greece, Russia, Germany, The Netherlands, Philippines and the United Kingdom on athletes in judo, karate, taekwondo, wushu, and pencak silat, with a possible new addition of arnis in the near future.

Dr. Pieter has published on martial arts in national and international scientific journals and has also presented at international scientific conventions. His most recent book deals with the scientific coaching of competitive taekwondo athletes and is published by Meyer & Meyer in Aachen, Germany. He is currently advising the British Taekwondo Control Board in its attempts to set up an instructor's certification program.

Dr. Pieter's background is in ITF (International Taekwondo Federation) and WTF (World Taekwondo Federation) taekwondo. Since the mid-1960s, he has taught and coached taekwondo in several countries in Europe, the USA, and the Philippines, and has recently retired to focus on his scientific research endeavors and consultancy work with athletes and coaches.

GIANINE ROSENBLUM, PH.D.
University of Medicine & Dentistry of New Jersey - RWJMS

Dr. Gianine D. Rosenblum received her masters degree and doctorate in psychology from Rutgers University. Dr. Rosenblum coordinates a mentoring program for young aggressive children and conducts research on the psychological development of adolescent boys and girls (at the University of Medicine & Dentistry of New Jersey). (Dr. Rosenblum is also a psychotherapist at the Center for Family Resources in Metuchen, NJ. and works with adults, adolescents and children coping with a variety of psychological issues.)

Dr. Rosenblum has been a practicing martial artist since 1990. Her husband Frank Bouchonville runs the Japanese Karate Center in Hillsborough, NJ and is the (New Jersey) Chief Instructor for Japan Karate-Do Itosu-Kai under Master Fumio Demura. Dr. Rosenblum works with her husband to incorporate an understanding of child development and the principles of learning into the teaching and curriculum at the Japanese Karate Center.

DERENDA TIMMONS SCHUBERT, PH.D.
Gresham, Oregon

Dr. Schubert is a Licensed Psychologist who has a specialty in child and family issues. Her doctoral degree is from DePaul University, Chicago, Illinois, and she completed her internship at the Morrison Center for Children and Family Services, Portland, Oregon. An active martial artist, Dr. Schubert also serves on the Board of Directors for Martial Arts Fitness Center, Inc., operated by her husband Ron. Dr. Schubert has been influential in assisting Ron and his instructors improve their ability to develop age specific programs for children.

Currently, Dr. Schubert is in private practice in the Portland, OR, area. She has worked with children and their families struggling with depression, anxiety, Attention Deficit Disorder, trauma, and life changes, as well as addressing the mental health issues of children with special needs and their family members. She conducts individual, family, and group therapy, and psychological testing.

SHARON B. SPALDING, M.ED.
Mary Baldwin College
Staunton, Virginia

Sharon Spalding received her B.S. from James Madison University and her M.Ed. from the University of Virginia. She is certified by the American College of Sports Medicine as an Exercise Specialist. Prior to her employment at Mary Baldwin College, she worked as an Exercise Physiologist for two Cardiac Rehabilitation programs, and as the Total Wellness Coordinator for a hospital-owned Wellness Center.

In 1989, she came to Mary Baldwin College, a small liberal arts college for women, as the volleyball coach. In 1990, she became a full-time faculty member.

In 1995, Ms. Spalding designed the fitness program for the Virginia Women's Institute for Leadership. This program initially was designed as an alternative to coeducation at the Virginia Military Institute, but continues today with a corp of 95 cadets and will graduate its inaugural class in 1999. Fitness is developed in this program through early morning physical training, monitoring of fitness levels with twice yearly strength and endurance tests, and individualized workouts.

Currently, Ms. Spalding continues to teach physical and health education courses, serves as the athletic director, coaches the volleyball team, and continues to supervise the fitness program for the Virginia Women's Institute for Leadership.

She resides with her husband, Phil, and two sons, Jason and Brandon.

TOM THOMPSON, M.S.
Dallas, Texas

Tom Thompson entered the health and fitness industry in 1990 after a 20-year career in commercial real estate. He holds a Bachelor of Science Degree in Business Management from LeTourneau University and a Master of Science Degree in Kinesiology from The University of North Texas. Mr. Thompson is also a faculty member of LeTourneau University, where he teaches a course he helped to develop entitled, "Lifetime Fitness for Executives."

Mr. Thompson was a member of the fitness staff at the world-renowned Cooper Fitness Center in Dallas, TX, where for six years, he was the head martial arts instructor and a personal trainer. He is certified as a Physical Fitness Specialist through the Cooper Institute for Aerobics Research. Mr. Thompson and his wife, Teresa, own and operate the Alpha Fitness Center in Dallas. In addition, he is on the faculty of Richland College and the Hockaday School as a self-defense instructor. He is an American-born instructor in Taekwondo, having begun his martial arts training in 1970 with American martial arts pioneer Allen Steen, and holds the rank of 6th-degree black belt. In addition, he is a 1st-degree black belt in Kobudo. He is also the founder and director of the Fellowship of Christian Martial Artists.

Tom and Teresa have two children, Eric and Rachel.

JOE LEWIS
Wilmington, North Carolina

Joe Lewis began teaching black belt instructor seminars in 1968. He has since taught tens of thousands of students all over the world. His studies include research with acclaimed self-esteem psychologist Dr. Nathaniel Branden. In 1975, *Professional Karate* magazine published Mr. Lewis' pioneering three-level system for teaching martial arts. The technical level involved mechanical skills using techniques. The second level integrated principles of combat tactics, and the third was the psychological level for using focusing skills, attitude strategies and mindsets.

He has been inducted into 12 international halls of fame, including the Black Belt Hall of Fame, both as "Fighter of the Year" (1974) and as "Instructor of the Year" (1985). Mr. Lewis' advice articles have appeared worldwide, including in two recent issues of *Parade* (circulation 37 million). Today, after three decades, he continues teaching his system, working with instructors including many world champions who have adopted it to teach their students.

BRIAN TRACY
Solana Beach, California

The author of the best-selling audio series, "The Psychology of Achievement" and "The Universal Laws of Success and Achievement," among many others, ACMA Board Member Brian Tracy is one of the world's most acclaimed and respected personal and professional development teachers.

Tracy began studying the martial arts in Montreal, Canada, in 1964, when he was 20 years old. During his extensive world travels, he has trained under six world champions in martial arts schools in such widespread cities as London, Paris, Berlin, Rome, Johannesburg, Bangkok, Tokyo, Vancouver and Mexico City. He has also competed successfully in national karate championships in South Africa, Canada and Mexico.

Over the years, Tracy has managed, and served as chief instructor for various martial arts schools. He has a great passion for the martial arts and believes that much of the success he has achieved in business and in life in subsequent years, has been as a result of the structure and discipline he learned during his thousands of hours of martial arts training.

DR. JOSEPH J. ESTWANIK
Charlotte, NC

Dr. Joe Estwanik studied orthopaedic surgery at The Cleveland Clinic and Bowman Gray School of Medicine of Wake Forest University In Winston-Salem, North Carolina. A dedicated physical culturist for some 36 years, in a typical week he might be weight training, practicing martial arts, bicycling, jogging, hiking, camping, pistol shooting, doing boxing aerobics or even open-water kayaking.

Dr. Estwanik is chairman and organizer of an annual Ringside Physicians Course located within the U.S. Olympic Training Center, Colorado Springs, Colorado. Formerly the National Medical Chairman for USA Boxing's Junior Olympic Boxing Program, Dr. Estwanik was appointed Chairman of the Sportsmedicine Committee for USA Boxing, allowing close, productive communication with coaches, athletes and officials.

His vast experience as a boxing safety consultant and ringside physician has led to his consulting ringside physician duties for the no-holds-barred events Battlecade Extreme Fighting, the World Combat Championships, and the Ultimate Fighting Championships.

Dr. Estwanik has written two combat-themed books: Boxing and Medicine (1995), a medical textbook, and Sportsmedicine for the Combat Arts (1998?), designed for the exercising general public. Dr. Estwanik holds two patents on high-tech gloves which are now being marketed and distributed. His designs apply the use of modern biomaterials and biomechanical principles to protect the hand of the puncher as well as we now protect the foot of the runner.

He currently lives in Charlotte, North Carolina, with his wife, Janice, and their three children, and balances his athletic pursuits by teaching nature photography.

TIM ROCHFORD
Sandwich, Illinois

Tim Rochford's teaching credentials include Personal Fitness Trainer certifications from the American Council on Exercise (ACE) and the National Strength & Conditioning Association (NSCA). Mr. Rochford currently has five instructor workshops accredited by the ACE and the NSCA for continuing education for fitness instructors. He has also produced a martial fitness workout program/home-study continuing education course (also accredited by ACE and the NSCA) available for fitness instructors.

He has created an aerobic/anaerobic workout, the Martial Fitness Workout Program, which utilizes movements, techniques and training methods from kickboxing, boxing, karate and self-defense training. This program has been designed to train a novice fitness instructor in safe and effective biomechanical technique execution, choreography, and proper methods in equipment use, from an exercise science perspective.

He began his martial arts training in 1978 at the Karate Institute in DeKalb, IL. He has achieved the rank of 4th-dan in Kajukenbo, and has owned and operated Health Kick Martial Arts and Fitness Center since October 1982, where he continues to be the head Martial Arts Instructor and Personal Fitness Trainer. ■

59.90 + 7.47   67.37 US

About The Authors

JOHN GRADEN
ACMA Founder/Publisher, ACMA Instructor Certification Manual

Author, publisher and pioneering martial arts lecturer, John Graden's efforts since 1995 have had a profound impact on the manner in which thousands of martial arts schools are operated in the U.S. and Canada.

Mr. Graden's two top selling books, *Black Belt Management* and *How To Open and Operate A Successful Martial Arts School,* are considered the quintessential references for martial arts school owners.

His position as the spokesman for the martial arts instructional profession was validated with his profile by the A & E Network in their landmark documentary, *The Martial Arts.*

In late 1994, Mr. Graden founded the National Association of Professional Martial Artists (NAPMA), for which he serves as Executive Director. Dedicated specifically to strengthening the professional skills of martial arts school owners, NAPMA has mushroomed to over 1,600 members throughout North America.

Mr. Graden launched two more significant support enterprises to fortify his industry leadership position. After intensely studying the techniques of the world's foremost motivational and business speakers, he initiated a second career as a martial arts business lecturer and has given over one-hundred presentations throughout the U.S..

In 1995, he capped his position as a martial arts teacher of teachers by publishing *Martial Arts Professional* magazine, the first widely accepted martial arts business journal. The slick monthly reaches over 20,000 American and Canadian school owners.

Today Mr. Graden's foremost goal—and greatest challenge—is to take the martial arts industry into the 21st Century by revolutionizing how the arts are taught to the public, through the creation of an unprecedented Instructor Certification Program. To accomplish this, he has created the American Council on Martial Arts (ACMA), whose Board of Advisors is composed of Sports Physiologists, Psychologists, and motivational, legal and fitness experts, all of whom also practice the martial arts. These Advisors have contributed their expertise to the *ACMA Certification Manual,* which equips martial arts instructors with state-of-the-art standards of teaching, communication and safety. He seeks to take the martial arts industry—and with it the public and corporate perception of them—to an unparalleled level of quality and credibility.

A former successful school owner himself, Mr. Graden was a five-time member of the World Championship U.S. Karate Team (1985-91). He is single and lives in St. Petersburg, Florida. ∎

JOHN CORCORAN
Editor, ACMA Instructor Certification Manual

Recognized as one of the world's premier martial arts authors and journalists, John Corcoran has been a prime force in taking modern martial arts literature into the major-league arena. In his 25-year literary career he has written millions of words about the subject in an acclaimed body of work encompassing books, magazine and screenplays.

Mr. Corcoran has authored six books to date, all but one with major New York publishers, which have collectively sold over a quarter-million copies worldwide. He is perhaps best known for his masterwork, *The Original Martial Arts Encyclopedia,* the definitive reference of the genre, which took ten years from concept to completion and has sold over 100,000 copies to date.

In addition, over the past 25 years Mr. Corcoran has served as an editor or founding editor of almost every influential martial arts magazine in the industry. Corcoran is currently Senior Editor of *Martial Arts Professional,* the industry's foremost trade publication. In 1977, he pioneered article syndication in his field and his stories have since appeared in six languages in over 70 countries.

Mr. Corcoran's writings on the subject have also extended into academia, motion pictures, and the mainstream media.

He was selected by the editors of both *The World Book Encyclopedia* in 1986 and Microsoft's "Encarta (Electronic) Encyclopedia" in 1996 to write their inaugural entries for martial arts. His mainstream articles have appeared in *Parade,* the Sunday newspaper supplement, and *Daily Variety.*

In 1995, Mr. Corcoran launched a national public-speaking sideline, teaching martial arts school owners publicity-procurement techniques, for the National Association of Professional Martial Artists. Overall, he has used the power of the media to bring thousands of martial artists to public attention, and a select handful—including superstar Jean-Claude Van Damme—to stardom.

Mr. Corcoran's literary mentors are the late great Academy Award-winning screenwriter Stirling Silliphant (*In the Heat of the Night*) and best-selling author Joe Hyams (*Bogie*). Legendary Heavyweight Karate Champion Joe Lewis has been his chief martial arts mentor since 1977. A veteran black belt in karate, he began his training in 1967. He is single and lives in Los Angeles, California. ∎

Let's Learn From The Past Lest We Repeat It!

BY JOHN CORCORAN

Don't tell me about training, buster! I'm from the "old school" of martial arts—and I've got the injuries to prove it! For years, in fact, you could hear the physical symphony of snap, crackle, pop whenever I moved. It especially terrified my dance partners.

It all started innocently enough. One time, when I was young and, in retrospect, astutely foolish, I enrolled in a karate class after seeing the flamboyant use of martial arts in a James Bond film. Most assuredly, I could have used James' help during my lessons—as a personal bodyguard. For, as it turned out, I signed up for lessons in 1967—at the tail end of that notorious period known as the "Blood-n-Guts Era" of American karate.

I was something of a 19-year-old skinny runt, standing only about 5'6" and weighing in at 120 pounds. The type of skinflint bullies traveled from out of state to line up for. When I put on my first gi, with its "high-water" pants flagging around my lower knees, I looked like a scarecrow on a popsickle stick.

The grueling training regimen of that era, as my co-author John Graden articulates it so well today, "Was not so much designed to build strong character, but to eliminate the weak ones." Most instructors were gung-ho ex-military types who ran their classes with brutal boot-camp regimentation. But I was gung-ho myself. I rode a bus five miles each way to get to class, and sometimes also had to walk about a half-mile, even in all kinds of inclement weather, to and from the bus stop to my father's home where I lived periodically. And it's not like I had much choice of changing schools for a more convenient location. In 1967, there were only about four or five karate schools in my entire hometown of Pittsburgh, PA.

Ah, the good old days! So scientific were the training methods of that time that, amazingly, I can still feel some of their peculiar lasting "benefits" even today—30 years later. How well I remember doing those character-building bare-knuckle push-ups on concrete floors; punching, bare-fisted, straw-wrapped *makiwara* boards till my fists ached; working up a good gi-drenching sweat during mid-winter in cold buildings with minimal heat; breaking boards—sometimes with bare-knuckled punches—that sometimes

didn't break, resulting in two swollen "egg knuckles" that never returned to normal size; and—my favorite—performing tens of thousands of repetitions using good old "bounce-stretching"—called "ballistic" stretching, for good reason.

Sure, you're thinking, everyone got hurt back then. And the truth is, only the strong did survive that prehistoric training, and it did forge us into stronger individuals, both physically and mentally. But as we know very well today, there's a radical difference between self-improvement and self-destruction—a distinction truly lost on old-school beginners and intermediate practitioners. Like gung-ho automatons, we just did what we were told. Example:

Sensei: "White belt, go run head first into that brick wall."

Beginner: "Yes, Sensei!"

Bonk!

Later, in our intermediate phase, we got smarter. We started to ask *why*. Example:

Sensei: "Green belt, go run head first into that brick wall."

Green Belt: "But Sensei, why?"

Sensei: Because it will strengthen your head butt."

Green Belt: "Yes, Sensei!"

Bonk!

Like so many of my peers today, I have some of those antiquated training methods I've cited above to thank for the torn ligaments in my knees, which is practically an industry standard among veteran black belts. As well, most of us suffer from a host of other unnecessary injuries from those early classes.

My nose, for example, is still cracked from one of my first sparring sessions: Me, a white belt with about three weeks of training, pitted against a bigger, stronger, more skilled green belt, who kicked me squarely in the face so hard I saw stars and my nose cracked and bled profusely. Some kind soul, probably *not* the instructor, threw some type of rag at me and directed me to wipe the blood off the floor so no one else slipped on it. My nose has been crooked ever since!

My second instructor was hardly better, which brings me to perhaps the lowlight of my entire martial arts training. I won't tell you his name in order to protect the guilty. He had this self-defense thing he did that he called, "Let's work out together." But his vision and execution of this "shared" concept confused me for a long time; most of the time it just hurt.

Our Equal Opportunity workout consisted of this. I would stand facing him, step forward and throw a simple reverse punch at his face with my right fist. He would block it and then beat the living daylights out of me with any number—and all manner—of hard-contact punches, kicks and chops all over my body. *Duh!* This is definitely where I became intimate with the phrase, "marriage to gravity."

The most memorable "Let's-work-out-together" workout led to my "Ben Gay Night of Terror!"

I came home that night with my then-fiancé, a green belt in the same class, and collapsed on the bed. My instructor had beaten me almost senseless. I was black and blue everywhere from head to feet.

I had a brilliant revelation on the way home from the school that night—"Honey, let's buy some of that Ben Gay stuff. The commercial said it's good for sore muscles." I had never before used a muscle ointment. Ignorant of its peculiar effect, I stripped and had my fiancé rub Ben Gay all over my body from neck to toes, both the back and front of me. *Double Duh!*

I quickly learned the science of cause and effect.

Cause: Never rub Ben Gay over your entire body.

Effect: When you do, it causes you to alternate between Hot Flashes and Cold Chills.

So bad were the Cold Chills my teeth were actually "chattering" audibly and I had to wrap a heavy blanket around me in a futile attempt to stop my body from shivering convulsively. About every 30 seconds, I was introduced to the "extreme" alternative. During the Hot Flashes, I broke into a feverish sweat and had to whip off the blanket and fight to breathe. I soaked the blanket and three towels with sweat before the dual effects began subsiding. The "Ben Gay Night of Terror" ended about a half-hour later.

This anecdote sure sounds funny in retrospect, but I can tell you now, folks, that I didn't know if I was coming into this world or leaving it. And boy, was I mad at that instructor! Had he and I and a gun been in the same room right then, I know only two of us would have left and it wouldn't have been him!

Here's the point behind all of my painful anecdotes. Let's learn from the past lest we repeat it. There are still, unfortunately, far too many instructors using frightfully outdated teaching methods. Maybe nothing as severe or brutal as in my era, but certainly antiquated compared to other modern fitness industries. The future—the time for change—is now.

In my 30+ years in the martial arts field I've watched our industry rise from a storefront novelty practiced by a few in rooms akin to dungeons, to a popular activity mass-marketed in fine schools to millions of people from all walks of life. I've applauded our victories and mourned our failures over the years. I'm proud of our spectacular strides in so many areas, but equally disappointed by areas suffering—unnecessarily—from stubborn stagnation.

One such area, standardized teaching practices, should now be brought up to speed. Many of you, through associations like the NAPMA, are now becoming black belts at business. So, isn't right now a great time to become a black belt at teaching, too?

I knew you'd agree. So please read this book and apply its modern principles. Your students will thank you instead of suing you.

Now *there's* a concept! Had I sustained my stupid injuries around the late 1980s or after, I probably could file a multimillion-dollar lawsuit for damages caused by instructor negligence. Heck, the trial for such a case might even air on "Court TV." I could become a courtroom star as I sing the blues about my black-and-blues. Good thing I'm a nice guy.

It's also a good thing I've spent some 25 years around Hollywood and the entertainment business. There I learned how to use "props" to not only look ten years younger than I am, but also hide the otherwise disastrous effects of those numerous martial arts injuries I sustained during the "good old days."

Now, at middle age, I'm finally gonna have to get my nose straightened too—the result of that green belt trying to remodel my face with his foot 30 years ago—since it mildly impairs my breathing capacity. No doubt a good L.A. plastic surgeon will charge me a few grand to help me smell the roses again.

Paying for my youthful ignorance has been an expensive education, folks. But—ha, ha—I no longer "clank" when I walk. And for darn sure I know how and where to use Ben Gay—sparingly! Now, if I could just perfect this last technique. . . *BONK!* ∎

INTRODUCTION

Traditional Techniques Versus Traditional Methods

BY JOHN GRADEN

With a literal translation of "military arts," the martial arts has been perceived as a self-defense-oriented exercise and artform that demanded the utmost in discipline and subordination. Indeed, in America, the vast majority of first-generation instructors in the 1960s received their training from the military while stationed in a Far-East country. Those classes reflected a strict military atmosphere and attitude and were taught by highly-disciplined adults to other adult men. It was only natural, that, upon arrival in the United States, these first-generation instructors continued to teach in the same manner they had learned.

This "hand-me-down" teaching method became what is known as the traditional, or "old school," method of teaching. It initiated the multi-generational cycle of, often, abusive instructional methods and a lack of professionalism that plagues the image of the martial arts instructor's profession to this day.

Naturally, since this was what was happening in martial arts schools, this is what was reflected in mainstream-media portrayals of martial arts instructors. The relationship between the students and instructor was typically portrayed as an absolute subordination. The "all-knowing" instructor had free reign to use any methods, no matter how brutal, to enlighten his pupil, whose only job was to submit without question. The master's philosophies of the martial way always seemed to be accentuated with some graphic method of inflicting pain or punishment.

Even one of the most progressive thinkers in martial arts history, the great Bruce Lee, in his legendary 1973 film, *Enter the Dragon*, demonstrated this teaching method. While working with a young student, he slaps the student on the head both for "Thinking," and as a reminder to "Never take your eyes off your opponent." In the following decade, virtually all of Jackie Chan's films included scenes of him submitting to outlandish and tortuous (though often hilarious) training at the hands of his "Master."

In 1985, *The Karate Kid* took a completely different approach. Rather than the super-human and often brutal master, Mr. Miyagi, the instructor in the film, was portrayed as a caring, compassionate teacher. The message connected on an emotional level with parents nationwide who recognized that martial arts could be an excellent supplement to their childrens' education. Schools, whose clientele had been almost exclusively adult, were inundated with children.

This influx dramatically changed the nature of the martial arts instruction profession. Instructors quickly discovered that the harsh military-like teaching style they had been taught, was often ineffective and inappropriate for the new young student. Instructors, seeking to stem the tide of drop-outs, were forced to turn to each other for help in creating a classroom-management system that would motivate children to stay in the martial arts instead of dropping out.

This led to a new and exciting period of sharing and networking. Rather than fighting each other as they had in the past, instructors began sharing ideas. While this was a step in the right direction, it was, for the most part, still hand-me-down teaching. The criteria for being a good instructor went from high *quality* of student to high *quantity* of students.

Any teaching method or gimmick that might result in higher retention was considered valid. This was a classic case of the ends justifying the means. Rather than doing what is right to move a student closer to being a competent black belt, schools, in order to maintain retention, began pushing students up the ranks regardless of competence. The result has been a significant drop in the quality of the black belt.

Instructors often placed the intangible goal of building a child's self-esteem ahead of the technical requirements of the rank. This "sidewalk psychology" placed the students' feelings in front of the students' performance. This created a vast inconsistency in the teaching methods of the more traditional "old-school" instructor, who tended to stick closer to prescribed technical-performance criteria to judge a student, and the new-school instructor, who tended to favor "effort" over technical performance. In both cases, most instructors were still teaching based solely upon what they learned from their instructor.

There is no educational standard to be a martial arts instructor. You could be a Ph.d. or never graduate high school. Most instructors either teach the way they were taught, because it happens to appeal to them, or teach the way other schools deemed "more successful," in order to imitate their success.

The result is an incredibly fragmented, hodge-podge of teaching methods. They range from ignorantly brutal to so safe and sterile as to resemble a pop-psychology seminar more than a training class for future black belts.

With the huge influx of children into martial arts schools, many instructors were unprepared to provide for the special needs of this group. Instructors raised in strict adult-oriented schools were often not prepared for teaching very young children or for working with their concerned parents.

Legislative attempts to regulate martial arts have been introduced in numerous states over the years. To date, they've all failed to materialize into law. Clearly, like scuba-diving, ski instruction, golf, personal fitness training and aerobics, the martial arts must institute some universal teaching methodology that can be followed regardless of style. This is the purpose of the ACMA.

Our goal with the American Council on Martial Arts (ACMA) is to provide the most modern, scientifically-proven "teaching methods" to allow you to be even more effective in teaching the "traditional techniques" of your system. The ACMA provides a universal teaching reference for all martial arts instructors, regardless of style.

For instance, an instructor may teach a traditional side kick in an inappropriate, unprofessional and unsafe manner — without even realizing it. This is the way he has always taught the side kick, and it's the way he was taught the technique. It's the school's traditional way of presenting the side kick. Though the mechanics adhere to the specific martial arts style he is teaching, the *presentation method* may be entirely inappropriate for his class' age or skill level.

The ACMA-certified instructor, on the other hand, would teach the same side kick, with the same style-requisite mechanics, but more effectively. That's because he would teach a traditional side kick by means of a much more age/skill-specific methodology.

Both instructors teach the exact same traditional technique with the same stylistic mechanics, but the presentation and teaching methodology may vary drastically. The result is, the students should be less frustrated, and less prone to injury or humiliation. Best of all, students should be more apt to stay involved with the school for a longer period of time and with higher skill retention, than with the instructor who teaches "the old-school way."

The ACMA is the best of both worlds. Instructors are able to teach their traditional style, but with the addition of new teaching methods proven to enhance student retention and motivation. This allows an instructor to maintain his traditional system, but offers the potential to increase student retention and the popularity of the school by using the most effective teaching methods known at this time.

Continuing education is required in any teaching profession. The subjects covered in the ACMA program are based on scientifically-proven strategies and techniques to maximize teacher effectiveness.

For example, subjects such as "How To Teach Martial Arts to Children with Attention Deficit Disorder" are usually not taught to instructors as part of their black belt test. Consequently, the methods used by instructors working with these children are inconsistent from school to school and, typically, incorrect for the special needs of hyperactive children. The ACMA program will teach instructors *exactly* how to work with these children.

We've worked very hard to compile an excellent Board of Advisors who've spent many hours working and reworking their individual chapters. I'd like to thank each one of them for their effort in making this the best manual possible, and for their patience in working with my co-author John Corcoran and me. With this publication, John has set a new standard in his already stellar literary career.

We're confident that the information in this manual will also set a high standard. A standard of competence, professionalism and safety never before realized *consistently* from school to school in this industry. That will happen with your support. Study hard and prepare for the certification exam. Most of all, take the information you learn from this text and apply it in your classroom. Your students will appreciate it more than anyone. ∎

THE SCIENCE OF TEACHING

Pedagogy (pronounced *ped'a-go-gee*), or the science of teaching, is in many ways the motivation and underlying theme in the creation of the ACMA program. This section provides many hands-on examples and illustrations to help instructors more effectively manage the martial arts classroom. This section will also address areas such as sparring that have, through the years, proved to be problematic from a classroom-management standpoint and consequently have resulted in a disproportionate number of drop-outs.

The combination of chapters within this section will help the instructor to clearly assess the needs of the students comprising a class and to formulate very specific classroom-management strategies to meet those needs.

How To Teach Martial Arts Skills

By Ann Boyce, Ph.D.

How To Teach Martial Arts Skills

Have you ever watched a student who was struggling to learn a front kick? At first, the attempts at the skill are highly erratic with no two attempts looking the same. The student may have a look of serious concentration and may talk to himself about the skill in an attempt to "figure out" how to perform the kick.

After the student "figures out" how to perform the front kick, the student continues to practice this skill. During this time, the skill performance improves with subtle changes made to the skill during practice. As practice continues over time, the front kick becomes more fluid and the student appears to pay less attention to the actual skill performance and more attention to other factors, such as when it would be advantageous to use the front kick in a sparring situation.

This scenario is an example of how students learn motor skills. What is important here is that you, the instructor, learn how to effectively guide your students through the three stages of learning:

1. Beginning Stage—Cognitive.
2. Intermediate Stage—Associative.
3. Advanced Stage—Autonomous.

(Adapted from the work of Fitts, 1964; Fitts & Posner, 1967).

Beginning Stage

As an instructor, it is your job to help students "figure out" how to perform a new skill (for example, front kick, choke-hold release, form, etc.). You can accomplish this by:

1. Giving a brief explanation of the skill with an accompanying demonstration.
2. Providing "cue words" that focus the students' attention on a few important things to remember when performing a skill.
3. Initiating student practice.
4. Giving feedback to students during their skill attempts. These four steps will help students develop "a plan of action" for executing a skill.

Further information on each of these steps will be provided later in this chapter.

It is important to remember that during this first stage, the students think about the movement a great deal, especially during the first few skill attempts. But, it is your responsibility to help them "figure out" how to accomplish the skill.

Generally, the beginning stage will only take a few minutes to accomplish, if you have followed the four steps. Obviously, it will take longer if you are teaching a more complex skill, because it will take longer to formulate "a plan of action," or if you are working with young students. Once students get the basic idea of how to perform the skill, they are ready to move on to the next stage.

Intermediate Stage

During the intermediate stage, the student needs to practice the skill and will need the continued support of the instructor in order to further refine the movement pattern/skill. The "plan of action" will be modified and refined as the skill performance improves. The instructor will note subtle changes in the skill and more consistent movements (meaning, less variety in the movement pattern).

In order for improvement to continue, students must have:

1. Continued opportunities for "correct" practice.

2. Feedback from the instructor on critical aspects of the skill and instruction on how to self-correct the skill.

3. Reinforcement and encouragement from the instructor.

An example of how to teach a student to self-correct a skill could be performed in this way. When learning a jab, the instructor could have the student look in the mirror to see: a) correct hand position; b) if the jab crosses the body; and/or c) if on the draw-back, the hand drops below the chin level.

An additional factor that will influence the student's rate of learning is the individual's level of motivation. This factor is generally beyond the control of the instructor, but it plays a key role in a student's development as a martial artist.

The time period for accomplishing the intermediate stage of learning will vary depending on the ability of the student, the complexity of the skill, the caliber of the instruction, and the opportunity for "correct" practice. In general, this stage is completed when the student consistently performs the skill with correctness and accuracy.

Advanced Stage

During the advanced learning stage, the student will consistently perform the skill at a high level of proficiency. The motor pattern is automatic and fluid with little time spent on consciously attending to the actual skill performance.

Instead, the student can concentrate on how and when to best use the skill in a competitive situation. It is the instructor's job to provide:

1. Practice conditions which are designed to test the student under competitive situations.

2. Feedback to students which facilitates further skill development. For example, feedback could focus on strategies related to a sparring situation, preparing for an upcoming belt test or competing in a tournament.

The student's level of motivation continues to be a key factor in the overall development. If motivation is lacking, then it will prevent the student from either reaching or maintaining a high level of performance.

In summary, it is extremely important for martial arts instructors to understand that motor skill learning proceeds from the beginning stage, where students begin to "figure out" how to perform the skill, to the intermediate stage, where they refine and practice the motor skill, to the advanced stage of where students consistently exhibit a high level of skill proficiency.

The role of the instructor varies from stage to stage. For example, at the beginning stage the instructor must help students to "figure out" how to perform the skill, while during the intermediate stage, the instructor helps the students refine the skill pattern by providing many opportunities for "correct" practice. And last, at the advanced stage, the instructor must assist the students in the development of a highly consistent, fluid motor pattern by providing opportunities for practice in real-world situations—sparring, self-defense scenarios and tournament competition. Information on how to effectively teach various martial arts skills and techniques will be addressed in the following section.

THE THREE STAGES OF LEARNING*

1. **Beginning Stage—Cognitive**
   A. Give a brief explanation with a demonstration.
   B. Provide "cue words" for important points to remember.
   C. Initiate student practice.
   D. Give feedback to students during their skill attempts.

2. **Intermediate Stage—Associative**
   A. Continue opportunities for "correct" practice.
   B. Provide feedback on critical aspects and instruction on how to self-correct the skill.
   C. Reinforce and encourage the student.

3. **Advanced Stage—Autonomous**
   A. Provide conditions designed to test the student under competitive situations.
   B. Give feedback to facilitate further skill development.

* Adapted from the work of Fitts, 1964; Fitts & Posner, 1967.

Teaching Fundamentals

In a typical martial arts school, students of differing ranks line up in belt order with the ranking belts up front and lower belts in back. Demonstrations are often given by the ranking instructor or one of his advanced students. These demonstrations are generally presented fairly quickly, with little explanation on the skill, and then students are instructed to begin practicing the technique as the instructor counts the practice cadence.

After observing this type of teaching situation, a few questions come to mind:

1. Who needs to see the skill demonstration the most?
2. Where are these particular students positioned in the class?
3. Who would benefit from a more detailed explanation of the skill?
4. Why are students of differing skill levels receiving exactly the same instruction?
5. If the beginning students in the back can't see the instructor, who will they watch and model?
6. Are the models of the less skilled students a good model for beginning students to imitate while they are attempting to learn the skill?

In the preceding scenario, several questions were raised relevant to effective instruction. The following sections will cover the fundamentals of effective instruction and give practical guidelines for instructors who seek to improve their teaching fundamentals.

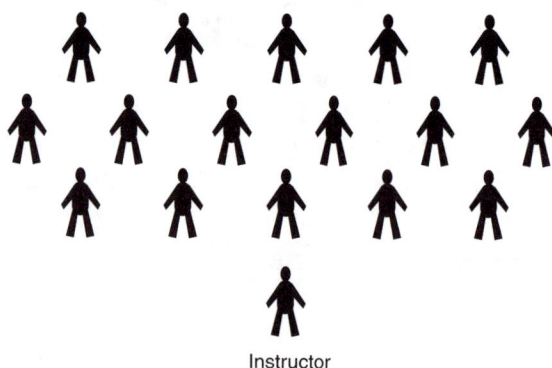

Instructor

Formations such as illustrated above provide each student with a sight-line to the instructor. Taped "X's" on the floor indicating where students should stand will assist the instructor in achieving a consistent line-up pattern.

Skill Explanations and Demonstrations

For inexperienced students, the instructor's role is one of helping them "figure out" how to perform a given skill. The term "inexperienced" can be applied to a rank beginner, or it also can be applied to an orange belt who is attempting to learn a jumping front kick because the student has no previous experience with this jumping type of kick.

Helping students "figure out" the motor skill can be initially accomplished through an explanation and corresponding demonstration of a given martial arts skill. When preparing to give an explanation and demonstration of any skill, the instructor must:

1. Get the students' attention before delivering any instruction.
2. Organize the students so that everyone can see and hear.
3. Utilize the KISS principle (Keep It Short and Simple)—spend no more than a minute on the explanation and demonstration of simple skills (for example, choke-hold release, round kick, etc.).
4. Remind students of a previously learned skill that is similar to the one you are currently teaching (for example, when the students already know the back kick, but you are attempting to teach them the spinning back kick).
5. Demonstrate the skill or have a student demonstrate it while you provide the explanation.
6. Demonstrate the skill several times and have students observe the skill from various viewpoints (from the side and front) to give them a better idea of what the skill looks like.
7. Provide a few "cue words" that relate to the key components of the skill which will help the students focus on what is important to remember when performing the skill. (For example, when teaching a front-leg front kick, the cue word could be "lift knee, extend, re-chamber, and down.")
8. Use mirrors during the demonstration and explanation phase to provide students with an image of their own performance.

For the best explanations and demonstrations,

there are several other factors that an instructor should consider.

First, who should demonstrate the skill? There are pros and cons to consider when selecting a demonstrator (instructor or competent student, or beginning student or video model).

In general, if the instructor demonstrates the skill, it helps to establish instructor credibility. In addition, because the instructor is highly proficient, the students will view a model who has perfect form, which will give them a good "snap shot" of how the skill should look. However, some students may not identify with the instructor due to his high level of proficiency and may not believe in their own ability to reach that same level of proficiency.

THE TYPES OF FEEDBACK

The types of feedback for martial arts instructors are:

1. **Augmented (external) Feedback.**
   A. Verbal Feedback.
   B. Visual Feedback.
2. **Intrinsic (internal) Feedback.**
3. **Skill Correction.**
4. **Motivating Students.**
5. **Teaching Students to Self-Monitor.**

Using a competent student or peer of similar age, gender and physical maturity may provide a model who is technically correct, as well as give the students someone with whom they can identify. However, if a student is unavailable, it is not recommended that the instructor enlist a student who is incapable of giving a quality demonstration, since it will not provide a suitable "snap shot" of what the skill should look like. In order for students to learn the skill, they need a model who performs the skill in a technically-correct manner. The use of videos is also a possible option for a demonstration, especially if the model is "believable."

Regardless of who the demonstrator is, select someone who can correctly perform the skill and who exemplifies the key components of the skill that you used during your explanation. The correct "snap shot" of the skill will help facilitate "correct practice" during the practice phase of instruction.

Second, should the skill demonstration be broken down into parts or should the demonstration show the entire skill? The answer to this question depends on the complexity of the skill and the ability level of the students. Some simple skills can be successfully learned from a demonstration of the entire skill. However, if the students aren't "getting it," then it is a good idea to break the skill down into its logical parts.

The use of "cue words" and the actions that correspond to those words are a good way to break the skill down. More complex skills will usually need to be broken down into parts in order to help students organize "action plans" for the execution of those skills. This is especially true when students are required to memorize a series of martial arts movements in a form. When this is the case, a "progressive part" method should be used to help students remember the series of movements.

This method allows students to "add on" movements to existing movements by putting skill sequences together. In this teaching method, the students receive skill explanations and demonstrations and then practice each series of movements before the next series of movements is presented.

For example, if the first movement sequence in a beginner's form involved an attention stance to a ready stance, then those two movements could be added to the second series of movements—the step back to a low block, step forward to a middle punch, to a step forward to a high block—which could then be added to the third series of movements, and so on until the form was finished.

An additional strategy, verbal rehearsal, helps students memorize the series of movements in a form. Have students repeat out loud the movements in a form as:

1. They practice the form.
2. They watch other students perform the form.

3. They are away from the school and think about the form.

The verbal rehearsal strategy also helps students when they are attempting to memorize a series of one-step sparring moves or combinations.

Third, how many times should the skill be demonstrated? The number of demonstrations depends on the complexity of the skill, with more difficult skills requiring a greater number of demonstrations. After the introduction of the skill, the instructor should continue to observe the students to decide if additional demonstrations are needed.

In summary, the use of the part or whole demonstration methods and number of demonstrations needed are dependent on the complexity of the skill, as well as the ability of the students. In most cases, it is recommended that skill demonstrations begin with the entire (whole) skill being demonstrated to give the learner a good idea of what the entire skill looks like. Thereafter, the decisions related to breaking the skill down or not, and the number of demonstrations necessary, are based on the skill's complexity and the ability level of the student.

Structured Practice

Practice is the single most important variable affecting learning (Schmidt, 1988). The instructor's ability to provide practice situations that emphasize "perfect (correct)" practice is paramount to the learning process. The old adage of "practice making perfect" is *partially* incorrect because the research on how students learn motor skills has found that "correct practice makes perfect."

"Correct" practice can

be achieved by providing:

1. An explanation and skillful demonstration of the motor skill so that the student has a clear idea of how to perform the skill.
2. Maximum opportunities for practice.
3. Specific and immediate feedback to the student so that errors can be corrected quickly.

Following the skill explanation and corresponding demonstration, the instructor must provide adequate practice opportunities so that the students can learn and perfect their martial arts skills. The challenge to the instructor is to structure practice in a way that makes learning new and/or difficult skills easy. This can be accomplished in several ways:

1. Teaching whole and part practice methods.
2. Selecting appropriate skill progressions.
3. Choosing a suitable teaching format.
4. Teaching for transfer.

Whole and Part Practice Methods

In the previous section on explanations and demonstrations, several ways to introduce skills were covered (whole, part, and progressive part). The *practice* of these skills also falls under those general categories (whole, part, progressive part), and the selection of the best method is still dependent on the complexity of the skill and the ability level of the student.

Before discussing each of these methods, a further understanding of what is meant by whole and part is needed. "Whole" can refer to a single skill (for example, a round kick), or whole can also refer to a series of skills (for example, a form or a series of movements in a sparring sequence—spinning front kick, jab, reverse punch).

In accordance with the two definitions of whole, "part" can refer to a single component of a kick (for example, the re-chamber position of the round kick), or it can refer to a single skill within a form (for example, round kick as the fourth move within the form).

The "part" method allows the instructor to break the skill or skill sequence down (for example, jab, reverse punch) into logical parts. In the part method, practice of each part of the skill is performed before

the parts are recombined into the whole skill. The advantage to using this method is that it breaks the skill down so that students can learn each part of the skill or skill sequence. However, the disadvantage is that too much emphasis on the parts can prevent the development of the fluid motion required for performance of the entire skill or skill sequence, whereas, the "whole" method presents the skill or skill sequence in its entirety.

If the skill is simple, the "whole" method is a great way to teach the skill. However, many martial arts skills and skill sequences are complex and foreign to most inexperienced students. Therefore, a combination of the whole and part methods may be the best course of action; it is referred to as a "modification" of the "whole-part-whole" method.

This method allows the instructor to structure practice so that the entire skill "whole" is taught first, and then teaching and practicing the component parts ensues. Once all parts are mastered then the whole movement is practiced again.

Another option, the "progressive part" method, has been previously covered in the "explanation and demonstration" section; it is basically an add-on process. Forms are the best candidates for this progressive part practice method.

The difficult choice of the best teaching method can be made easier by asking two questions. Is the skill or skill sequence too complicated to be taught as a "whole"? How can the skill or skill sequence be broken down so that it can be learned without sacrificing the long-term goal of fluid motion when all the parts are recombined?

In summary, the recommendation is to teach a skill or skill sequence as a whole, if the students can learn it that way. If the skill is complex, then a part or progressive part or modified whole-part-whole method should be employed. For complex skills, skill demonstrations and explanations should cover the whole movement or the series of movements first, with the practice phase using one of the part methods so that students can learn the skill or skill sequence. Always relate the parts to the whole movement so that students understand how the parts of the skill or skill sequence fit together.

Appropriate Skill Progressions

One of the keys to effective teaching is deciding what to teach and then deciding on the order that skills should be taught. The instructors selection of skills to be taught should be based on the his expectations of students at different skill belt or belt-stripe levels. Most schools have clear expectations of what martial arts skills a white belt should be able to perform in order to be promoted to the next level or belt. If this is not the case, then the instructor should determine the skills and be able to clearly articulate those expectations to students and the parents of the students.

In general, skill progressions should be taught from simple to complex. The instructor should be able to determine which skills are more difficult than other skills and devise a plan for teaching skills and skill sequences in a logical skill progression. It is obvious that a sparring situation is far more complex than performing a stationary kicking or hand technique in the air. However, it does ask the question, how does a student progress from performing basic techniques to surviving a sparring situation?

Since martial arts ultimately involves physical contact, instructors must carefully plan the students' progression from basic skills performance to performing in a sparring situation. It is critical to structure practice progression in a way that minimizes injury. For example, an instructor might teach the skill progression in these ways:

1. Start with basic kicking and hand techniques (for example, stationary front, round and/or side kicks and jab and reverse punch), where form is emphasized and the skills are practiced in the air.

2. Once the fundamental skills are mastered, then the kicking and hand techniques are expanded (for example, the front kick is expanded to step-up and back-leg front kicks). These kicks are also performed in the air while moving a limited distance.

3. Kicking and punching combinations are introduced (back-leg round kick, jab, uppercut) while students perform them in the air in front of a mirror. This provides not only an opportunity for practice, but also an opportunity for self-correction.

4. Single skills (for example, a side kick) and, later, combinations of skills are performed against large stationary shields or long bags, contacting the objects using light to medium force.

5. A partner moves with a shield as a student practices single techniques and then combinations, so that the student learns to adjust the techniques for variations in distance and movement.

6. Large shields are replaced with smaller hand targets, and accuracy as well as force are now emphasized. At first, the targets are stationary and then the partner moves the targets.

7. Students now practice predetermined instructor-specified techniques and combinations with a partner, using light force. Blocking techniques are introduced and practiced (this practice stage lasts a long time and students now wear protective gear throughout the remaining steps).

8. Using light force, partners practice techniques and combinations of techniques with each other using both attacking skills (for example, kicks and hand techniques) and defending skills (for example, blocks and footwork).

9. Using light to medium force, partners practice both attacking and defending techniques.

This progression is intended to gradually introduce the students to the physical contact that is a part of martial arts training. This suggested progression is not the only way to introduce a student to sparring and other instructors may have additional steps. However, the instructor is ultimately responsible for the safety of his students.

One final note on skill progressions. Throughout the example on the progression from the performance of basic skills to participating in sparring, specific variables were altered to make the practice either easier or more difficult. Examples of these alterations included: a) moving vs. stationary kicking and/or punching; b) small vs. large targets; c) practice solo vs. practice with a partner; d) performance of a single skill vs. a series of skills; e) kicking or punching in the air vs. kicking or punching an object; f) using low vs. medium force; and g) slow vs. medium vs.

high speeds.

Using a combination of these variables during practice can help an instructor adjust the level of difficulty for students while they are attempting to practice and learn martial arts skills. By manipulating the level of difficulty, the instructor can adjust the complexity of the skill to account for individual differences among students. For expanded lists of variables, instructors could review: 1) Graham, Holt/Hale, & Parker (1993) (see Appendix A); and 2) Rink (1993) (see Appendix B).

Teaching Formats

Organizing students for practice often falls under two general teaching formats:

1. Whole Group Practice.
2. Modified Stations Practice.

One practice format is not inherently better than the other, it really depends on the instructor's underlying purpose(s) for the practice session as well as the skill level of the students. The whole practice format involves all of the students performing the same skill(s); whereas, the modified-stations format is designed to have small groups of students working on different skills simultaneously.

For example, the modified-stations format could involve several locations in the school where specific groups of students work on skills related to their martial arts abilities. In this case, the white belts could practice the white belt form while the yellow and orange belts practice one-step sparring.

If the group of students are all at the same skill level, lack motivation to work on their own, or the instructor has the same skills planned for all students, then a whole-group format might be the appropriate choice. However, if the students are at different skill levels, can work on their own, and/or the instructor wants to cover different content with the students who are at different belt levels, then a stations format might be more appropriate.

This is not to say that the practice formats must be the same throughout an entire session. An instructor might start off with a whole group format, then switch to a stations format and then finish the class

session by returning to a whole-group format.

In summary, the choice of session formats are based on:

1. The skill level(s) of the students.
2. The ability of students to work independently.
3. The content (skills) that the instructor wants to cover in the class session.

One final question. If the students are at different skill levels (belt levels) within the same class, why would an instructor cover the same skills with these students?

Teaching for Transfer

One way to make the learning of new or complex skills easier is through teaching for transfer. Transfer is defined as "the gain or loss in the capability to respond to one task as a result of practice or experience in some other [task/skill]" (Schmidt, 1991, p.218). Many previously learned skills may have similar component(s) to new skills, and one way to capitalize on the student's previous learning is to point out similarities between the new and old skills.

For example, let's say that you are attempting to teach a spinning back-hook kick and the student has already mastered the front-leg hook kick (especially the components of the whipping action of the leg and the foot/heel position). In addition, the student has already learned a side kick (especially the component of the extension portion of the skill). If you combine the similar components of those two skills (front-leg hook and side kicks) with a turn or spinning action of the spinning back-hook, then the student may be able to perform the spinning back-hook kick. This process may be further facilitated with cue words such as "spin," "extend" (the side kick) and "whip through" (hooking action).

Transfer can be facilitated by focusing on positive transfer situations where the elements of two skills (old and new) are similar and contribute to the learning of the new skill. In order to accomplish this, the instructor should:

1. Figure out the similarities between the old and new skill.
2. Explain and demonstrate the similar components.
3. Use cue words that emphasize the similarities of the old and new skill as well as accentuate the key movements in the skill.
4. Make sure that the old skill components have been learned well enough to make a positive contribution to the learning of the new skill.

Feedback

The "correct" practice of skills can be accelerated by immediate and specific feedback delivered by the instructor. One of the most important roles of the

instructor is to evaluate the student's skill performance and to give feedback about the correctness of the skill attempt. This role is especially crucial when an inexperienced student is attempting to perform new skills for the first time. The inexperienced student may not be capable of evaluating his own skill performance, even though he will be receiving internal feedback resulting from the skill performance.

Basically, there are two types of feedback:
1. Augmented (external) Feedback.
2. Intrinsic (internal) Feedback.

Augmented feedback is information that the student would not normally receive as a result of the skill performance. Two examples might be: a) Verbal feedback that is provided by the instructor on some aspect of the skill performance (for example, when performing a back-leg round kick, "keep the knee bent longer as you are spinning, then extend the leg to the target"; and b) visual feedback that is provided to the student by viewing his performance on a videotape or in a mirror during the movement's execution (for example, look to see if you are striking with your heel when performing a foot stomp).

Intrinsic feedback is information that the student receives as a normal consequence of a movement. For example, the student can "feel" if his foot made solid contact with a shield or can "see" if the foot landed with accuracy on the target.

Feedback can serve several functions:
1. To provide information on how to correctly perform during the next skill attempt.
2. To motivate the student.
3. To provide a mechanism for students to self-monitor their own skill practice.

Instructor Feedback: Skill Correction

As stated earlier, one of the instructor's primary roles is to provide feedback to students who are attempting to learn a skill. This feedback should function to correct the past skill attempt and to give information to help students perform the skill in a more correct manner on the next attempt.

When delivering feedback to students, the instructor should consider the following recommendations:
1. Give feedback on aspects of the skill that aren't

already known. For example, if the student missed the target during a kicking drill, he already knows that; instead, tell the student that he is standing too far to the left or right of the target.

2. Be positive. Start off with a statement that reinforces what the student is doing right and then move to the correction phase of the feedback. For example, on an inside crescent kick, the instructor might say, "Good, you are delivering the kick toward the center line of the body, but you need to strike the target with the side of the foot instead of with the heel."

3. After giving feedback, don't walk away from the student. Stay there and check to make sure that the student is attempting to make the correction to the skill that you just suggested.

4. Give brief and concise feedback related to the cause of the error. For example, don't focus on the fact that the student just was hit in the face during a sparring situation; instead, tell the student to keep his hands up.

5. Provide the student with immediate and specific feedback on the skill.

6. If there are many components wrong with the skill, focus on the *major* skill problems first and, after the student corrects that problem, then move on to the minor corrections. For example, since stance is very important to the execution of many martial skills, that is usually a good place to start.

Instructor Feedback: Motivating Students

Feedback can influence motivation, which in turn can affect the student's desire to further develop his martial arts skills. Feedback (intrinsic or augmented) should give the student a good idea of what his present level of performance is and how much improvement is needed in order to achieve a goal (for example, the perfect front kick). Instructors who provide quality skill-related feedback as well as encouragement to their students, can positively impact the student's level of motivation.

However, when a student is not improving, then this factor will negatively impact a student's motiva-

tion. In this case, the instructor must seek to give the student concrete suggestions on how to improve performance. If this is not done, then the student will either try harder or give up completely. Remember that once a student reaches a high level of proficiency, the progress the individual makes is measured in small increments.

Feedback: How to Teach Students to Self-Monitor

Students are constantly receiving internal (intrinsic) feedback throughout and immediately following the execution of a skill. For example, a student can be taught to not let his back hand drop during sparring practice, if the instructor has taught them to "feel" the gloved-hand touching his chin during defensive situations while sparring.

Many skills have corresponding feedback related to how the skill should *feel*. This type of internal feedback can be extremely useful when working with more experienced students as well as inexperienced students, if the instructor takes the time to teach them about the "feel."

For example, an experienced student might ask, "When should I release the kick on a spinning back kick in order to hit the shield with a lot of force?" The answer is related to the amount of pressure built up in the lower back (internal feedback), similar to a twisted rubber band. Basically, the kicking foot stays on the floor until the pressure in the lower back becomes uncomfortable, and at that point the kick is delivered.

Students can also be taught to use mirrors to self-monitor movement (augmented feedback), if they are taught what to look for during the movement's execution.

For example, a student could look for the following skill components when performing a side kick in the air: a) heel of supporting foot pointed toward target; b) knee of kicking leg raised; c) chambered foot position of raised leg; d) full extension of leg; e) heel strike; f) re-chambered position with knee pulled back toward body; and g) return to fighting stance.

Both types of feedback (intrinsic and extrinsic) can provide students with information on how to correctly perform a skill on their next skill attempt. A lot of feedback can be gained from skill practice, if the instructor takes the time to focus the students' attention on particular aspects related to how the skill should feel and/or how the skill should look.

In summary, feedback serves several functions:

1. To provide information on how to correctly perform during the next skill attempt.
2. To motivate the student.
3. To provide a mechanism for students to self-monitor their own skill practice.

Guidelines and examples have been given to illustrate the recommended ways to use feedback to improve skill development. In general, augmented feedback delivered by the instructor should be positive, immediate and specific. It should focus on the cause(s) for the error and provide the student with a concrete idea of how to correctly perform the skill on the next skill attempt.

Feedback's important role as a motivator should not be overlooked. A well-timed "attaboy" or "attagirl" may be just what's needed to help students persist at a difficult skill.

Lastly, it is recommended that the instructor spend time teaching students how the skill should feel and look, so that the feedback can be properly used to make them more successful martial artists.

Summary

In order for an instructor to successfully teach students martial arts skills, he must first understand how students acquire motor skills. From this understanding, the instructor can then begin to plan for effective class sessions that focus on students' learning and success.

The teaching fundamentals can best be summed up from the literature on teacher effectiveness, which states that the best teachers provide "a lot of practice, practice with success in a structured learning environment" (Berliner, 1984; Gage, 1984; Graham & Heimerer, 1981; Rink, 1985; Rosenshine, 1983; Siedentop, 1983).

Practice with an emphasis on "correct practice" can be influenced by effective skill explanations and demonstration, lots of structured practice and quality feedback. ∎

TEACHING TECHNIQUES TO MANIPULATE THE DEGREE OF DIFFICULTY

This is a Modified List of Variables from Graham, et al. (1993) Textbook. These variables can be used to manipulate the difficulty of the task/skill when teaching students:

- Speed (fast, medium, slow). For example, kick or punch at the differing speeds.
- Force (light, medium, strong). For example, use different forces when kicking and punching.
- Directions (up/down; forward/backward; right/left; clockwise/counterclockwise).
- Level (low, middle, high). For example, a front kick at a high vs. a low level.
- Pathways (straight, curved, zigzag). For example, practice offensive and defensive moves while moving in a curved pathway.
- Accuracy (far, near).
- With people (leading/following; unison/contrast; partner/solo/group).

OTHER MANIPULATION OPTIONS

This Modified List of Variables is from Rink (1993) Textbook. These variables can be used to manipulate the difficulty of the task/skill:

- Increasing or decreasing the size of the whole to be handled by the learner. For example, a longer vs. a shorter form.
- Adding or subtracting movement to a stationary skill. For example, add a jab and reverse punch to a stationary front kick.
- Increasing or decreasing the force requirements such as the height or distance involved in producing or receiving force. For example, high roundhouse kick with medium force.
- Receiving an object from different levels or from different directions, such as to the side of the receiver. For example, blocking a high front kick; moving away from a spinning back kick by sliding to the side.
- Increasing or decreasing the size of target.
- Requiring a higher or lesser degree of accuracy in the placement of a kick or punch.
- Involving more or less interaction with people. For example, offensive vs. defensive moves with a partner or shadowboxing using a mirror.
- Using larger vs. smaller or heavier vs. lighter equipment. For example, kicking against a shield or long hanging bag.
- Increasing or decreasing the speed of the object to be received or redirected.
- Involving sideways or backwards movements. For example, when sparring, move to avoid being hit.
- Increasing or decreasing the speed of the skill. For example, kick or punch with greater or lesser speed.
- Combining skills or breaking skills down.
- Using skills in a competitive or self-testing situation.

References

Berliner, D. (1984). The half–glass: A review of research on teaching.

In P. Hosford (Ed.), Using what we know about teaching. Alexandria, VA: Association for Supervision and Curriculum Development.

Fitts, P.M. (1964). Perceptual–motor skills learning.

In A.W. Melton (Ed.), Categories of human learning (pp. 243–285). New York: Academic Press.

Fitts, P.M., & Posner, M.I. (1967). Human performance. Belmont, CA: Brookes/Cole.

Gage, N. (1984). What do we know about teaching effectiveness? Phi Delta Kappan, 66(2), 87–93

Graham, G., & Heimerer. E. (1981). Research on teacher effectiveness. Quest, 33(1), 14–25.

Graham, G. Holt/Hale, S., & Parker, M. (1993). Children moving: A reflective approach to teaching physical education (3rd ed.). Mountain View, CA: Mayfield Publishing Company.

Rink, J.E. (1985). Teaching physical education for learning. St. Louis, MO: Times Mirror/Mosby.

Rink, J.E. (1993). Teaching physical education for learning (2nd ed.). St. Louis, MO: Times Mirror/Mosby.

Rosenshine, B. (1983). Teaching functions in instructional program. Elementary School Journal, 83, 335–351.

Schmidt, R.A. (1988). Motor control and learning: A behavioral emphasis (2nd ed.). Champaign, IL: Human Kinetics Publishers, Inc. Schmidt, R.A. (1991). Motor learning and performance: From principles to practice. Champaign, IL: Human Kinetics Publishers, Inc. Seidentop, D. (1983). Developing teaching skills in physical education. (2nd ed.). Palo Alto, CA: Mayfield.

Additional Resources

Christina, R.W., & Corcos, D.M. (1988). Coaches guide to teaching sport skills. Champaign, IL: Human Kinetics Books.

Harrison, J.M., Blakemore, C.L., Buck, M.M., & Pellett, T.L. (1996). Instructional strategies for secondary school physical education (4th ed.). Dubuque, IA: Brown & Benchmark.

Martens, R., Christina, R.W., Harvey, J.S., & Sharkey, B.J. (1983). Coaching young athletes. Champaign, IL: Human Kinetics Publishers, Inc.

Martens, R. (1990). Successful coaching: NFICEP edition (2nd ed.). Champaign, IL: Human Kinetics Publishers, Inc.

How To Structure Your Curriculum

By John Graden

How To Structure Your Curriculum

Phase One: Learning the "Black Belt Attitude"

Phase One is the first year of a student's career as a martial artist. The basic premise is that it's more important to have a less–than–perfect orange belt *in* class than to try to perfect a student and have them drop *out*. The focus at this level is in building the student's enthusiasm for the martial arts, for his school and for earning a black belt. Most of all, you have to motivate the student to want to keep coming back to class.

This is also a period of education and indoctrination for the student into the traditions of the martial arts. The key is to de–emphasize the physical demands and emphasize the mental benefits of the training. Your job at this stage is to build your student's confidence so he can see himself earning a black belt.

Your goal is not to perfect the students' front kick in the first month. The key is retention. You can only help the students who are *in* class. You can't help the ones you drove off with demands that were not in line with the students' confidence, skill or conditioning level.

The emphasis in beginner classes should be about 90% mental skills and 10% physical skills. This doesn't mean the student will be meditating for 90% of the class. It means the focus of your teaching will be in helping the student *learn how to learn*. Teach your students how to try without getting discouraged— how to stay focused and recover from making a mistake in class. Teach them not to look for 100% improvement overnight. Instead, help them realize that progress will come in 100 different areas 1% at a time.

Most of all, teach them how to take these principles out of the classroom and into their lives. This is the essence of the black belt attitude. The black belt attitude is an attitude of high standards and 100% effort. Excellence is defined in the black belt. How would a black belt sit in school and listen to a teacher? How would a black belt perform his job? Would a black belt complain about a problem or take action to resolve a challenge?

The black belt attitude is one of positive self-expectancy. This is an attitude that says, "There are rewards for my hard work."

Phase Two: Good Form

Phase Two is year two of the student's road to black belt. Now you have a student who is in better shape. His conditioning should be improved along with his understanding of the disciplines of the art. These students have been training with you for a year. Now they are ready for a somewhat more intense experience. You have to be cautious here because their confidence is fragile. Much of their confidence in their abilities and future is tied directly to their trust in you.

At this stage, you can turn the heat up some and run a more physically and technically demanding class. Good form is the emphasis at this stage. Feet should be bladed on kicks and wrists flat when punching. Nevertheless, you want to keep the motivation level high, so a 50/50 balance between physical and mental skills seems to work real good here for retention.

Phase Three: Preparation for Black Belt

Phase Three is years three, four and five. Now the student should be in good shape with good technique. He is in preparation for his black belt exam,

though it may be two or three years away. Now, we have to begin the process of developing tenacity, toughness and survival skills befitting a black belt.

The difference now is that these students should be ready for it. They should be in shape. They've been with you for over two years and they are hungry for some advanced training. Give it to them.

Increase your physical demands, but always preframe it by telling them how proud you are of them and that you are going to bring them all the way home to black belt. Tell them you believe in them and expect the highest effort and performance. However, you cannot make demands beyond the skills, strategies and tactics you provide them.

This is an important point. Prepare your students for the demands. Give them sparring strategies for being exhausted. Teach them how to run and then to shadowbox or practice forms or combinations after the run, so they get used to digging deep and discovering the spirit of the arts.

Real confidence as a martial artist comes when you have been tested. Not by some external exam board, but by your own internal doubts and fears. Typically, these arise when faced with a tougher, stronger, faster opponent, and when faced with exhaustion against an opponent that won't quit. That's the key. That's the bottom line. Not everyone can win every fight.

Teach your students at this level that survival is the key. Survival builds confidence. To know you can face overwhelming odds and not quit. To know, even if you are exhausted and facing a tougher opponent, that although you may not win, you can keep that opponent from hurting you. You can defend yourself. That's the essence of self–defense. That's a black belt.

To get a group of students to advance to this level is not easy. Sure, we all have the killer jocks who seem to eat this stuff up. But, can you take a group of 30 brand new students of all ages, athletic backgrounds and confidence levels into white belt class and then, three to five years later, have ten or 15 new black belts? That's the mark of a pro.

Not everyone can be a black belt. Some people are just not going to make it. However, your job is to get 100% of the students, who by any stretch of the imagination could make it to black belt.

Like most things, the longer–term your perspective in nurturing a student, the better. Curriculum must increase demands gradually. The opposite is a common error. Unsuccessful schools tend to overload new students with material and then taper off as they progress through the ranks.

The results are new students feeling overtaxed as they are constantly introduced to new, sometimes overwhelming challenges before they can absorb them. Then, when they get to the brown belt level and are ready for big challenges, the curriculum has run out of material. The result is boredom and drop out.

Study your curriculum to see if you too are overloading the requirements at the front end and are too light on those at the back end. Are you overwhelming your white belts and boring your black belts? Most curriculums are. The problem is that there is a common instinct within martial arts instructors to teach the curriculum the way they were taught. This is also a mistake.

You can, while operating within the confines of a particular style, vary the order and the timeline of the material in that style, in order to enhance retention. The only two belts that matter are white belt and black belt. All the rest are "tutti–frutti" belts, so far as I'm concerned. They are designed for curriculum control and motivation. That's all.

How you design your curriculum between white and black belt is very important. You must feed your students material like it was a food supply for a three–year refuge in the mountains. You have to make it last. Each year, as part of your goal-setting process, take another close look at your curriculum and make the adjustments you feel are best for the student. ∎

How To Reduce Student Drop Out

By John Graden

How To Reduce Student Drop Out

Entertainment's Influence on the Martial Arts

Since the release of *The Karate Kid* film in 1984, millions of people have joined martial arts schools. Unfortunately, due to unprofessional teaching, unsafe and outdated practices, millions of people have dropped right back out again.

The Karate Kid was followed by its three sequels, during which time the *Teenage Ninja Mutant Turtles* films, TV show and merchandising shot to American entertainment prominence. The *Turtles*, in terms of merchandising, were bigger than the Cabbage Patch Dolls! After that came more success and exposure with the "Mighty Morphin' Power Rangers" phenomenon. Since then, virtually every action program on television includes martial arts scenes, as do most action films.

No other physical activity has received as much mainstream media and entertainment exposure as the martial arts. Certainly, how the martial arts was displayed was frustrating to many of us. Clearly, the entertainment industry was interested in exploiting the most violent aspects of the arts. Although, in *The Karate Kid* and the "Power Rangers," there was always an attempt at introducing a positive, philosophical message amidst all the mayhem.

Still, most kids and, in fact, most adults, were not drawn to the arts because of a positive message. They were drawn and excited by the action. This is not by any means a new trend. Many current veteran instructors were originally inspired by the first wave of "Chop-Socky Kung-Fu" films, led by Bruce Lee in the early 1970s. On a higher note, the "Kung Fu" television series certainly inspired many of us to get involved.

But despite the strong philosophical messages that infused the show with substance, I seriously doubt it was Caine's mumbled wisdom that prompted us to seek out a martial arts school. As interesting as his philosophy of peace and tranquility was, we sat through it patiently in anticipation of the point at the end of the show when he kicked a cowboy through a window. The kick is what got us excited. That's what sent us out to seek a sensei, sifu or sabanim.

Unfortunately, that excitement and anticipation of learning the martial arts often turned to frustration and quitting when faced with the realities of the "dungeon dojo," that to this day, is still the prevalent class of school in America.

The Dungeon Dojo

A dungeon dojo is one that is typically small, smelly and soiled. The instructor doesn't teach as much as command. The demands on the new student far outweigh his confidence or skill. The atmosphere in the school is intimidating. The result, of course, is a massive drop-out rate. These are schools that have been in business for as much as 20 years, yet still have less than 100 students. As many students are dropping out as are dropping in.

Our estimation is that, in the last 20 years, the above paragraph describes the martial arts experience for *over 10-million people*—most of whom dropped out, never to return. Not only were these people failed, but the entire martial arts community suffers to this day because of that enormous loss of participants. Imagine how many great martial artists would have come out of those programs had their experience been more positive. Where would the arts be today in society?

We all agree that martial arts is good for people and for the community. The more people learning and living the principles of respect, self-control and discipline, the better for everyone. With that in mind we have to ask ourselves, "If martial arts is so good for people, why aren't more people involved?"

We know a lot of people enroll in martial arts classes. The questions are: Why don't they stay with it? Why do we drive them off? Why do more than half of the students that begin training drop out within the first year? If the benefits of martial arts training are so good, why aren't more people sticking around to enjoy them?

The real solution-oriented question is, "What can we do with our program to help them feel more comfortable with its demands?" This manual and the ACMA program is a step toward answering that question.

People Are Busy

First, let's recognize that people are busy and have an incredible number of choices demanding their time and attention. In the case of an adult student, work, family and social activities all beckon. For kids, the choices are endless. For their parents, the demands of the kids financially, combined with the stress of being the house taxi to and from every activity including martial arts classes, make the elimination of one of those stresses ever inviting.

As martial arts professionals, we are under great pressure to continually motivate the students to stay involved and resist the temptations to move onto another activity that may be more enjoyable or that they feel they are better at.

Remember, many of our instructors learned in the military from instructors who really didn't want to teach them anyway. That type of dungeon dojo atmosphere was used by tough, highly-disciplined adults for other tough, highly-disciplined military students. They were not designed for eight-year-old kids or moms who haven't exercised in 20 years because they have been raising a family.

Or, most of all, they were not designed for time-stressed people who have a full menu of other activities to choose from. Just because we were raised in a dungeon dojo doesn't mean that was the right way to teach. How many of your classmates are still in the arts? I would guess very few.

Again, if martial arts is so good for people,

why aren't more people involved? What can you do to keep them involved longer?

Why Students Get Bored

After working with thousands of schools, we've come up with what we feel is a good list of the most common reasons students get bored and drop out of martial arts schools. This list is by no means complete since students may have many reasons, including personal situations, that lead them to drop out. Our goal here is to try to draw attention to the common problem areas that instructors can control.

1) The Instructor Fails to Communicate Student Progress

Students must feel progress! A great example of the power of progress is the efforts of someone attempting to lose weight by dieting. All a dieter needs is someone to comment on his slimmer appearance to motivate him to keep dieting. Likewise, your students need to know how they're doing and you must try to phrase your feedback to them as positively as possible.

Too often, martial arts instructors, because of the exacting nature of the skills, become hypercritical. They become experts at citing what's wrong with someone's technique rather than what's right with it. Instructors must communicate some progress to the student while at the same time suggesting how to improve a technique. Explain to the student "What to do" rather than "What not to do."

Solution: Some instructors have been successful with a strategy of Praise-Correct-Praise. An example would be to replace a command such as, "Your knee's too low!" with "Your side kick is coming along. Be sure to get your knee up like this to make it even better. You'll get it. Keep practicing."

In this example, we've replaced an impersonal comment with a personal observation and communication of the student's progress and combined it with a helpful tip to improve performance. Certainly, this requires a little more effort on behalf of the instructor, but keeping students in class and watching them grow through the ranks is well worth the effort.

Let the students know you recognize their efforts and appreciate them.

2) The Program Does Not Have Clear, Compelling Goals

How can you expect students to overcome obstacles or distractions without a compelling goal? There must be a strong reason for them to pull themselves off the couch twice or more a week and go to class. We all need goals, and students are no different.

This is why a set, posted testing schedule is so critical. In the past, instructors made the mistake of waiting until enough students were ready collectively before scheduling an exam. This can be very frustrating for students. For one, under the collective exam policy they don't have a specific timeline to work with. They could test next week, or they could test in three months. This is not very motivating. And it is particularly difficult for a student who fails an exam or misses some classes due to vacation or illness. They may have *months* to wait before they have a chance to advance again. Goals must be measurable and have specific deadlines.

Solution: Schools that have replaced the above collective-testing program with a more structured, monthly testing cycle have experienced great improvements in retention and overall student satisfaction.

Equally important to instituting goals in your program is your process of teaching your students the importance of and strategies for goal-setting. Use the black belt goal continually in classes to keep them focused. Finish class by congratulating the group for coming that night and remind them that it will not always be easy to make class, but that goals worth having are goals worth working for. That's what makes black belt so special. Martial arts is about discipline, and the first discipline is to come to class.

Lack of a compelling goal is all it takes for a student to accept an invitation to a movie instead of attending class. Having clear, definable and scheduled goals is also all it takes to prompt that student to go to class and reschedule a movie night with friends.

3) The Classroom Lacks Excitement or Enthusiasm

One of the great revelations of the past 20 years is that the martial arts can be taught effectively, indeed, *more* effectively, in an atmosphere that is enjoyable to the student and the instructor. One of the practices carried over from the military-trained instructors that first brought martial arts to America was a hyper-strict, oppressive classroom environment. Students were treated as though they were getting ready to go to war. Most, of course, were not.

When going to martial arts class becomes more stressful than going to work, students drop out. This is why instructors have effectively implemented a classroom atmosphere that is an enjoyable experience. People will always prefer to do something they enjoy. Instructors who do not allow laughter, or fun within the school, will typically deal with a significant drop-out rate.

Solution: Today's instructors encourage clapping, high fives and verbal support among the student ranks. Still, many instructors feel such activities undermine the seriousness of the martial arts and are signs of weakness. However, one look at the practice sessions of some of the toughest sports in the world provides clear evidence that enthusiasm and excitement are signs of confidence and commitment. Football, basketball and hockey all high-five, clap, and slap each other on the rear. While we don't encourage that last example, the first two have fit in perfectly in classes around the country.

4) Too Much Repetition

ACMA Board member Joe Lewis tells a great story of his first night in karate class in Okinawa in the mid-1960s. Lewis, who at the time was a 200-pound bodybuilder, said the first thing they did in class was form a circle while in a horse stance and work on middle-range punches. Lewis, who prides himself on physical prowess, said he was going to show those "little guys" how hard he could punch. So he started blasting out powerful, but crude, to be sure, white belt-level punches. What he didn't anticipate was that the drill lasted for *2,000 punches.*

He said he could barely get out of bed the next day. While it is certainly funny to imagine a white belt Joe Lewis *crawling* out of the bed from soreness, what if he quit as a result? How many other potentially great or even average martial artists have quit because the instructor was more of a professional "counter" than a teacher?

Many instructors seem to excel in the art of dramatic counting more than education. These are instructors who rely on dramatic voice inflections and volume as they simply count off repetitions, "Ooone! Twoo! Threee! Fourrr! Fiiive!"

This is not teaching. This is counting. While you must work a technique enough to create a skill, too much repetition results in students not learning any skills, because they drop out.

Solution: You must become creative in your teaching so that techniques can be repeated, but in a variety of fun and interesting drills.

A great example is to take a technique like the round kick and work it ten times on each side in the mirror. Then work it ten times on each side against a partner, for accuracy and application, and finish with ten times on each leg against a target. That's 60 kicks in an exciting, interesting class application.

5) Student Doesn't Receive Enough Encouragement

Students have to believe they can be black belts. While many of your more athletically-confident students will believe it from day one, the majority will have some doubts.

Solution: You must encourage them. Tell them they are on track and that you are proud of their progress. Let them know that you are their "success coach" and you're behind them all the way. Recognize even the smallest improvements as a way of communicating progress.

Point out their strong points to the rest of the class. If they have a good reverse punch, pull them up in front of the class and use it as an example for the rest, and finish with a round of applause for the performer. Few things will encourage a student faster than that level of recognition.

6) Curriculum Overwhelms White Belts and Bores Black Belts

While we all understand that, just because we were taught a certain way doesn't make it right, this applies to more than just teaching methodology. It can also

apply to how you present your style of martial arts.

In most systems of martial arts, the beginner ranks are virtually overwhelmed with confusing, difficult and seemingly (to the student) purposeless techniques. As the student progresses through the ranks, each belt often holds less and less new material to learn. Indeed, often, at the black belt level, the exams are years apart and the only new material is one or two advanced forms.

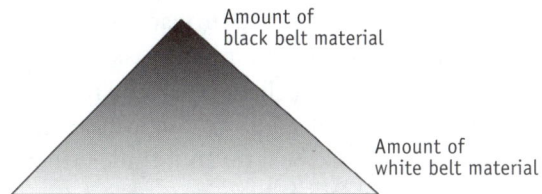

This pyramid structure illustrates the tapering off in the amount of new material taught to a student as he progresses through the ranks in a typical curriculum.

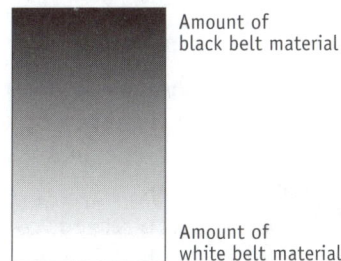

This vertical rectangle illustrates a curriculum that is more consistent through the ranks. This is less apt to overwhelm white belts and bore black belts.

Beginners can get frustrated with all the material that's demanded of them so early. Particularly when the material doesn't match up with their expectations of what they were hoping to learn. For instance, an adult who wants to learn self-defense may get frustrated and quit if class is more focused on the stances and basic classical blocks of a traditional system.

Conversely, a student who actually works his way up through the ranks to black belt may be disillusioned when, as a new black belt, most of class is spent working on under-rank material because there isn't that much left within the system or within the skill of the master instructor. The student has outpaced the program.

In this scenario, the curriculum for the system might look something like a pyramid. The base, with all the techniques, is at the bottom (white belt), while the tip has very little new material (black belt).

Solution: Schools have had great success, while maintaining the integrity of their systems, by adjusting the curriculum to more of a long, tall box that's even from top to bottom.

Regardless of what techniques are required for students to earn a black belt, they can be adjusted in the timeline from white belt to black belt, to make the curriculum more interesting and easier to learn. For instance, while the six basic blocks are required, is it important that students learn *all six* in the first month? Couldn't the blocks be spread out a little so they aren't so overwhelming?

This approach is important. You must maintain the integrity of your style, but, simultaneously, set it up so that even more people will enjoy it—and therefore won't drop out. Your program should not encourage discouragement by its design. Still, your black belts will end up with all the material, as before. The difference is you may have *more* black belts.

7) Sparring Too Much Too Soon.

Sparring is one of the biggest areas of fear and concern for the beginner. Many of our backgrounds were composed of intense sparring sessions in the blood-n-gut's tradition.

As much as we love to spar and value it as a major requirement for black belt, it has *nothing* to do with inspiring beginning students. The most effective method of introducing students to sparring is outlined in an entire chapter later in this book (*see Chapter 11: How to Teach Sparring Safely*).

But, too many beginning students, enthused and inspired about martial arts, have dropped out when they reached the belt where students begin to spar. Typically, this is within three months of joining the school. This is *way* too soon.

Most people, particularly females, are taught to *never hit someone*. The thought of actually hitting someone is against their values. This takes time to overcome without losing the student. Often, in beginning sparring classes, you'll actually see someone

tentatively punch his opponent and then apologize when it actually hits. This is a clear indication that this person is not yet ready to spar.

Most schools feel, and we agree, that sparring is essential to self-defense and earning a black belt. However, there simply *should be no rush* to get the student to this stage. By slowly introducing sparring, through a set program as described in this book, you'll have more students enjoying sparring for the rest of their life, because they didn't drop out by sparring too soon.

Sparring too soon is a leading cause of student frustration and drop-out.

The longer term your perspective in dealing with students, the better. If you can approach the process of teaching a student with the idea that, if you are able to keep them coming to class, you have three to five years to get them ready for their black belt exam. This attitude fosters a patient, long-term approach to working with students. The result is less drop outs and more people enjoying the benefits of martial arts. ■

INTRODUCTION TO PHYSIOLOGY

Despite the wide range of styles and techniques taught in the martial arts, the human body responds well only to healthy activities and responds poorly to unhealthy activities. The proper execution of flexibility exercises, calisthenics, warm-ups and cool-downs and other subjects included in this section are all universal in nature.

Virtually every martial arts class includes these components. However, the degree of proper and safe execution of these components varies drastically from school to school. The goal of this chapter is to help the martial arts instructor to learn and, in turn, follow these guidelines for properly executing these components in a consistent manner in each class.

How To Conduct A Proper Warm-Up

By Sarah Chung, M.A

How To Conduct A Proper Warm-Up

Anyone who has ever participated in physical activities class or just any type of martial arts lesson, has heard the phrase, "You've got to warm up before you exercise." But what does "warming up" mean? What types of warm-ups are best? How can you tailor a warm-up to best suit the martial art you teach? How long should a warm-up last? Is warming up really that important? Is stretching the same as warming up?

This chapter will address these questions to enable you to incorporate the best warm-up routine for your students.

What Is "Warming Up?"

Warming up is exactly that—it's the process of increasing blood flow and muscle temperature, increasing respiration and heart rate, and guarding against muscle, tendon and ligament strains. It's pos-

Traditional stance movements can be part of an effective warm-up for the knees and ankles.

sible to warm up your whole body or parts of your body. Studies have shown, however, that warming up the *whole* body, as opposed to specific parts, is the only beneficial method.

There are two ways to warm up:
1. Active Warm-Up.
2. Passive Warm-Up.

Active warm-ups are accomplished by any physical activity similar to the exercises or activity you will be performing in martial arts, involving the large muscles of the body—mainly, the arms, legs and back. Passive warm-ups, on the other hand, can be accomplished with hot baths or showers, steam rooms or saunas.

Always include a stretching program toward the end of your warm-up.

The warm-up should consist of the following, all applied with gradually increasing intensity:
1. Stretching Exercises.
2. Calisthenics.
3. Sport-Specific Activities.

Many students find it is more effective to stretch *after* warming the muscles with calisthenics or sport-specific exercise (for example, skipping with or without rope, light kicking drills, etc.).

Purpose of Warming Up

Every practice should begin with a ten to 15 minute warm up. Warming up your body before exercising produces many benefits that can help a person achieve maximum value from martial arts class, including:

1. Stimulating joint lubricants so muscles and joints are more pliable, thus lessening the risk of injury to muscles, tendons and ligaments. This derives from warming up with limbering exercises and mild static stretches. "Static" stretching uses slow, rhythmic movements to desired positions to stretch the muscles (See Chapter 6: Proper Execution of Flexibility Exercises).

2. Promoting nerve-impulse conduction for quick reaction. In the martial arts, by using exercises such as punching, blocking, kicking or attack-and-defense techniques—in which efficient speed is required—warming up will actually increase performance.

3. Gradually warming up the heart and muscles,

safely preparing them for more vigorous activity such as speed-kicks.

4. Increasing the rate of chemical reactions in the body. These reactions, in conjunction with the increased oxygen levels, further speed up the quick production of energy.

5. Raising blood flow to the muscles. Increased blood volume supplies muscles with needed oxygen and nutrients for maximum performance.

6. Psychologically preparing for further martial arts activities such as board-breaking, bag-kicking, self-defense and sparring.

You should begin each training session with a warm-up designed specifically for your martial arts class. In low-energy, high-skill martial arts such as tai-chi, the warm-up should include stretching and skill rehearsal. In high-energy martial arts such as tae kwon do, aikido, judo and karate, etc., the warm-up should raise the respiratory and heart rates and body temperature, and involve stretching and technique rehearsal.

During an adequate warm-up is also a good time for students to review and practice important psychological skills (imagery, relaxation, concentration) and to review their strategies for the oncoming workout. Meditation before the warm-up is also a good example for psychological preparation.

Stretching
(also see Chapter 6: Proper Execution of Flexibility Exercises)

The stretching part of a warm-up reduces soreness and the risk of injury and increases the range of motion (ROM) around joints. Martial arts instructors should begin the warm-up on a comfortable surface and have students slowly stretch the lower back, hamstrings, and other muscles susceptible to soreness or injury.

Do *not* use old-fashioned bobbing-and-bouncing movements to stretch (called "ballistic stretching")— they cause a reflex muscle contraction that makes stretching difficult and risks injury. Many of the torn ligaments plaguing veteran black belts and instructors today are a direct result of years of ballistic stretching.

Students should extend each stretch until they feel slight discomfort, hold the position for eight to ten counts, then relax. Another effective approach is the "contract-relax technique": students stretch, hold, and relax, then they contract the muscle for several counts and immediately stretch it again.

WARM–UP GUIDELINES

1. Warm up first, regardless of the duration of the martial arts activity.

2. A warm–up should occur from the "inside out" and have three components:

 a) cardiovascular (heart and blood vessels);

 b) stretching; and

 c) sport–specific activities.

3. Warm up 8–to–15 minutes before the main workout.

4. The amount of time spent on the warm–up will vary depending on:

 a) the fitness level of the class;

 b) age of the students;

 c) type of martial arts program (beginner, intermediate, advanced, self–defense, forms/patterns, full–contact sparring, etc);

 d) type of equipment available; and

 e) school workout–area size.

5. Warm up rhythmically prior to static stretching.

6. Proper stretching is very important in preparing for activity and should concentrate on the muscle groups you are going to use.

7. A good stretch should be felt but never hurt.

8. Include a balanced combination of cardiovascular fitness and stretching for the entire body.

9. Exercises included in the warm–up may be of lower intensity and mimic movements that may be performed later in your exercise session.

10. How you do the warm–up and the time you take is important.

Five to ten minutes of easy stretching is usually adequate.

Students should stretch any muscle that gets sore or is more easily injured when stiff and cold. Warm muscles are easier to stretch, so if you want to emphasize improved flexibility (as needed in judo, karate, tae kwon do, aikido, etc.), do additional stretching after some warm-up.

Correctly-performed, mild static stretching will increase the capacity for performing full range of movement. This allows one to exercise efficiently with less risk of injury to muscles, ligaments and tendons.

Here's how to proceed:

1. Begin a slow and easy stretch without bouncing.
2. Stretch to the point of mild tension and hold the position.
3. As the muscle relaxes, increase the stretch slightly until the point of tension is reached again.
4. If tension is painful, ease off slightly.
5. Breathing should be slow, rhythmic and controlled.
6. Proper body alignment during the stretch is necessary to prevent injury and to allow for the elongation of the muscle.
7. The student should begin a stretch by inhaling, then exhaling slowly while moving into the proper position.

The length of time that an individual stretch is held will vary according to whether or not one is stretching at the beginning of exercise, when the muscles are not thoroughly prepared, or at the end of exercise, when the muscles are warm. For warm-up, hold each stretch approximately eight to ten seconds. Once the muscles are warmed up, hold each stretch for eight to 15 seconds.

Avoid stretching muscles that are cold prior to performing preliminary limbering exercise.

Calisthenics (also see Chapter 5: Proper Execution of Calisthenics)

After stretching, move on to calisthenics—beginning with slower movements before doing vigorous ones like jumping jacks—to increase respiration, circulation and body temperature. After five minutes, the students should be warmed up enough to practice skills. Start out easy; don't begin

Light, low kicking as a warm-up.

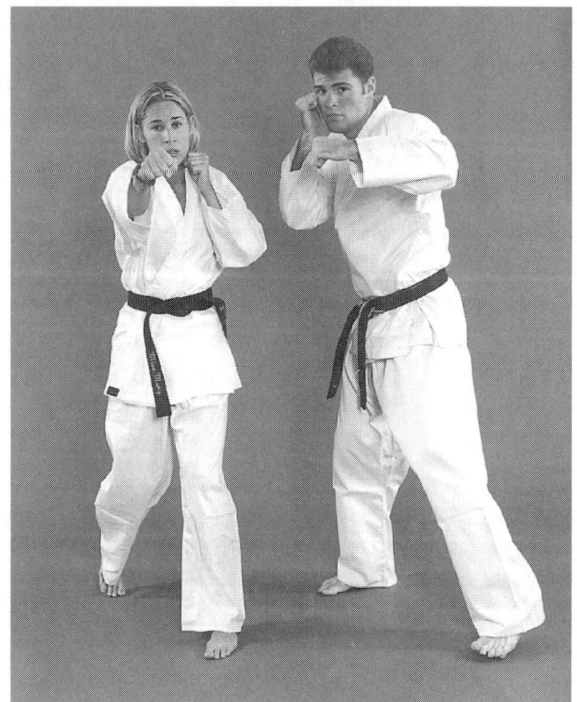

Freestyle shadow-fighting is an excellent warm-up.

contact drills or violent moves until students are well warmed up.

Use limbering exercises, which are multi-joint exercises that incorporate large muscle groups and are performed at a smooth and moderate pace. They help prepare the students' body for more vigorous exercise by increasing the range of motion of the joint and its attachments, raising muscle and body temperature, increasing circulation to the tissues surrounding the joints, and maximizing the effective function of the nerves and muscles (neuromuscular).

Limbering exercises can serve as a rehearsal of similar moves that may be performed later at a higher exercise intensity. An example of this kind of warm-up procedure could be:

(a) Walking
(b) Light jogging (regular or in place)
(c) Running back and forth, or in a circle or in rows;
(d) Light calisthenics (a few jumping jacks, squats, sit-ups, push-ups, etc.);
(e) Low-level physical-specific activity such as light punching to the air, side-stepping foot work, evasive body motions;
(f) Skipping or bouncing in place; and
(g) Full stretching.

If your students get too tired during warm-ups, have them do less strenuous warm-up exercises.

Customizing Warm-Ups

Active warm-ups can be conducted in a:
1. General Form.
2. Specific Form.
3. Combination of the Two Forms.

Limbering exercises may be categorized as either general or specific, depending on the activity.

General warm-ups are exercises that incorporate large muscles of the upper body such as the back and chest, and lower body such as hip, hamstring and calf muscles, and require working at a light pace for five to ten minutes. Such activities are walking, jogging, skipping, jumping jacks, etc. These help to gradually warm up the heart and blood vessels (cardiovascular)

system and lessen the risk for abnormal functioning of the heart such as heart attack and stroke.

A general warm-up should always be performed *prior* to stretching and resistance training.

A specific warm-up involves the same muscles you are planning to train in your exercise session. Some examples are light punching, blocking, kicking, light non-contact sparring and self-defense prior to the main workout or practice session.

There is no difference in performance for those people who practice general versus specific warm-ups. Either form, general or specific, may be performed if the purpose of a warm-up is achieved in training. Remember that certain activities require complex skills, such as, for example, a spinning hook kick, or throwing or jumping movements. Therefore, it would be better to participate in a warm-up activity specifically related to the martial arts events prior to intense training and competition for them.

Summary

Warming up is necessary for increased physiological function, preparing the body for optimal performance and lowering the risk of injury, in order to promote physical, technical and psychological readiness. Warming up should be an essential part of your overall fitness routine. ■

The Proper Execution of Calisthenics

By Sharon Spalding, M. Ed.

The Proper Execution Of Calisthenics

The martial arts participant has the ability to develop all of the components of fitness, since moderate to vigorous exercise is performed in most classes. A martial artist must concentrate on three fitness components:

1. Muscular Strength.
2. Muscular Endurance.
3. Flexibility.

Muscular strength and muscular endurance are important to withstand the resistance offered by opponents. Participants must also develop flexibility so that they can bend and twist with ease when executing martial arts movements.

Calisthenics are a series of rhythmic exercises which use the body's own weight as resistance in order to develop muscular strength, muscular endurance and flexibility. A martial arts instructor who uses safe, properly-executed calisthenics in his class will assist students in increasing their personal levels of muscular strength, muscular endurance and flexibility.

Warm-Up Phase of Class and Calisthenics

An active warm-up of jogging/running in place or footwork drills, combined with proper stretching which holds static stretches for 10-60 seconds, should precede the use of calisthenics in the martial arts class. ("Static" is a type of stretching in which the muscle to be stretched is held motionless and stretched via flexion of the opposing muscle group.) In the active warm-up and stretching phase of class, the instructor should concentrate on warming up and stretching those muscles that will be used during the class session. In most classes, the full body is involved so all major muscle groups should be properly warmed up and stretched. If, for example, a particular class will be focusing on kicks, make sure that extra attention is given to the lower body.

Once the class has completed a warm-up and stretching, calisthenics can be used to develop the fitness components of muscular strength, muscular endurance and flexibility. For students in your classes, inadequacies in these fitness components will limit their ability to perfect the martial art they are attempting to learn.

Specificity and Progressive Overload

The instructor should choose calisthenics that develop the muscles used in the martial art being practiced. In making the choice of calisthenics to be used, the instructor should ask himself what muscle group(s) is being developed with each exercise. Keep in mind that the principle of "specificity" tells us that *only* those muscles groups stressed during the exercise will become stronger.

A second principle instructors should remember is "progressive overload." Muscles become stronger as they respond to a greater workload than is usually demanded of those same muscles. With repetition of the greater workload, the muscles will adapt to the stress and become stronger. When using calisthenics, progressive overload is accomplished by increasing:

1. The intensity or difficulty of the exercise.
2. The duration of the exercise.
3. The frequency of the exercise.

Safety Issues in Calisthenics

Some calisthenics that are used in classes are unsafe or inadvisable. Yes, you may recognize some of these exercises from the list below and may have even used them yourself. Just remember that there are safe alternatives that develop the same muscle groups, but pose less of a threat to students' safety.

The following exercises should *never* be used in classes:

1. Full Squats. Those that involve deep knee bends. The knee should never be flexed beyond 90 degrees when performing the squat as a strength-building exercise. An alternative would be to use squats where the weight is in the heel, and the buttocks does not drop lower than the knees. A few cues to give students in your class would be, "Keep your weight back," "Sit back" and "Your knees should not be coming out over your toes."

2. Straight-Leg Sit-Ups. This type of sit-up places too much stress on the lower back. An alterna-

tive should be performed with the knees bent. The hands should not pull on the neck or pull the head forward, if placed behind the head. Hands placed on opposite shoulders with the arms across the chest are even better for the neck.

3. Straight-Knee Toe-Touches. Those in which one bounces to touch the floor. This also places extra stress on the lower back and, when performed ballistically (bouncing), stresses the hamstrings (the muscles in the back of the thigh).

Alternatives, if using this as a stretch, is to perform it in a sitting position; reach to the point where the stretch is felt and hold for at least 10 seconds. If used as a calisthenic (like a windmill), keep a bend in the knees and use a slow cadence.

Another safety issue when using calisthenics is that a muscle or muscle group cannot repeat an exercise if the muscle or muscle group is too weak to perform one repetition. An instructor should *not* have students with weak upper-body strength performing full-body push-ups when they cannot perform one full-body push-up correctly. This would also be the case with students who have weak abdominals and hip flexors (the muscles that help the upper body bend forward at the waist), who are instructed to perform many sit-ups and, because of their lack of strength, cannot properly perform just one sit-up.

In both of these cases, the exercise can be modified so that the student is training the desired muscle but not straining. Also, the difficulty of the exercise can be gradually increased, per the progressive-overload principle.

Let's take the push-up as an example. I'm sure that it is much easier for the instructor to demonstrate what a proper push-up looks like and have all students perform it in the same way. In reality, unless all of your students have the same upper-body-strength level and can properly execute the push-up, they will not all develop the upper-body muscles and may even injure themselves.

As an instructor, you could use a progression to help those weaker students work up to a full-body push-up without unnecessary strain and soreness.

Step #1: Wall push-ups. Have the student stand an

Starting position for push-up
(L: full push-up; R: modified push-up on knees)

arms length from the wall. While keeping the legs and back straight, the student will lean forward to touch his nose to the wall and then push back to the starting position.

Step #2. Next, use a horizontal surface to put the hands on and gradually decrease the height of the horizontal surface. Example: Push-ups using a table, then a chair, then a bench or box lower than a chair.

When doing these, it is important that the body be held straight and tight from the shoulders to the ankles, as the body is lowered and again as it is raised to the starting position.

Step #3. Next, have the student perform push-ups on the floor from the knees. Again, the student should concentrate on having a straight, tight body from shoulders to knees.

Step #4. Full-body push-ups keeping the body straight from shoulders to toes, head in line with the body, and lowering the body until the upper arms are parallel to the ground.

Of course, variations of full-body push-ups can also be used for stronger students who can perform full-body push-ups correctly and with proper form. These would include wide-arm push-ups, diamond push-ups, fingertip push-ups, and lowering the chest to the ground. But remember, students must be able to perform the basic push-up correctly before performing these variations.

The same principle applies to abdominal exercises. An instructor cannot expect all students to be able to perform bent-knee sit-ups. Other variations include:

1. Curl-ups in a bent-knee position, where the

student just curls his/her shoulders off the ground. The arms can be crossed over the chest

Contracted position for crunch sit–up or curl–up.

Contracted position for both–knee to both–elbow sit–up.

with the hands resting on the opposite shoulders. The hands can also be just touching the side of the head next to the ears.

2. Curl-ups with the lower leg resting on a chair or bench while the student lies back on the floor.
3. Full Sit-Ups. But remember, these train both the abdominals and the hip flexors. So now the instructor must incorporate progressive overload for the hip flexors.

In using progressions for calisthenics, students in a class would perform the variation that they can correctly execute. They will still develop the muscle group(s) even though they may be using a variation, but more importantly, will do it in a safe manner.

When choosing other exercises to be used as calisthenics, remember to consider which muscle you are trying to develop, and pay attention to proper body mechanics. Try to avoid exercises that exaggerate the normal curves of the spine or put undue strain on any joint, especially the knees.

POINTS TO REMEMBER ABOUT PROPER USE OF CALISTHENICS IN CLASS

1. Always have an active warm–up and a static-stretching session before moving onto calisthenics.
2. Remember the principles of specificity and progressive overload.
3. Choose safe exercises to be used as calisthenics.
4. Make sure all students are performing the exercise correctly. If they cannot, modify the exercise.
5. Lead calisthenics in a slow, controlled manner.
6. Strength gains can be realized with a low number of repetitions (15–20) when performed correctly and on a regular basis.
7. Calisthenics do not need to be performed to exhaustion; the resulting muscle soreness from this practice may turn beginners away from pursuing fitness through the martial arts.
8. As the class moves into drills for the martial art being taught, the resistance offered by opponents will also improve muscular strength and muscular endurance.

Instructors must also keep in mind that regardless of the exercise used, repetitions must be kept at a reasonable number. Properly-performed calisthenics done at a slow, controlled cadence with proper form, can develop muscular strength and endurance with as little as 15-25 repetitions. To develop the muscles used, these calisthenics should be done every other day at first.

If students are not in your class every other day, they should be encouraged to perform these at home on their own. This is even more reason for the instructor to teach proper form and cadence in the martial arts class.

Summary

When teaching a class, instructors must consider the fitness level of each individual student. Students who overtrain may become injured or ill. Developing strength through safe, properly-executed calisthenics will keep students in your classes and help produce many future martial artists. ■

The Proper Execution of Flexibility Exercises

By Tom Thompson, M.S.

Proper Execution Of Flexibility Exercises

For many years, in addition to martial artists, the subject of flexibility has been the focus of athletes, coaches, and the academic and scientific community. Research studies in the area of flexibility involve such topics as: injury avoidance, flexibility hypertrophy (increase) and atrophy (decrease), muscular fitness, and flexibility exercise.

Flexibility refers to the range of motion of a joint or a series of joints. There are three factors that influence flexibility:

1. The amount of connective tissue around the joint.
2. Structure of the joint.
3. Muscle, tendon and ligament elasticity.

Flexibility improvement is the result of an increase in the elasticity of the muscles, tendons and ligaments. There are several factors that will affect flexibility. They include:

1. Age.
2. Gender.
3. Level of physical activity.
4. Type of physical activity.

Stretching exercises can improve flexibility; however, they may *not* be effective in reducing the potential for injury from physical activity. Failure to stretch may appear to increase the potential for injury, but there is little evidence from research literature that supports this idea. Therefore, the primary purpose of stretching exercises is to achieve the goal of obtaining and/or maintaining flexibility. Children should develop flexibility in order to better maintain their flexibility as an adult.

Types of Stretching

Ballistic stretching utilizes "dynamic" movements, such as bouncing up and down, to stretch the muscles. This type of stretching is counterproductive since the muscle is forced to stretch against itself. This type of stretching can lead to injury because the elastic limits of the muscle may be exceeded. Ballistic stretching exercises are *not* recommended by the American Council on Martial Arts for flexibility development.

Some examples of ballistic stretching include any flexibility exercises that use rapid (dynamic) movement to the point of the stretch and returning rapidly (dynamic) to the point of exercise origination.

"Static" stretching uses slow, rhythmic movements to desired positions to stretch the muscles. Once the position is reached, the position is to be held between 15 and 30 seconds, then slowly released. The stretching positions should be performed only to the point of stretch.

This type of stretching exercises should not develop a feeling of pain, rather a feeling of mild discomfort. Static stretching exercises (Figs. 1-1 to 1-16) result in little or no muscle soreness, low incidence of injury, and require only a small amount of energy expenditure.

Static stretching exercises are recommended by the American Council on Martial Arts for flexibility development.

Stretching exercise programs should include warm-up/cool-down segments (see Chapters 4 and 7). The warm-up elevates the heart rate and increases circulation to the working muscles. The muscles become saturated with both blood and oxygen. This process will develop enhanced range of motion, and the muscles become prepared for the activity. The cool-down segment helps to prevent or minimize muscle tightening after the activity.

The warm-up and cool-down segments should use continuous, rhythmic movements that progress from a low to a moderate intensity level.

It's also very important to note that a warm-up should *precede* the stretching portion of the class. It is a common and dangerous mistake for instructors to begin a class of "cold" students with stretches. The muscles must be prepared prior to stretching.

Stretching Guidelines

The following guidelines for stretching exercises should be followed for safe and effective results:

- Warm-up *before* stretching for five-to-ten minutes.
- Stretch to the point of discomfort (not pain).
- Hold each stretch for 15 to 30 seconds.
- Perform stretching with slow and steady movements.
- Avoid *all* bouncing movements.
- Cool-down *after* stretching for eight to ten

minutes. (The first section of class following the stretching exercises can involve activities that permit a cool-down process.)

FACTORS LIMITING FLEXIBILITY

Flexibility is affected by the following factors:

1) Internal Factors

A) Structure of a joint (some joints simply aren't meant to be flexible).

B) The internal resistance within a joint.

C) Bony structure of a joint.

D) Muscle, tendon and ligament elasticity. (Muscle tissue that is scarred due to a previous injury is not very elastic. Ligaments do not stretch much and tendons should not stretch at all).

E) Physical impairment.

2) External Factors

A) Age (pre-adolescents are generally more flexible than adults; joint stiffness can be attributed to soft tissue changes that occur with age (Johns & Wright, 1962).

B) Gender (females are generally more flexible due to childbearing functions).

C) Level and type of physical activity (since martial arts utilizes techniques that require flexibility, the proper execution of flexibility exercises is paramount).

Flexibility Exercises

The following flexibility exercises are designed to improve and maintain flexibility in the entire body. These exercises are not martial arts-specific; however, the lower-body exercises are very beneficial for martial artists.

- **Press-Up (Cobra) (Fig. 1-1).**
  1) Lie on your stomach with hands at shoulder level in push-up position.
  2) Raise your trunk off the floor by gradually straightening your elbows.
  3) Keep your hips on the floor, and your back relaxed. Do not arch your neck backwards.

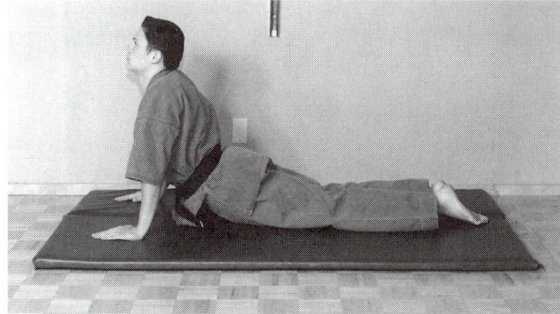

Figure 1.1

- **Mad Cat (Fig. 1-2).**
  1) Position yourself on your hands and knees.
  2) Arch your back and bend your head down as you arch.
  3) Let your back sag while bringing your head up.

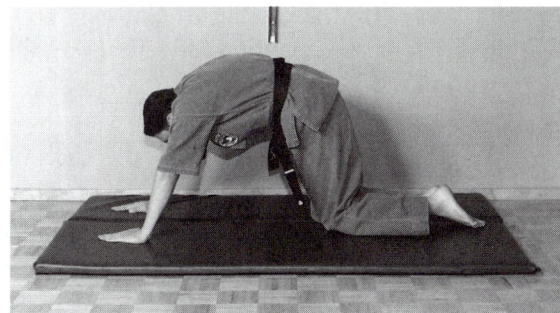

Figure 1.2

- **Iliotibial Band Stretch (Side of Thigh) (Fig. 1-3).**
  1) Lie on your back with both legs straight.
  2) Cross one leg over while keeping your knee straight.
  3) Grasp your thigh with your opposite hand and pull your leg down toward the floor until you feel a stretch on the side of your thigh.

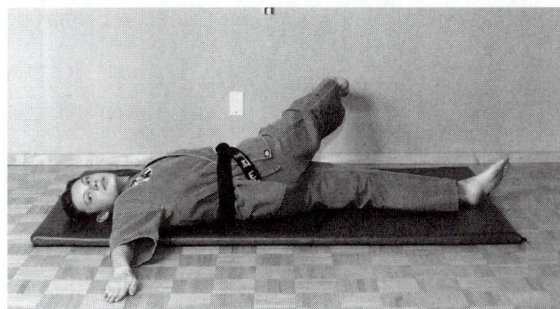

Figure 1.3

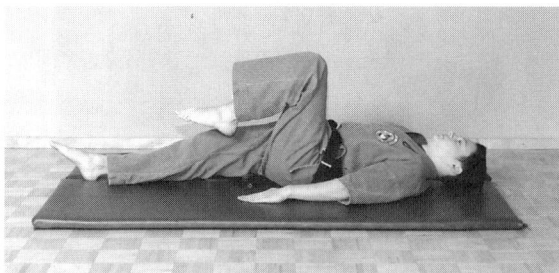

Figure 1.4

- **Knee To Chest (Fig. 1-4).**
  1) Lie on your back with one knee bent and the other leg straight.
  2) Pull the bent knee toward your chest, while keeping the other knee and your lower back pressed into the floor. (Tip: When pulling, be sure to place your hand behind the leg just above the knee of the leg with the bent knee).
  3) Return to starting position and repeat with the opposite leg.

Figure 1.5

- **Double Knee To Chest (Fig. 1-5).**
  1) Lie on your back with both knees bent.
  2) Pull both knees to your chest. (Tip: When pulling, be sure to place your hands behind the legs just above the knees).
  3) Return to starting position. This exercise may be repeated.

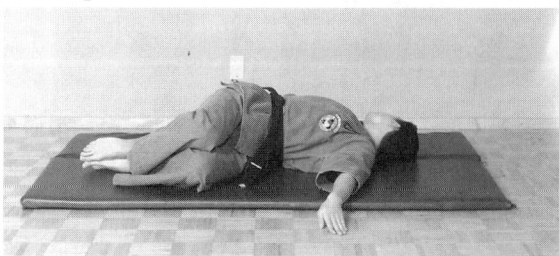

Figure 1.6a

Figure 1.6b

- **Lateral Trunk Stretch (Fig. 1-6).**
  1) Lie on your back with both knees bent.
  2) Let both knees fall to one side, while rotating your head to the opposite side.
  3) Return to the starting position and repeat to the opposite side.

Figure 1.7

- **Piriformis (Buttock) (Fig. 1-7).**
  1) Lie on your back with your knees bent. Cross your right foot over left knee.
  2) Place both hands behind your left knee and pull left knee towards the left shoulder.
  3) You should feel the stretch in the right buttock.
  4) Return to starting position and repeat to the opposite side.

Figure 1.8

- **Hamstring Stretch (Fig. 1-8).**
  1) Sit on the floor with your legs together.
  2) Bring your right foot to your left knee. Your right knee should rest on the floor.
  3) Slowly reach forward to grasp your left foot.
  4) You should feel the stretch in the left hamstring. (Tip: This exercise is suggested to replace the "Hurdler Stretch". Research indicates that the Hurdler Stretch can cause injury to the lower back).

Figure 1.9

- **Adductor stretch (Fig. 1-9).**
  1) Sit with your back straight. Bend your knees, placing the soles of your feet together.
  2) Bring your feet in towards your body. Place your hands on thighs above your knees.
  3) Push your thighs toward the floor. You should feel the stretch in the inner thigh.

Figure 1.10

- **Hip Flexor Stretch (Fig. 1-10).**
  1) Start on your hands and knees. Bring one foot forward, even with your hands.
  2) Straighten the opposite knee behind you.
  3) Lean your trunk forward as your back knee moves towards the floor until you feel a stretch in the front of your thigh.

Figure 1.11

- **Quadricep Stretch (Fig. 1-11).**
  1) Stand next to a wall or balance bar.
  2) Bend one knee as far as you can, and grasp your ankle with your hand.
  3) You should feel a stretch in the front thigh.

Figure 1.12

- **Standing Calf Stretch (Fig. 1-12).**
  1) In a standing position, lean against a support, such as a wall, with both hands.
  2) Place one foot in front of the other, keep the rear foot pointing straight ahead, heel down, and the knee straight.

3) Shift your weight forward by bending the front knee, until you feel a stretch in the calf of your back leg.

4) Repeat with the rear knee bent to stretch the lower calf.

Figure 1.13

• **Overhead Latissimus Stretch (Side of Back) (Fig. 1-13).**
1) Interlock your fingers with the palms facing up.
2) Push your hands upward above your head.

Figure 1.14

• **Posterior Shoulder Stretch (Fig. 1-14).**
1) Place one hand on top of your opposite elbow

2) Pull your elbows across your body. Repeat for opposite shoulder.

Figure 1.15

• **Prayer Stretch (Fig. 1-15).**
1) Begin on your hands and knees. Arch the back toward the ceiling and slowly sit on your heels.
2) Hold the stretch for 15 seconds.
3) Walk hands to one side for 15 seconds.
4) Walk hands to other side for 15 seconds.

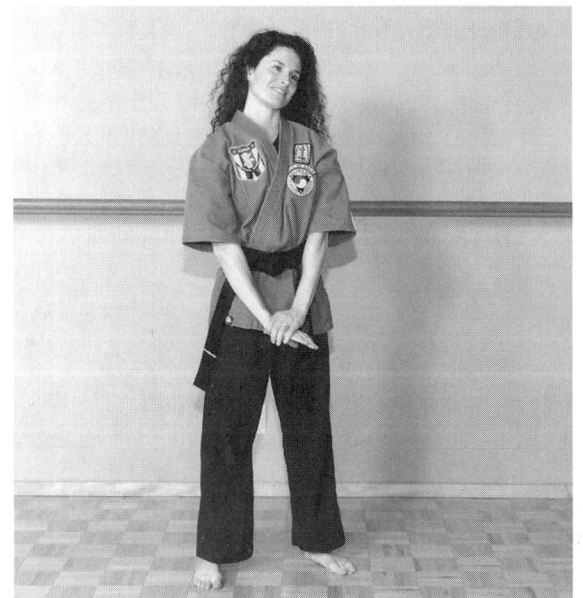

Figure 1.16

• **Neck Stretch (Fig. 1-16).**
1) Bring your ear to your shoulder.
2) Depress opposite shoulder by pulling down at wrist in front or behind trunk.
3) Return to the starting position and repeat to opposite side.

Summary

Exercises for flexibility help to develop full range of motion for a joint or series of joints while maintaining suppleness of the tendons, ligaments, and muscles. The factors that affect the flexibility of a joint are bone structure, amount of tissue at the joint, and the elasticity of the muscles, tendons and ligaments. Age, gender, and the level of physical activity will influence flexibility.

Ballistic stretching exercises may contribute to injury and are counterproductive to joint-elasticity improvement. Static stretching exercises are recommended by the American Council on Martial Arts.

Stretching exercises should not be painful. Stretching exercises should include a warm-up/cool-down segment. Stretching exercises are essential for martial arts activity. The proper execution of flexibility exercises can permit the martial artist to develop flexibility without the risk or fear of injury from them. ■

References

Anspaugh, D.J., Hamrick, M.H., Rosato, F.D., (1997). Wellness, 3rd edition, New York, Mosby.

Institute for Professional Development and LeTourneau University, (1997). Lifetime Fitness For Executives.

The Cooper Institute for Aerobics Research, (1989). Physical Fitness Specialist Course.

Johns, R.J. & Wright, V, (1962). Relative importance of various tissues in joint stiffness. Journal of Applied Physiology,17, 824-828.

How to Conduct a Proper Cool-down

By Sarah Chung, M.A.

How to Conduct a Proper Cool–Down

Just as every practice begins with a warm-up, the activity portion of practice should conclude with a cool-down. The cool-down is just as important as the warm-up. Abruptly halting vigorous activity causes pooling of the blood, sluggish circulation and slow removal of waste products. It may also contribute to cramping, soreness, or more serious problems such as fainting. A cool-down will also help to prevent muscle soreness, as it contributes to the removal of lactic acid from the muscle and will prevent blood pooling in the legs.

What Is a Cool-Down?

A cool-down should be composed of only light activity and stretching, and should take place immediately after the main martial arts workout. This kind of exercise continues the pumping action for muscles on veins, promoting both blood circulation and removal of metabolic waste (product from chemical reaction of the body, such as lactic acid).

General movement activities with a comfortable range of motion (ROM), similar to those used in the warm-up, should be used in the cool-down. Deep breathing and relaxed movements should be encouraged. The breathing rate should be back to normal by the end of the class.

Some examples of recommended cool-down exercises are:

1. Easy jogging.
2. Performing light- or slow-movement patterns for about five minutes.
3. Sit-ups.
4. Heel- and toe-raises.
5. Footwork.
6. Light air-kicking for about five minutes.
7. Full stretches.
8. Light calisthenics.

A proper cool-down should last five-to-ten minutes in a light and relaxed mood, long enough to gradually decrease the students' body temperature to normal.

Because the muscles are very warm at the beginning of the cool-down, performing stretches to improve flexibility can be very effective. Stretches can be done effectively after working specific muscle groups, after the muscle strength and endurance components of martial arts class.

However, this can often interrupt the flow of the class if the time is taken to do them thoroughly.

Stretches done in the cool-down to improve flexibility should be held for a minimum of 20 seconds and, preferably, 30 to 60 seconds. Stretching should be done on the muscles that were primarily used during the class.

Stretching will also reduce the chance of delayed muscle soreness the following day.

Slow kicking from a kneeled position is one example of a cool-down exercise. This figure illustrates the chambered kicking position followed by the extended side kick in the figure below.

Stretching is safer if it is:
1. Limited to a single muscle group.
2. Does not require flexibility in other joints.
3. Allows for intensity variations.
4. Does not require excessive balance.

The cool-down and relaxation portion of the class is intended to return the body's systems to normal. Heart rate, blood pressure and respiratory rates should decrease and body temperature should drop slightly. The exercises of the cool-down will gradually diminish the intensity of strenuous work and permit the return of both the circulation and various body functions to the pre-exercise level, especially after strenuous workouts.

An effective cool-down should also help students feel relaxed, calm and tension-free. Incorporating breathing exercises and mental-skills training into the martial arts program is a way to improve the overall well-being of the students. Regardless of the techniques used in the cool-down component, relaxation (reduction of muscular tension) enhances

COOL–DOWN GUIDELINES

1. Cool-down is always done at the end of the class.
2. The cool down should last from 10 - 15 minutes.
3. The amount of time spent on cool-down will vary depending on the:
   a. Fitness level of the class.
   b. Age of the students.
   c. Type of martial arts program (beginner, intermediate, advanced, self-defense, patterns, full-contact sparring, etc.).
   d. Type of equipment available.
   e. Facility size.
4. The needs and goals of the students will also dictate the emphasis placed on the cool-down.
5. A lesson plan is very helpful.
6. It is important to plan in advance and practice the cool–down techniqes and routines beforehand.

the outcome of the effort. A participant can use physical and psychological techniques to relax overall, or to relax specific muscle groups during the cool-down.

Some martial arts instructors use techniques to encourage relaxation before actually performing stretching exercises and controlled breathing during stretching. Several techniques physically reduce tension in a muscle, thereby enhancing relaxation.

Psychological relaxation techniques, such as "mind-over-body" techniques to control muscle tension, combined with efforts to create an environment more conducive to whole-body relaxation, have also been used to improve flexibility. Controlled breathing may facilitate relaxation and stretching, especially if it is combined with imagery. Imagery should involve the desired outcome—in the case of cool-down stretching and relaxation, lengthening of connective tissue in the muscles, and students' satisfaction as well as self-confidence.

Controlled breathing can also help prevent breath-holding, which may cause immediate problems for people with circulatory disorders. Encourage exhalation during a stretch of short duration or instruct the students to breathe normally during a longer stretch. To prevent hyperventilation, the period of exhalation should be longer than the period of inhalation.

Mental-skills training at the end of the class, such as meditation, yoga and positive affirmation, are recommended to enhance performance. As a result, a lesson plan is a must. ■

MODIFICATIONS

To meet the challenge of providing a workout for students with a variety of abilities, fitness levels and goals, instructors should develop basic routines and modifications to meet diverse needs. Exercise modifications are guided by three important questions:

1) Are the movements safe?
2) Will the modifications be effective for delivering an appropriate training effect?
3) Are the modifications appropriate given the person's abilities, level of conditioning, and movement characteristics?

Understanding General Adaptation Syndrome*

By Willy Pieter, Ph.D.

Understanding General Adaptation Syndrome

Introduction

Preparing martial arts students for improved performance requires systematic and methodical planning of their training. Training may be defined as "a process of stimuli that is goal-oriented and planned to enhance athletic performance." Although various stimuli may be distinguished, such as the psychological and technical, the emphasis in this chapter will be on the physical; for example, those that will bring about changes in physical appearance and in the efficiency of the muscles (strength) as well as the lungs and heart (endurance). In other words, from a physical/physiological perspective, training will affect the athlete's physique (less fat, more muscles), the athlete's bodily functions (more endurance, lower resting heart rate), and the athlete's flexibility.

In order to optimize the martial artist's training, the instructor needs to know how to physically stress the student in such a way that his health is not jeopardized. The instructor needs to know how to manipulate work and rest periods to enhance the student's adaptation to training, which is called the "training effect."

For instance, running will improve the student's endurance, while strength training will improve his strength. Kicking and punching will likewise improve the speed and force of the kicks and the punches. These improvements are called "training effects." A training effect is what you get when you practice. Whenever you work out, you'll get an effect. To continue this effect and to improve on it, you need to apply the next load after the student has recovered from the present workout.

If one stops kicking or punching, so-called "detraining effects" will occur. In other words, when one stops training, the gains in performance will be lost. This is called "detraining effects." However, before detailing how to improve performance and how to avoid detraining effects from occurring, the General Adaptation Syndrome (GAS) concept needs to be addressed.

GAS is a model to explain the reactions that people display as a result of long-term stress, although it can also be shown as a result of short-term stress. Stress can be defined as "the response of the body to any demand placed upon it." In martial arts training, this demand is of both a physiological as well as psychological nature.

For instance, after a particularly hard training session, the student or athlete will feel tired. The training is the demand placed upon the body, which resulted in the athlete's being tired (the short-term response).

From a psychological point of view, the student will have to motivate himself to continue until the end of the training session, which is also a form of stress. The longer the student is engaged in systematic training, the more physiological and psychological stress he or she will endure. If this is not carefully monitored, staleness or burnout will result.

The student's response to fatigue can be considered the first phase of the GAS; for example, the alarm stage, or "fight or flight" reaction. The student can decide to stop for awhile to catch his breath (flight), or to continue with the training until the end of the session (fight). The more often the student shows the fight reaction, the sooner the body will adapt to the training stress, in which case he has entered the so-called "resistance phase." The student or athlete will not get as tired anymore after the same kind of workout and will be able to withstand an even higher level of training stress.

Another example of this stage can be seen when strength training. A martial arts student involved in the beginning of a strength program may have a problem lifting 60 pounds, but after a week or two, this weight will be lifted more easily. It may even be possible for the weight to be increased by five pounds, for instance, which is a higher level of stress. By the same token, in martial arts training the student may only be able to execute five or six kicks or throws with full speed and power before getting tired. After a week's training, however, he will be able to perform 10 or 12 of these techniques.

Although the student will show an increasing ability to "resist" higher levels of stress as a result of his body's adaptation in the resistance stage, there will come a time that his energy levels will be depleted, which is aptly called the "exhaustion phase." Any new stress placed upon the student, however light, will result in an excessive and strong resistance. If no adequate measures are taken, the student or athlete will not only show a decrease in performance, but may drop out of martial arts training.

In the remainder of this chapter, the three stages of GAS will be illustrated in relation to training effect and recovery from training.

THE THREE STAGES OF THE GENERAL ADAPTATION SYNDROME

The General Adaptation Syndrome has three distinct stages, which define a martial arts student's response to training:
1. Alarm Phase/Fight or Flight Reaction.
2. Resistance Phase.
3. Exhaustion Phase.

Training Principles

To aid the instructor with a more systematic approach to training, certain training principles need to be adhered to. These principles are:
1. Specificity.
2. Overload.
3. Progressive Application.

The principle of "specificity" of training dictates that the instructor overload the training components that are most important to the martial arts involved. For instance, when developing endurance in martial arts, in most cases the workouts should be geared toward overloading both aerobic and anaerobic endurance. On the other hand, there are also martial arts for which the aerobic system is more important.

Aerobic endurance refers to that type of endurance for which a (large) contribution of oxygen is needed, such as in distance running. In the martial arts, this is typically seen in forms or in martial arts training in general, for instance, but it also plays a role in competition in between bursts of attack or defense, which in turn are examples of activities for which anaerobic endurance is necessary.

Anaerobic is the type of endurance for which there is *no* major contribution of oxygen needed. As a result, anaerobic endurance is characterized by brief periods of activity, as opposed to aerobic endurance, which may last for hours.

Training overload is accomplished by:

1. Frequency.
2. Duration.
3. Intensity.
4. Mode of training.

"Overload" involves volume ("frequency" and "duration") and "intensity" of the training stimuli to bring about physiological adaptations. "Volume" of training refers to the *amount* of training. For instance, the total number of miles covered running in a week to train aerobic endurance. In martial arts, the total number of kicks, punches or throws could be recorded and added to represent the volume of martial arts training.

"Frequency," "duration" and "intensity" will be dealt with below.

"Overloading" should be done in a progressive manner that is gradual and discontinuous in nature. This implies that periods of high-intensity training should be interspersed with recovery periods of decreased volume and intensity, because it is during this time that adaptation occurs. This adaptation is called the "training effect," that is, the effect that the training has on one's body so that more training of a higher intensity can be endured.

For instance, a training effect has occurred if a student does not get out of breath anymore ("alarm stage" of the GAS) after executing one complete martial arts form, and instead can do the same form twice or even three times without becoming tired. That student has adapted to the stress and can now move on to the next level and a higher form of training intensity ("resistance phase" of GAS).

Overloading means that the training load should be increased to meet the new training status of the athlete. For instance, during strength training, suppose the martial arts student is able to bench press 60 pounds. After one or two weeks, a training effect will occur in that he will have gained strength. In order to accommodate for this strength gain, the load should be increased by ten pounds, for example, given the same number of repetitions.

So, if the object is to *gain* in strength, the system (for example, the muscles) has to be overloaded. If the object is to *maintain* strength levels, no overload is necessary.

Overloading applies to any of the physiological or psychological aspects trained:

1. Strength.
2. Endurance.
3. Speed.
4. Concentration.

For instance, in terms of speed, one could record the number of punches thrown in ten seconds. After a week, one could try to improve on that by doing one extra punch within those ten seconds.

Progressive overload that is discontinuous in nature has to do with alternating work and rest periods. The training load, which should increase progressively, is applied during the work periods, whereas the training effects take place during the rest periods. If the interplay between work and recovery periods is not carefully planned, the athlete will become overstressed, which will eventually lead to a decrease in performance and even health problems.

Both the work and rest periods may be manipulated by alternating heavy and light workouts and by short or long periods of rest. However, the recovery periods should not be too long, since any training effects may disappear that way. Fig. 13.1 shows the relationship between training or workload and recovery.

A certain workload will temporarily lead to fatigue (see Fig. 13.1), which, in turn, will have a negative effect on performance; meaning, performance will decline. This is the alarm stage of GAS. After that, recovery will set in and lead to a higher performance level than before, which is the training effect. The recovery is the resistance stage of GAS.

The new training load should be applied during the time the training effect occurs and preferably at the highest point of this effect. However, determining this highest point is not easy. It depends on the training status of the student and the experience and knowledge of the instructor/coach. If no training stimulus is applied, performance will deteriorate until it reaches the level *before* training started (see also Recovery and Detraining Effects subheading later).

There is no clear example of the third GAS stage in this case. The exhaustion stage will be more clearly seen later (see Fig. 13.4 under Recovery and Detraining Effects).

"Frequency" of training refers to how often the martial arts student trains. It is usually expressed in terms of number of days per week. A minimum requirement to get a training effect is to practice three days a week. If the frequency is reduced to two days per week, for instance, it will take longer to produce a training effect.

For elite athletes, this minimum requirement is not sufficient anymore, unless it is used to recuperate from very intensive workloads. For an elite martial arts athlete, frequency may involve four to six days of training per week.

"Duration" of training refers to the duration of a single training session, but also to series of training sessions. For instance, a typical martial arts training session may last for two hours, while running to improve aerobic endurance in martial arts may have a duration of 30 minutes.

"Intensity" refers to how "heavy" a training session is. Depending on the exercise, intensity may be expressed as heart beats per minute (bpm) or as a certain resistance to move, such as in strength training. Intensity may also reflect the number of repetitions a weight is lifted, or the number of laps run, or the number of repetitions to run a specified distance, such as ten times the 100-meter dash, or the time exercised.

In martial arts training, heart beats per minute may be used as an indication of intensity, such as

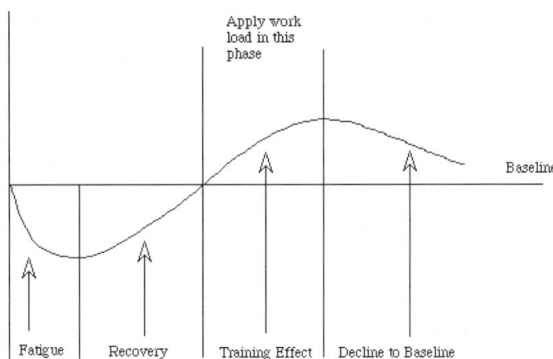

Figure 13.1

when executing a form. Alternatively, one could choose the number of times the students will have to perform certain techniques before a break is allowed. To increase the intensity, the instructor could shorten the break period. To decrease the intensity, the break could be lengthened, or the number of techniques executed could be decreased.

When using heart rates to represent training intensity, the so-called "Karvonen formula" is typically employed. This formula requires the athlete or coach to assess the athlete's resting heart rate and his maximal heart rate (max HR) in beats per minute (bpm). Maximal heart rate may be found by subtracting one's age from 220. The Karvonen formula is as follows: HRex = HRrest + % (HRmax - Hrrest) where HRex = exercise heart rate and HRrest = heart rate at rest.

Heart rate at rest may be taken before training by having the athlete lie down in a supine position for about ten minutes after which the heart rate is taken. It may also be taken in the morning before getting out of bed, in which case it is sometimes called the morning heart rate or the morning pulse. Applying this formula to martial arts training would give the following exercise heart rate for a 20-year-old student with a resting heart rate of 60 bpm, a maximum HR of 200 (= 220 - 20) and training at 80% of max HR: HRex = 60 + 0.80 (200 - 60) = 172 bpm.

"Mode" of training is simply the exercise employed to bring about any training effects. For instance, to improve aerobic endurance, running, swimming or bicycling may be used as the mode of training. To improve kicking force, martial arts will be the mode of training, while improvements in strength may be done by engaging in a strength-training program, or one could use a heavy bag in martial arts, which is a form of martial arts-specific strength-training.

Although training has to be progressive in order to result in any training effects, there will come a time that improvements will start to show a leveling-off (the law of diminishing returns), preceded by smaller increments of improvement compared to the beginning of training (see Fig. 13.2). In other words, the longer the student is in training, the more difficult it will be to improve performance. As can be seen from Fig. 13.2, over the same amount of time (Period 1 and Period 2), less training effect has resulted from training during Period 2 compared to Period 1. The instructor or coach will have to be very creative in manipulating the training stimuli and training principles that will lead to the desired training effects.

A strength program using different machines (free weights, nautilus, etc.), and endurance training on a different surface (for instance, instead of running on a track, running on the beach) are two examples of how this may be done. Working out with other martial arts instructors, coaches or students/athletes, from the same or a different style, may also be considered. Another example would be to kick with one's boots on while training outdoors, or to punch while holding an elastic surgical tube in one's fists.

TRAINING PRINCIPLES

To aid the martial arts instructor with a more systematic approach to training, certain established training principles need to be adhered to. They are:
1. Specificity.
2. Overload.
    a. Frequency.
    b. Duration.
    c. Intensity.
    d. Mode of Training.
3. Progressive Application.

Recovery and Detraining Effects: Recovery

As cited above, the main goal or purpose of training

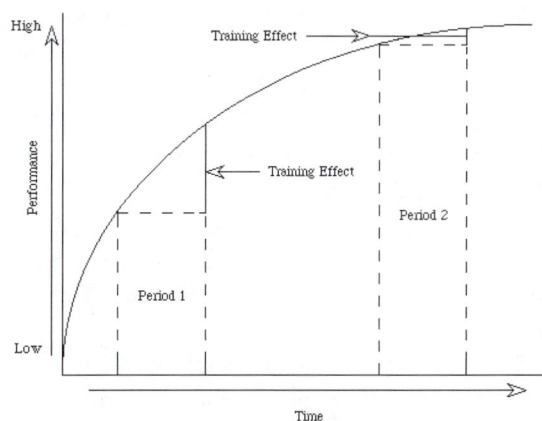

Figure 13.2

is to improve the student's or athlete's performance. The aforementioned principles of training are based on the knowledge that the human body adapts itself to the situation it is subjected to (GAS or General Adaptation Syndrome). In order to achieve a training effect, the student or athlete surrenders his body to ever greater demands.

The link between training and recovery periods, and the importance of adequate rest, are illustrated in Figs. 13.3-13.5.

In Fig. 13.3, the workload is applied after the training effect is on the decline, which will result in a performance level that will be an extension

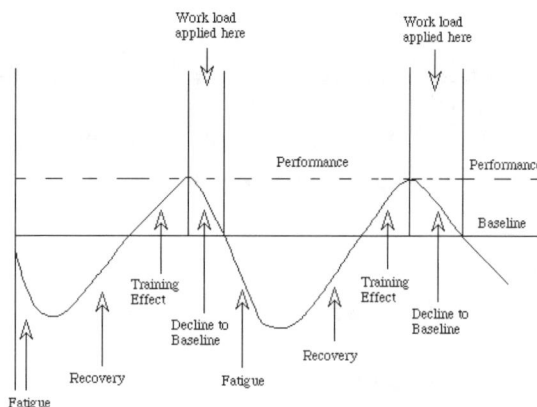

Figure 13.3

of the previous level; that is, the training load did not have any training effect whatsoever. Instead, the next training load needs to be applied during the period of the training effect. If it is applied after that, it will *not* lead to any increased performance.

For instance, if the martial arts student works out on Monday and the next training session is not until Friday, any training effect that may have occurred will be on the decline. Similarly, if the martial arts instructor waits too long to continue kicking drills during a workout, the work load would then have been applied after the training effect was on the decline.

Fig. 13.4 shows the vital importance of adequate rest. If the stimulus is applied before the body is fully recovered from the previous training load, the result

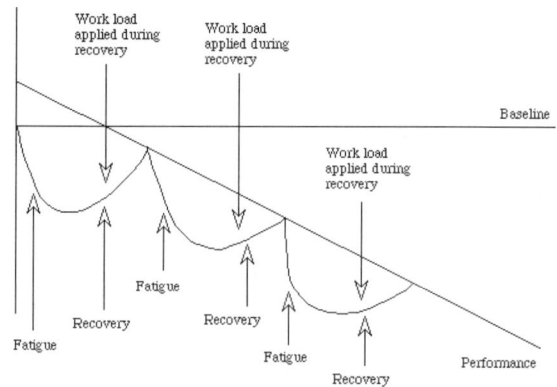

Figure 13.4

will be a decrease in performance. No training effect will occur.

For instance, if a student is showing obvious signs of fatigue and the instructor still insists on having him do all-out kicking drills or full-power forms, the training load will defeat its purpose. The student is tired and therefore in the alarm phase of the General Adaptation Syndrome and, as mentioned above, added stress will lead to a decline in performance.

If the workload is systematically applied before adequate rest, the result will be a burnt-out student or athlete, who will not only experience a decrease in performance, but who will also have a higher chance of getting injured, which, in turn, will interfere with his training. This is a vicious circle that can only be broken by forced rest.

The decline in performance is typical of the third stage of GAS, the exhaustion phase. The cumulative effect of the training stress, applied at the wrong time, for example, before the student or athlete was fully recovered from the previous training load (stress), eventually led to the exhaustion stage (long-term response to stress).

Fig. 13.5, finally, displays the adequate connection between training load and recovery that will lead to increased performance. The training effects will get a chance to be cumulative after the appropriate timing of the training stimuli. The workload may also be increased to lead to the desired effects, which could not be done in the previous two cases.

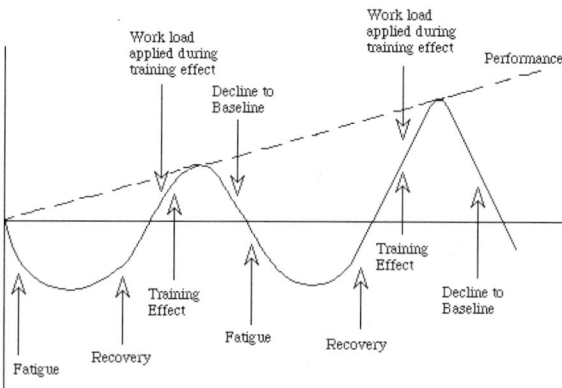

Figure 13.5

Unfortunately, it is not possible to indicate the precise duration of the rest or recovery periods. First of all, the recovery depends on the preceding training stimulus. A strenuous workout will need a longer recovery than a training load that was done at a low intensity. For instance, after a forms workout at 60% of maximum heart rate (HR), a relatively short recovery period will suffice. After an intensive anaerobic workout at 95-100% of maximum HR, however, such as kicking and punching the heavy bag for two or three minutes continuously, a much longer recovery will be needed. Of course, the training status of the student or athlete also plays a role. The better trained the student is, the longer it will take for him to get tired.

Secondly, the recovery period depends on the athlete's ability to recuperate. If he is still fatigued from the preceding training load, regardless of its intensity, a longer recovery may be in order.

Thirdly, job- and study-related stress may influence the recovery periods as well. Personal factors and sickness also exert their own specific impact on the recovery process of the student or athlete.

A rule of thumb is to advise both the student and instructor to listen to the former's body. If the student or athlete does not feel 100 percent, a decreased training load should be applied.

Another preventive measure is to alternate heavy and light workouts. Heavy and lighter workloads can also be used during any single training session. For instance, one could choose to alternate the exercise heart rate between 65% and 90% of max HR during a two-hour training session, instead of keeping it at 90% of max HR throughout.

To summarize, there is a delicate balance between work and rest in the athlete's training. It should be remembered that it is during the recovery period that any training effect will occur. If the workload is applied after the training effect has disappeared, the resultant improvement in performance will be destroyed. If the training stimulus is applied before the athlete has had a chance to recover from an (intensive) workout, performance will decrease.

Alternating heavy and lighter workouts may be employed to ensure an effective balance between training load and recovery. Depending on the training objective, full or partial recovery periods may be utilized.

Detraining Effects on Students and Athletes

Although an interval of rest is advised for competitive martial arts athletes prior to competition, the so-called taper-off period, this time-off from training, if continued indefinitely, will eventually lead to so-called "detraining effects"; that is, any effects of training will disappear. In fact, if martial artists do not engage in *any* form of training at all, their health may be severely compromised.

The effects of detraining on a short-term basis, such as in a taper-off, however, are less severe than one would tend to think. In fact, research has shown that swimmers experienced an improvement in performance after reduced training as well as an increase in muscular strength. Of course, this does not necessarily imply that the same effects will also be observed to the same extent in athletes from other sports or in the martial arts.

Short-term inactivity showed no significant effects on loss of muscular strength up to four weeks after cessation of training. Reduced training does not seem to have any major effects on anaerobic endurance either, although complete inactivity, such as immobilization (for example, the wearing of a total body cast) may affect this type of endurance within the first two weeks. Since the taper-off period for martial arts athletes is not characterized by complete inactivity, this finding is not relevant for martial arts coaches.

Speed and agility are less affected by training than strength, for instance. Therefore, potential losses in speed and agility during the taper-off period will be even less than for strength or anaerobic endurance. Flexibility, however, should be maintained year-round, since it is lost as well as gained rather quickly. It should come as no surprise, then, that flexibility is maintained throughout the taper-off period.

Aerobic endurance will deteriorate faster than any of the other training factors, even within some three weeks after bed rest. Any decrease in aerobic endurance during the taper-off period will be negligible, though, since the taper will consist of reduced training and only a few days of no training, which are not exactly similar to three weeks of bed rest.

The longer the student has been in training, the longer it will take to lose the gains from systematic training.

Detraining Effects on Martial Arts Instructors

One of the unfortunate characteristics of many veteran martial arts instructors is long-term detraining as a result of the GAS. This can often be recognized in instructors with excessive fat and a generally unhealthy appearance, even though they are active with their classes. These instructors continue to perform the same routines with classes year after year. They perform techniques, walk through forms and do light sparring with their students.

All of these activities are done at low levels of intensity. This is a classic example of the GAS at work. The instructor's body has long since adapted to the stress of these techniques. As a result, the positive physical benefits are greatly diminished for him.

It is highly recommended that martial arts instructors vary their workouts and class-training participation in order to continually take the body through alarm, resistance and, most of all, exhaustion, so they can continue to enjoy the benefits of martial arts training.

Contrary to the aforementioned short-term periods of relative inactivity, however, those that are more long-term will not only have adverse effects on one's martial arts skills, strength, endurance or flexibility level, but may also lead to undesirable health effects. One of the major health risks that is associated with long-term inactivity is the accumulation of fat. Fat deposited in the abdominal area has been found to be particularly detrimental.

Carrying an excess of body fat is called "being obese." Scientific research has revealed that obesity is associated with such conditions as heart disease, hypertension, diabetes, and stroke. In fact, it has been suggested that functional losses as a result of long-term inactivity resemble those found in elderly people! By the same token, elderly people who have stayed physically active, have been shown to have physical and physiological characteristics of those 15 to 25 years younger.

In addition to the health risks of carrying an excess of body fat, martial arts instructors/coaches are typically considered role models for their students and athletes, especially the children and youth among them. Being a role model includes setting an example as a proponent of a healthy lifestyle.

Ways to Help Offset Long-Term Detraining Effects

It is realized that it is not easy to reverse losses in endurance, strength, and so on. To change one's lifestyle does not happen overnight! An integrated program of physical exercise, nutritional considerations and behavioral change seems to be most effective.

For instance, one could choose to start working out again for two or three days a week. After five or six weeks, this could be increased by one day, and so on, until one is active for six or seven days a week. Exercises to improve, and later maintain, flexibility should always be included in the program, as this training factor is lost rather rapidly as cited above.

One way of starting to exercise again, for instance, is to do forms, although forms training can always be part of one's daily routine. Whatever the exercise, it should definitely include aerobic activities, hence the suggestion to do forms, for aerobic work has been shown to help reduce the aforementioned negative health outcomes. The intensity of the workouts could start at 40-50% of max HR, which can be increased as one's endurance level improves.

It is certainly not necessary to adopt the same training regimen as a competitive martial artist. It is more important to stay active. After all, one does not work out to prepare for any competitions, but to beat physical inactivity that has been linked to adverse health effects.

A restricted caloric intake could supplement one's physical training. Avoid the use of tobacco, alcohol and drugs, which are considered to be destructive habits. Instead of eating ice cream for dessert, for instance, one could choose to have fruits. Avoid excess (saturated) fat in one's diet, as this has been associated with an increased health risk. Choose a diet that is low in cholesterol, moderate in sugars and salt, with plenty of grain products, vegetables and fruits.

If one is in doubt about what to eat, consult a registered dietitian, preferably one who is familiar with the dietary habits of one's culture. For instance, Filipinos have a different diet than Germans, so if one has, say, a German diet, consulting a dietitian familiar with this diet would be an advantage.

Behavioral changes start with knowledge of the health-risk factors. Read articles, journals and/or books on the topic or talk to people with the appropriate background. Have confidence that one will succeed in bringing about the changes that will lead to a healthy lifestyle. One way to build one's confidence is to set short-term, realistic and attainable goals. These goals should be considered as guidelines and should be modified as one's situation changes.

For instance, with an improvement in one's endurance level, it will be possible to increase the intensity of one's training session, which will require a set of different goals. Confidence and adherence to the training program are enhanced by realizing that gradual improvement is an accomplishment in itself. Do not compare yourself to others. Everybody progresses at his or her own pace.

It is suggested to include breathing exercises such as meditation in one's martial arts training program to offset detraining effects and to facilitate adherence, self-confidence, motivation, enjoyment, variety and relaxation. Proper breathing also reduces one's stress levels. Excess stress has been found to be a health hazard, for it predisposes the individual to ulcers, hypertension, heart disease, depression, headaches and other health disorders.

In terms of the General Adaptation Syndrome (GAS), long-term detraining effects will lead to a severe decrease in even baseline performance. Similar to the exhaustion phase of the GAS, which is characterized by a decrease in performance (see Fig. 13.4), a lack of training stimuli will also lead to a decline in performance. So much so, that one's health may be jeopardized.

In other words, the martial artist needs to be subjected to adequate training stress. For the martial arts student or athlete, this means training stimuli that will gradually lead to improved performance without burnout; while for the martial arts instructor/coach, this means a training load that will ensure the maintenance of his health. ∎

This chapter is partially based on Systematic training in taekwondo, in Pieter, W. and Heijmans, J. (1997), Scientific Coaching for Olympic Taekwondo, Aachen: Meyer & Meyer.

How To Teach Kicking Safely

By Tim Niiler, M.S.

How To Teach Kicking Safely

As I was first learning the martial arts (in my case, Shaolin kung-fu), a great emphasis was placed on kicking skill almost from the beginning. In addition to the essential types of kicks such as the front, crescent and side, I was taught many jumps, spins and sweeps as part of my basic training. If you can remember how hard it was just to perfect your side kick, you will realize just how difficult learning all of this simultaneously was, from both a mental and physical standpoint. It is no small wonder that I have been dealing with knee problems for most of my martial arts career.

Since learning a large number of kicks was deemed to be essential, so was flexibility training. It is not with fondness that I recall the forceful stretching, often using ropes to gain leverage, which was required to condition me so that I could kick higher in all directions.

Such drills left me in a condition where I could scarcely limp home on an almost daily basis. Alas that my teacher at the time was only a great fighter and not a skilled trainer. He only wanted the best for me.

Although I would like to say that such extreme methods have been left in my past, I still see equally primitive methods of helping students improve their kicking being propagated today. Many students use stretching devices without a true understanding of what they are doing or how they are doing it. Likewise, many instructors are teaching the unsound methods of old when "no pain-no gain" was the slogan. Although practice will often force us to endure discomfort, my counter to the first slogan is that "perfect practice makes perfect." I can think of many ways to create pain without gaining from it.

Kicking is often especially difficult to learn without pain or even injury, although it does not need to be. Kicking is found in most martial systems and can be very effective as a weapon when utilized properly. It is also something which causes many beginners great anxiety as they rightly perceive it to require flexibility of a sort which is not common among non-martial artists. Beginners are equally anxious due to the need to balance on one leg while kicking with the other.

So kicking requires the learning of new mechanics, as punching or blocking does, but it requires physical conditioning and balance training as well. It is these latter factors which result in most beginners' ability to master the techniques of the upper body more quickly.

This chapter will focus on the issues surrounding kicking safety. Motivation for this will come from a discussion of kicking-related injuries. Injuries inflicted by kickers will not be discussed here, since this is a subject beyond the scope of this chapter. Modes of training beginner and advanced students will be outlined with specific examples from training programs. Lastly, I will discuss teaching the more difficult spinning and jumping kicks and factors which are important to understand.

Kicking Injuries

I am constantly amazed at all the ways in which people discover how to hurt themselves. Kicking is one of those activities which, with respect to this, the sky is the limit. Kicking may involve just about any muscle of the leg, and as such, injuries may occur just about anywhere.

Several very comprehensive surveys of injuries in the martial arts have been conducted (Birrer and Halbrook, 1988; Birrer & Birrer, 1982; Birrer & Birrer, 1981; Birrer, et al., 1981; Kurland, 1980). Unfortunately, this data has not been broken down by the specific activity which caused the injury. Rather, the favorable manner of reporting seems to be by category (sparring vs. solo practice), injury site (ankle, knee, hip) and type of injury (sprain, strain, break, etc.).

Thus, we generally do not know the reason for the occurrence of self-inflicted injuries in the martial arts due to kicking. Nearly all studies to date have focused on injuries due to sparring and not from other causes. It is also thought that of the injuries obtained in solo practice, the majority of them are strains and sprains (Kurland, 1980). Other types of injury from solo practice include bursitis, tendonitis, and fatigue fractures (Birrer & Birrer, 1981; Birrer, et al., 1981; Kurland, 1980).

With regard to kicking, injuries may occur due to three general factors:

1. Body alignment.

2. Under-conditioning.

3. Over-training.

Other more commonly identified causes, such as improper warm-up or excessive power, have been classified under the above categories. Each category and the more common injuries are related below.

Unfavorable body alignment usually creates injuries in conjunction with excessive or repeated loading of a joint. ("Loading" is the application of force to a body part. Loading of joints occurs every time you throw a kick or even when you take a walk.) This happens because the joint in question cannot properly handle loading due to awkward positioning.

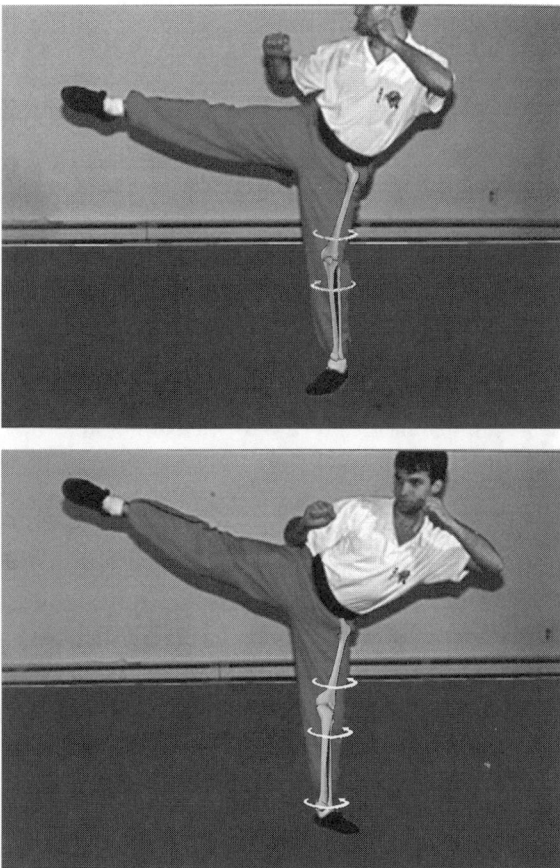

Figure 1. The rotational motion of the upper body can cause tremendous stress of the knee joint when the support foot is not rotated properly. TOP: Improper rotation leads to excessive rotation of the femur (thigh bone) on the anchored tibia (shank bone). BOTTOM: Proper placement of the foot eliminates this problem and allows the leg to rotate as one unit.

Examples of bad alignment range from locking out joints during kicking to a poorly-positioned support foot in a kick which requires rotational motion.

The second case is worth additional discussion. When the support foot is not rotated with the body in certain types of kicks (crescent, roundhouse and side, for example), this can force the large bone of the leg, the femur, to rotate with respect to the tibia (Fig. 1). Such a rotation creates large rotational forces within the joint capsule of the knee. Resulting injuries can be as severe as a ruptured anterior cruciate ligament. The anterior cruciate ligament is the ligament in the knee which prevents the tibia from moving forward with respect to the femur at the knee. (See Fig. 2: Cutaway of knee.)

Another common case of bad alignment occurs when the hip is flexed and internally rotated (Fig. 3). This type of alignment can lead to strains of the hip flexors and abductors and in some cases has been responsible for ilio-tibial band syndrome (Fig. 4).

Under-conditioning is another common cause for injury. Typically, injury will occur when a martial

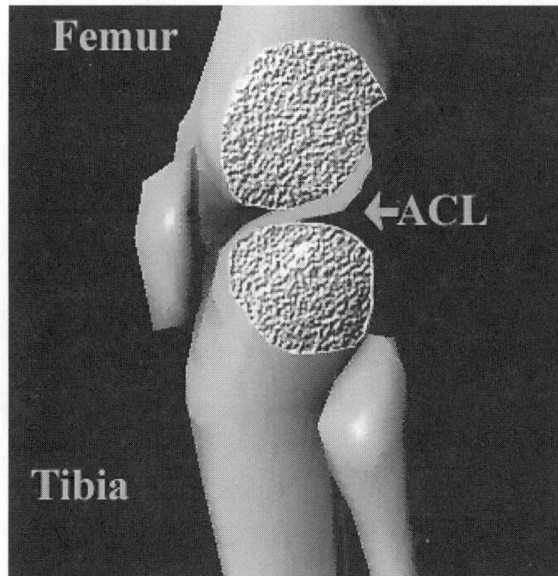

Figure 2. Cut-away of knee showing the Anterior Cruciate Ligament (ACL). The ACL is the ligament in the knee which prevents the tibia from moving forward with respect to the femur at the knee.

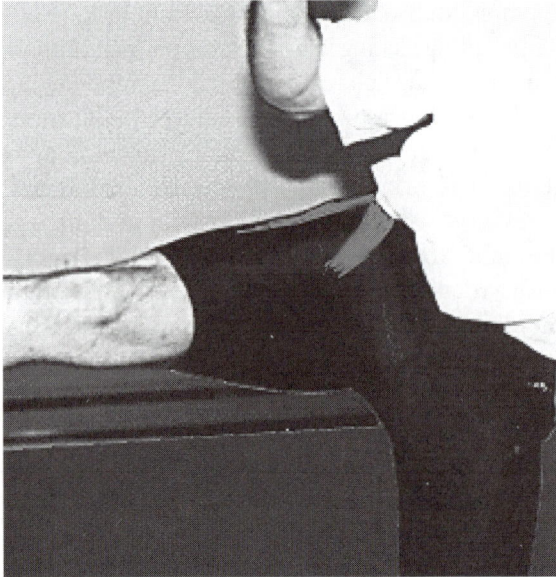

Figure 3: Stress is on hip flexors and abductors when leg is flexed and internally rotated. Repetitive snapping motions which put the leg in this position can lead to a popping in the hip and pain in the hip area.

Figure 4: The ilio-tibial band is located along the outside portion of the thigh. When repeatedly tightened without proper stretching, this can become inflamed and create pain anywhere from the knee to the crest of the hip.

Figure 5: Example of the normal range of motion (ROM) of the knee. LEFT: the fully flexed position and RIGHT: the fully extended position

artist attempts a technique which his body has not been trained to tolerate. A prime example of injury in this category is a range of motion (ROM) related injury (Birrer & Birrer, 1981). ROM is defined as the comfortable range through which the muscles may move a joint (Fig. 5). When the ROM is exceeded, the associated muscles may be strained. At worst, a tear in the muscle or its tendon may result. ROM injuries are most often encountered due to inadequate warm-up. Warm-ups, when done properly, increase ROM. Martial artists who are injured in this manner classically try to kick full range of motion and full speed before warming-up.

Another type of injury due to under-conditioning relates to direct loading of tissue. A simple example of this is the person who can only bench press 100 pounds trying to press 300. It is obvious he will be injured. In the context of the martial arts, such an injury often occurs in jump kicks.

Recently, one of my own students injured himself in this way. While landing from a tornado kick, a wushu kick which requires a jump off the right leg followed by a right 360-degree inside crescent kick and a right-leg landing, his leg gave out (Fig. 6). While the landing was technically perfect, his conditioning was not. His parents later confided to me that he had only been training twice a week, far too little for this sort of jumping.

What many people in the martial arts forget is that a large part of the training is to condition

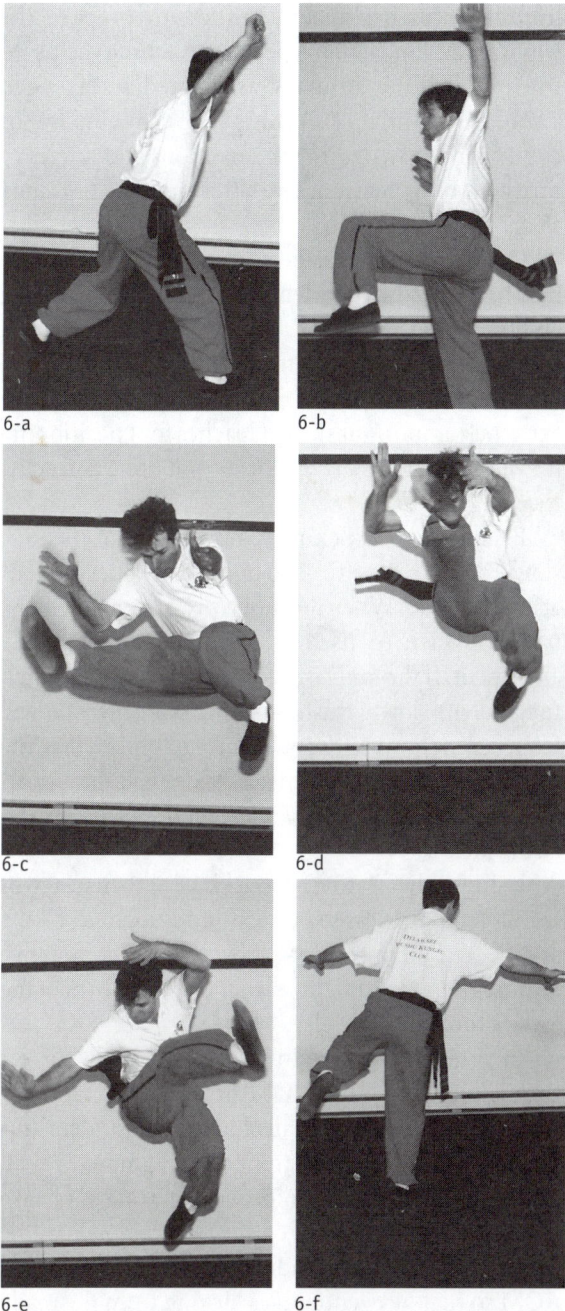

6-a 6-b

6-c 6-d

6-e 6-f

Figure 6: Key positions of the jump inside (tornado) kick. Both takeoff and landing are done with the right leg which exposes it to enormous stress.

muscles, ligaments and bone to withstand commonly-applied forces. Simply knowing how to do a technique is not enough.

Overtraining is the other major cause of injury in kicking. Overtraining may take the form of too many

repetitions of a kick in a single workout, or simply not enough recovery time in between workouts. In both cases, the culprit behind the injury is the body's inability to repair itself fast enough. Working out causes micro tears to the muscles and, dependent on the type of workout, can also create micro-scale damage to the bones or ligaments. When a martial artist has sufficient recovery time after a hard workout (usually about 48 hours), it is possible to work out hard again without damaging the body.

Unfortunately, when there is insufficient recovery time, a number of things happen. As living tissue bears force, it begins to weaken. The first line of defense is the muscle which absorbs most of the force. When the muscle grows tired, the bones and other connective tissues take the load. As the time of loading or number of repetitions increase for the same amount of force, the possibility of injury increases as well (Fig. 7) (Nordin & Frankel, 1989). When the muscle still takes the primary load, the injury is a tear. When the bones and connective tissue bear the load, the injury is a fracture or sprain.

Knowledge of kicking injuries and their common causes is essential for martial arts instructors and coaches. This information allows the skilled instructor to identify and prevent problems before they happen. More importantly, when an injury does occur, the instructor will be more likely to react in a proper manner.

Training Methods to Minimize Injury

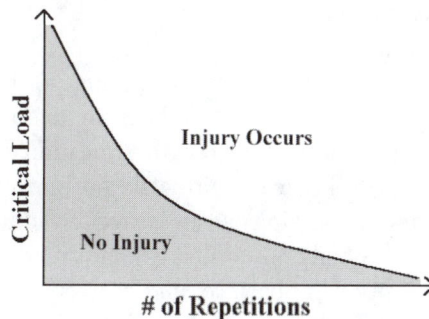

Figure #7 Curve showing (solid line) the amount of loading required to create an injury as a function of repetitions, and (dotted line) the probability of injury as a function of repetitions.

Now that the general injuries due to kicking have been discussed, it is possible to relate training strategies to avoid them.

One of the most important steps in practicing any sort of kicking is the warm-up, since warm muscles are more elastic and less likely to be strained. It is recommended to start with joint rotations at the hips, knees and ankles, since this will lubricate the joints and thus lessen the possibility of injury. This is to be followed by a low-intensity aerobic activity such as jogging in place or jumping jacks, although any number of calisthenics may suffice (Kurz, 1994).

Another way which is recommended (Kurz, 1994) is to use a technical warm-up. This is a low-intensity, low-speed workout which makes use of techniques from the martial curriculum. Kicks which meet the low-intensity and speed criterion are ideal for preparation to kicking training. Such kicks should also be done at waist level or lower and with *no* power at this phase. This sort of warm-up serves to activate the specific muscles which are to be used in the later training. Novices may substitute simple knee raises at this point.

When the warm-up has been completed, it is essential to stretch. A properly constructed technical warm-up will, by its very nature, include an entry into stretching. In general, it is important to set the ROM utilizing "static active" stretching, a type of stretching in which the muscle to be stretched is held motionless and stretched via flexion of the opposing muscle group. This type of stretching prevents the stretch reflex and thus allows the individual to stretch without reflexive tightening.

Advanced forms of this are sport-specific and mimic the actual fully-extended kicking positions. This sort of stretch should be held for five to 20 seconds depending on the strength of the individual. Care should be taken to ensure that the position of the support foot and kicking foot are correct. In addition to helping flexibility, this drill is good for increasing strength, improving balance, and correcting body alignment in kicking.

Besides static active stretching, dynamic stretching—or stretching using controlled swinging of the limbs—is further recommended to prepare the legs for action. This type of stretching helps to prevent kicking injuries associated with speed alone. Dynamic stretching should consist of controlled leg swings in the directions and ranges of motion over which the kicking is to occur (Kurz, 1994).

Once stretching has been completed, other drills may be used to help students to improve their kicking ability. While normal padwork will always help a student, using padwork to introduce a student to a kick may save hours of practice later. Padwork is extremely important since it teaches foot positioning for the contact foot. If the kick is not done correctly, the student will feel it.

Beginners to a kick may move through the kick slowly so as to have time to adjust their kicking foot against the pad. When the foot is properly aligned, the pad may then be used to teach the student body alignment. If the body is incorrectly positioned when the student slowly pushes on the pad, then he will feel a lack of power, loss of balance or both. Thus, the pad is the ultimate tool to aid students in foot positioning, body alignment and general internalization of the kick.

Using padwork to teach kicking is the first step of a multi-step process to perfecting a student's kicking ability. The slow type of padwork described above requires that the student learn the proper form of the kick before anything else.

In order to be certain that the form is correct throughout the entire ROM of the kick is another matter entirely. This entails having the student understand the timing of the body alignment. Such understanding may be improved by working backwards from the point of contact on the pad. While keeping the speed low, gradually increase the student's ROM so that he eventually is kicking from the ready position, hitting the pad, and returning to the ready position.

Once the student displays adequate form and timing, you may then put him in the class lineup for repetitions. At this point, students should strive for repetitions only and not speed or power. Repetitions which are done correctly tune the muscle memory. They will also increase strength in the appropriate areas.

This part of training is called "building a base." Building a base conditions the body to increase the ROM and strength in a kick, in a manner which decreases the likelihood of injury.

An important question is, "How much base do I need to build?" This answer will vary from student to student since each has his own physical ability. As with all exercise programs, in the martial arts it is important to start small and then work up. One guideline is to have the students be able to do a certain fixed number of repetitions comfortably and without strain before moving onwards. Once this number is reached, then encouragement to kick higher or faster may be warranted.

In order to go higher and faster, a student needs to increase both his strength and flexibility. While both may be improved via kicking, other exercises are often quite important. For martial artists, a number of exercises fit the bill.

To increase the power of kicks, a type of power training called jump training, or "plyometrics," is in order. This sort of training typically involves jumping, but really is any sort of activity in which the muscles explode out of a flexed position repetitively. Kicking out of stances is one way in which to do this, which is totally consistent with most martial arts curriculums. However, the traditional rapid jumping off of and then back onto a short bench will also serve.

Another drill for students which may be modified according to skill level is having them throw a certain number of kicks with a leg within a specific time span. A beginner may only be able to do seven kicks in ten seconds, whereas a very advanced student might do 15. As with all exercises, these drills may be graded according to ability.

Along with strength training of this nature, additional stretching increases ROM. Dynamic stretching is recommended for this since kicking involves dynamic flexibility. Students who wish to really increase their flexibility should be stretching upwards of four to five times a week.

Advanced Kicking Techniques

This section will discuss safety in teaching two of the most dangerous types of kicking to learn, spin kicks and jump kicks. The first is dangerous since it requires the practitioner to spin to the blind side, maintain balance, and not twist or torque anything while doing so. Jumps are dangerous mainly due to the forces involved with takeoffs and landings, although balance is also an issue here. The key to safety in teaching these kicks is to use the principle of progression: start with something the student knows and build on it. Progression enables students to expand their comfort zone slowly and also results in better body mechanics in the long term.

To a beginner, spin kicks are scary. The usual fear is that they will not be able to keep their balance as they go around. Others feel that adding a spin to an otherwise difficult kick will take superhuman effort. The first step in teaching these kicks is to make them accessible to students, that is, remove the fear factor. One very effective way to do this is to teach "turning" kicks first. This type of kick is simply a kick to the rear from a standing position. This sort of kick familiarizes students with turning the head first to focus and then gets them orienting the body correctly.

The next step is to teach the spin without the kick. I usually teach my students a pivot of the front foot followed by a turn of the head. When done properly, the body swings around on its own. More importantly, well-taught pivoting skills will keep students from twisting their knees or ankles as they spin. When the student is comfortable with both of these skills, it is then possible to combine them into a real spin kick (Fig. 9).

Jumping kicks are also problematic since they may present a mental as well as physical challenge to the novice jumper. As with spin kicks, it is necessary to segment the kicks into their components in order to provide a progression in the training.

The student should first show proficiency in the ground-based version of the kick before even attempting the jump. The next step is to familiarize the student with any differences in the footwork between the ground-based kick and the jump. This is crucial since the footwork sets up the position of the rest of the body. When this has been accomplished, jumping without the kick may be tried.

Jumping drills of this nature train the student's landing ability, balance and sense of well-being while airborne. Without this last quality especially, the student will not be mentally prepared to execute a proper kick. Lastly, the actual jump kick should be tried (Fig. 10).

The jump kick itself should be executed in such a way that the apex of the kick matches that of the jump. In addition to making for a more powerful kick, this will ensure that the student does not land out of position. Practice for this may include any number of drills. One of my favorites is a plyometric exercise which involves stepping up onto a low chair and kicking at the same time (Fig. 11). This strengthens the coordination between body motion and kick as well as increasing power in the legs.

A second drill which helps students to learn the feel of the kick involves a spotter who helps the student through the kick while providing an extra push (Fig. 12).

Students who are learning jump kicks should spend time actively working to reduce their landing forces. Kicking on the way up and not on the way down will enable the student to focus on the landing at the appropriate time. The landing itself should be done with a slightly flexed landing leg, since flexed joints will absorb the impact of landing better (Niiler, 1997). Additionally, the student should actively control the ankle of his landing leg so as to avoid "limp" landings. Landing with a loose ankle drastically increases the rate of loading and thereby also increases the possibility of injury (Niiler, 1997, Gross & Nelson, 1988). Likewise, leaving the ankle loose is liable to end in a sprain if the foot's alignment is not perfect.

Many martial artists traditionally do not wear shoes during their practices. This can become an issue for jump kicks, since shoes can cushion the landing and help prevent injuries such as bruises to the bottoms of the feet and *plantar fascitis*, a painful irritation of the connective tissue in the sole of the foot.

Some schools use floor mats to decrease the impact of bare feet on hard surfaces. While this solution may be preferable to wearing practice shoes to many mar-

tial artists, it does carry risks. Unless a student consciously keeps a firm ankle when landing, landing on soft surfaces has been shown to increase the rate of loading. It is thought that this is because people expect the padding to totally absorb their impact and thus keep their ankles "limp". Students landing on hard surfaces with bare feet will unconsciously try to land more softly and, as a result, will have a lower rate of loading, although their landing forces are usually higher. Shoes tend to provide the best of both worlds as they lower both landing forces and the rate of loading (Pink & Jobe, 1997).

Conclusions

Even with the best of training, injuries will probably occur. However, the well-trained instructor will create conditions inside the studio that minimize the factors which can lead to injury. No instructor can read a student's mind or tell exactly what that student's physical abilities are, so general safety measures are called for. The most general of training principles introduced here is progression—the slow introduction and adjustment to a technique.

Other principles which are equally important are maintaining proper body alignment, establishing the proper conditioning, and not overtraining. Ultimately though, patience, empathy and understanding on the part of the instructor will be instrumental to providing a safe training atmosphere for kicking or any other martial technique. ■

Figure 9: Teaching a spin kick in stages.

Top row: Regular side kick,
2nd Row: Turning side kick
3rd Row: Spin without a kick,
4th Row: Full spinning side kick.

Figure 10: Teaching a jump toe tap kick (Similar to jump front kick) in stages

Inset below: Completed jump kick
1st Row on right: Regular kick on ground
2nd Row on right: Walk through showing takeoff foot work
3rd Row: Adding the jump and landing but without the kick
Bottom Row: Now adding the full jump kick.

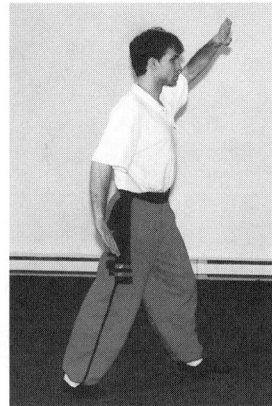

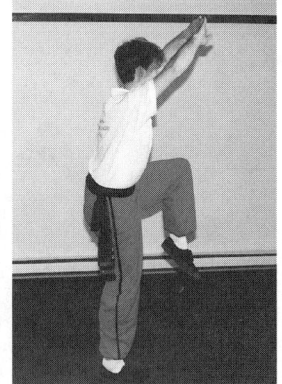

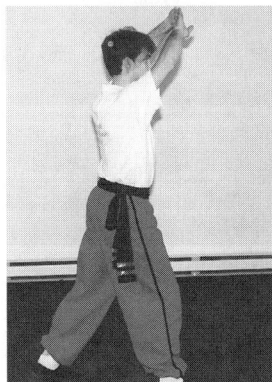

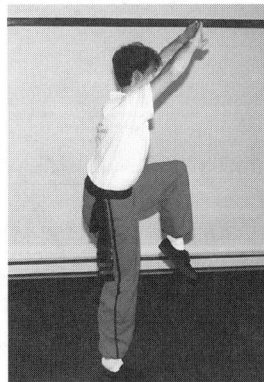

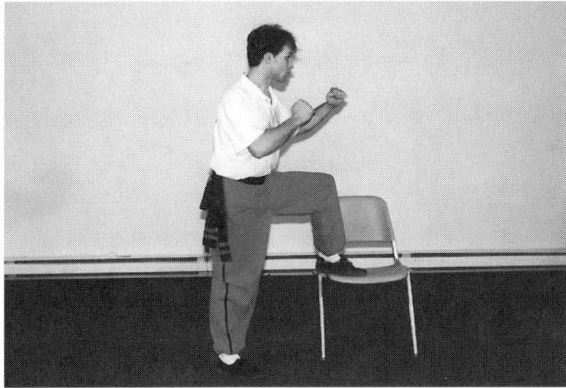

Figure #12 (a) Preparation for the drill.
(b) The jump and spot for a jump toe tap (jump front kick).

*Figure #11 (a) Preparation for the drill. (b) The step up. Note
that the support leg is not straight. (c) The kick. The support leg
has straightened at the same time the kick has extended. This
drill is good for developing timing in forward jumping kicks.*

References

Birrer, R.B., Birrer, C.D. (1982). Martial Arts Injuries. The Physician and Sports Medicine. Vol. 10, No. 6.

Birrer, R.B., Birrer, C.D. (1981). Medical Injuries in the Martial Arts. Springfield, IL: Thomas Books.

Birrer, R.B., Birrer, C.D., Duk, S.S., Stone, D. (1981). Injuries in Tae Kwon Do. The Physician and Sports Medicine. Vol. 9, No. 2.

Birrer, R.B., Halbrook, S.P. (1988). Martial arts injuries: The results of a five year survey. The American Journal of Sports Medicine. Vol. 16, No. 4.

Gross, T.S., Nelson, R.C.. (1988). The shock attenuation role of the ankle during landing from a vertical jump. Medicine and Science in Sport and Exercise. Vol. 20, No. 5.

Kurland, H.L. (1980). Injuries in Karate. The Physician in Sports Medicine. Vol. 8, No. 10.

Kurz, T. (1994). Stretching Scientifically: a guide to flexibility training. Stadion.

Niiler, T.A. (1997). Landing Impact Loading and Injury Risk in Chinese Wushu. Masters Thesis. Newark, DE: University of Delaware.

Nordin, M., Frankel, V.H. (1989) Basic Biomechanics of the Musculoskeletal System. Philadelphia, PA: Lea & Febiger.

Pink, M.M., Jobe, F.W. (1997). The Foot/Shoe Interface. In Running Injuries. Ed. Guten, G.N. Philadelphia: W.B. Saunders Company. pp. 20-29.

How to Teach Self-Defense Safely

BY TOM ROCHFORD

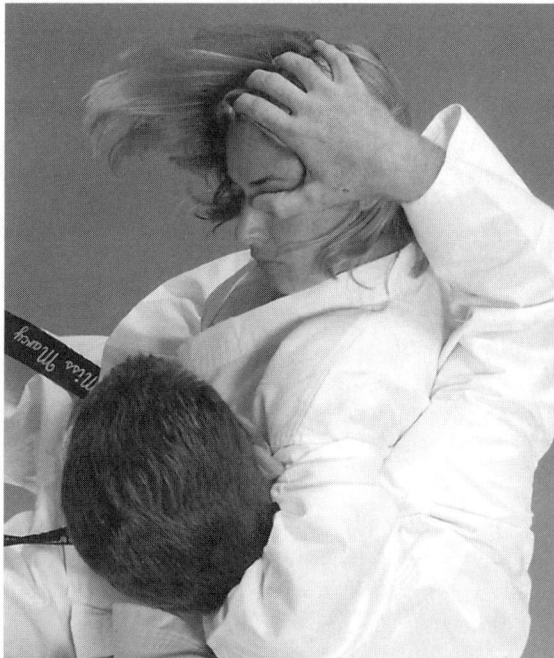

Also: Psychological Issues In Teaching Self-Defense To Women

By Gianine D. Rosenblum, Ph.D.

How To Teach Self-Defense Safely

One of the main responsibilities of today's martial arts instructor is to provide students with practical, realistic and effective self-defense training, all within a safe environment. Teaching students to physically defend themselves in appropriate situations, especially without placing them at risk of injury, can be a key to the overall success of the instructor's program. Most students have other personal and/or professional responsibilities (family, school and/or work) that hold a higher level of priority in life than does self-defense training. The ability to successfully meet and complete these responsibilities should not be compromised by a self-defense training program taught in an unsafe manner.

The ultimate goal of teaching/learning self-defense is to provide a vehicle by which the student can/will achieve a higher level of physical, emotional and mental confidence and self-esteem, thus feeling a greater level of personal safety. The ultimate goals for self-defense training are to:

1. Develop the quickest possible reaction time (response) to a physical attack.
2. Maintain physical balance through all self-defense movements and techniques.
3. Learn/execute self-defense techniques and movements:
    A) With the greatest possible speed;
    B) With the highest potential power level;
    C) In the shortest timeframe possible (efficiency of movement);
    D) With the least amount of effort;
    E) In rapid succession; and
    F) To the proper (most vulnerable) targets.

Martial arts instructors must strive to reach each of these goals within the safest possible environment for the student.

This chapter will attempt to provide guidance and information intended to assist the martial arts instructor with certain aspects of self-defense training within the martial arts classroom. Other chapters within the Certification Manual will detail related concepts, which should also be considered as factors in planning and performing a safe self-defense training program.

What Is Self-Defense?

Self-defense instruction, as taught in the martial arts classroom, is the process of developing and improving the knowledge and skills required to recognize, avoid and/or deal with negative conflict or confrontation. In this chapter, self-defense can be defined as the practice of escapes and/or counters against a specific attack.

Of course, the ideal solution to any problem would be completely nonviolent and nonphysical. Unfortunately, that scenario cannot always be achieved. So the martial arts instructor also has the job to physically prepare the student for physical confrontation. This preparation process must involve actual and practical physical application of techniques and movements associated specifically with self-defense.

THE ULTIMATE GOALS OF SELF-DEFENSE TRAINING

1. Develop the quickest possible reaction time (response) to a physical attack.
2. Maintain physical balance through all self-defense movements and techniques.
3. Learn/execute self-defense techniques and movements:
    A) With the greatest possible speed;
    B) With the highest potential power level;
    C) In the shortest time frame possible (efficiency of movement);
    D) With the least amount of effort;
    E) In rapid succession; and
    F) To the proper (most vulnerable) targets.

The martial arts instructor has many different "tools" available which can be used to begin and continue the training process. Forms, sparring, choreographed self-defense scenarios, equipment training and free-style sparring are methods by which the actual learning process can be executed. Within each method, a progression of difficulty should be gradually (depending on the capability of the individual student) applied to the training. This allows the student to safely learn and improve the required skills for self-defense.

Physical Conditioning

When teaching any physical activity, an instructor should consider each individual student's current physical capabilities. Self-defense training is no different, as the following two factors will greatly influence instruction, initiation and progression:

1. The level of physical conditioning.
2. Skill levels and coordination.

It's quite obvious, for the safety of the student, that certain medical factors must also influence the intensity level or method of the training activities. But medical subject matter is beyond the scope of this inaugural Certification Manual.

A student's current fitness level should be another consideration when self-defense training (or any other physical activity) is being performed. Fatigue must be a major consideration in the efforts for injury prevention.

Another type of conditioning, potentially having an effect on safety, is that which is achieved through the repetitive physical experience with a particular training method. Students (specifically their physical bodies) should be allowed to acclimate to a particular type of training mode or method.

A practical example of a negative scenario would be a situation where a beginner-level student—with minimal (or no) technique performance training and no previous experience of working with equipment—is allowed to perform powerful, uncontrolled strikes on a heavy bag. Improper form and improper use of the training equipment could very easily result in physical injury to the student.

Physical Skill and Coordination Progression/Plan of Progression

Every new student has different levels of coordination and individual skill depending on his past level of activity and athletic participation. The potential amount of improvement in skill level and physical coordination will also vary for each new martial arts student. Not everyone can or will reach the same high

level of physical ability, or we would all be Bruce Lee.

Almost everyone had to learn to crawl (slow movement, requiring little balance) initially. But, as a child develops coordination in the involved muscle groups, the crawl speed is progressively increased until he is walking (requiring a greater level of balance), and then running (requiring even greater levels of coordination and balance), and so on.

Safe self-defense instruction should progress in the same manner. The rate of progression in skill and coordination levels will most certainly be different from student to student. Remember, some toddlers walk before they reach one year old, others don't walk until they are beyond that age. Likewise, some students will progress through the beginning stages of learning self-defense much more quickly than others.

Physical skill/coordination is learned and practiced. As a movement becomes familiar, through performance practice, to the body and to the brain, five things occur:

1. Balance is more easily maintained.
2. Reaction time decreases.
3. Speed of movement increases.
4. Movements become shorter.
5. Potential power generation is increased.

Physical skills are best taught ("best," meaning the safest *and* most easily learned) by breaking the specific skill down into the smallest possible, practical component of the complete technique or movement. The amount of breakdown required will depend on the students' current level of skill and coordination and their potential for learning. The components should be performed at a speed which allows the student to properly control the form.

As a component is learned and improved in execution, another component can be added and practiced and improved, until the complete technique or movement is learned and proficiently executed by the student. At each stage of learning, the execution speed should be at a level in which the technique/movement can be performed with the proper form, which helps to minimize injury risk.

This plan of progression allows the student to gradually develop other vital aspects of performing self-defense techniques, including:

1. Proper form in technique execution.
2. Accurate focus.
3. Control of techniques and physical balance during movement.
4. Complete mental concentration.

As each of these areas begins to improve with the repetition, the total proficiency (reaction time, speed, power, rapid succession, etc.) of the technique/movement execution is enhanced.

Balance

Maintaining physical balance is a prerequisite for executing the most efficient (quickest, fastest, shortest, with least amount of effort) and/or powerful physical movements and/or techniques possible. It's also a prerequisite for safety in movement. This applies to self-defense training activities as well. Maintenance of balance will minimize the risk for injury (due to falling, unfocused strikes, excessive stress placed on joints, etc.) to the person performing a movement, as well as, in the case of partner-training, to the person who might be on the receiving end of a particular technique.

Balance is not a naturally occurring skill. If it was, we would not have to progress through the stages as an infant of sitting up, walking and running. As an individual grows up, he will acquire and possess varying levels of balance awareness. This is mainly due to the physical-movement environment which he experiences throughout life. Someone coming into a martial arts class with several years of experience in a gymnastics program, for example, will normally have greater balance awareness than someone who has very little or no physical-activity experience.

Balance can be "learned" and must be practiced in order to improve.

Escapes

Escapes from grabs and/or holds are an important aspect of self-defense training, also requiring much practice. This type of training requires physical contact between two or more students. Here is another situation where the planned-progression concept can and should be used.

To escape from a grab or hold, the person being held or grabbed must execute an action which will cause the person doing the holding to momentarily release or loosen his grip. A target which would cause a person to release or loosen a grab on someone, must be an area which is easily accessible and very vulnerable to immediate pain or discomfort. The student learns these loosening-technique target areas and is required to practice various techniques which would be effective in achieving the intended goal—escaping the grab or hold.

The "planned-progression" concept should once again be used in this training situation. Slow, controlled movements (striking, pressure, pinching, etc.) are performed against the intended target areas. As the student improves in familiarity with the target areas and focus/control of the technique being used, the speed of the movement can be increased.

In the case of a pressure- or pain-point counter-technique, a method by which *all* students can inform each other of an extreme level of pain or pressure being exerted, is crucial to safety. When the attack technique and the counteractions are performed slowly and controlled, they should be executed to the degree where the student experiences the effect (pain, pressure, etc.) of the technique on the body.

Some examples of attack techniques to use in this context are: a) chokes; b) bear hugs; c) headlocks; and d) arm bars. Some examples of counter-techniques could be: a) Thumbs to the eyes; b) pinching the inside of the thigh; and c) "grabbing" the Adam's apple with the fingers.

The "pressure/pain" signal should be used to demand immediate relief of the technique causing the pain or pressure. Signal methods should be defined by the instructor and universally used, so that the meaning will be clearly understood by all students. Instructor-defined signal methods will ensure consistency and a lower chance of mistaken meaning by the students, which could result in a delay of releasing pressure or pain, thus increasing the chance for injury. It would be wise to use a couple of options for methods, in case the particular attack prevents the use of one of the signal methods.

An example for this would be the attacker using both hands to execute an attack technique, which could prevent him/her from using a hand tap to inform the defender to relieve pressure from the countermovement.

Reliable suggestions for signals would be to use one of three methods:

1) Voice Command (choose one word to use).
2. Hand Tap (define the target for the slap—attacker tapping him/herself or the victim).
3. Foot Tap (to the ground).

One of these three areas is usually free to move or create sounds during any self-defense counter-technique.

Teaching Strategies for Student Motivation and Safety

Many ideas have already been presented in this chapter for maintaining student safety. Student motivation can also be a factor affecting safety during training. Students who are motivated are also more focused and attentive to what they are doing. This high level of concentration should translate into a greater awareness of the physical actions being performed and what effect they may have on a training partner or others close by.

Initially, students should be matched together (when the planned progression of training reaches the partner-training stage) according to similar physical size and skill level. This situation promotes safety in that one student will not likely physically dominate another student due to greater size or skills. However, as students' abilities improve, they should be subjected to training with others of various sizes and skill levels. This will make them better prepared to face any potential foe on the street.

Create scenarios where the student is forced to react to different stimulus. This will keep the minds focused on what is being done, whereas consistently working with the same partner in the same training method (the same stimulus) can create a "no-mind" scenario, where the student becomes so familiar with the actions and reactions of his consistent partner that the level of mental awareness declines, thus compromising the safety status of both students. Provide students with the chance to practice with different "opponents," within the planned progression model.

Also, use a variety of training methods that will enhance mental awareness and keep the student motivated and safe. Game-like training creates a fun atmosphere which can be more easily controlled by an instructor. Some examples of training methods are:

1. Partner Training

Rotating to a new partner when signaled by the instructor.

2. In-Line Training

One person stands facing a line of opponents. As the student completes the self-defense technique, the next opponent attacks. The tempo of this method must be controlled by the instructor.

3. Circle Training

One student is positioned in the center of a circle formed by the other "attacking" students. Assign each "attacking" student an identification tag (number, name, color, etc.). Initially, the circle remains stationary, but as skill levels increase the circle can begin to move in one direction. Further increases in skill level can be challenged by having the "defender" student in the center of the circle close his eyes until the attack is signaled.

The instructor calls out the ID of an "attacker," who responds with an attacking signal (a *kiai*, or loud yell, is a good and practical signal) *before* the actual attack can take place. This provides a bit of a safety time-margin for the defender to respond to the oncoming attack.

The key is to offer a variety of training methods through which the student can learn self-defense and gain proficiency in execution, while always maintaining a practical level of safety.

Age-Specific Considerations for Self-Defense Training

Age, in relation to emotional/mental maturity level and physical condition, can definitely have an affect on the safety considerations for self-defense training and should influence the methods of instruction as well as the content of the class.

Self-defense training can be divided into three age-specific groups:

1. Children
2. Adults.
3. Older Adults.

Children

The main safety concerns involve both the physical conditions and mental capabilities of children. Instructors must remember that children's bodies are not fully developed until the mid to late teens. Some of the physical stresses placed on the immature muscles, bones and connective tissue of a child, during repetitive self-defense technique and movement training, can possibly be the cause of two types of injuries:

1. Acute Injuries (which occur immediately when the stress is experienced).
2. Chronic Injuries (which occur after a period of repetitive stress).

The mental maturity of a child should also be an influence on how self-defense training is performed. Outside of class, a child may not possess the ability to truly comprehend the serious consequences which could result from using his self-defense training improperly. Telling children, repetitively, about the "proper" times to use physical self-defense techniques can help to increase their understanding of the possible negative results of such action.

Inside of class, the instructor needs to maintain total control of the children's actions when practicing self-defense techniques, in order to prevent or minimize the chance for injury. The ability to monitor the whole class, at all times, is very important.

Adults

Teaching self-defense to adults can be an interesting task. Instructors need to be able to evaluate each individual's current and potential physical skill level and abilities. They also need to be aware of certain personality characteristics of adult students.

For example, the competitive adult may not recognize possible physical limitations he may have and may try to "keep up" with other students in all activities, increasing the risk for injury. Or, aggressive adults may not settle for the planned-progression learning method, even though their potential for learning and improving may require a slower progression than others, thus increasing the risk of injury to themselves and to those who are training around or with them. The introverted adult may have difficulty, due to his inhibitions, in giving full effort to the learning process and the practice of techniques.

Also, at the beginner-level stages of partner training, because of the adults' greater sense of awareness about their own physical abilities and personality traits, it is advisable to match training partners according to physical size, physical ability and personality trait. Personality traits should have a large effect on how closely monitored and controlled a set of partners will be. For example, two aggressive and/or competitive people, paired up, should obviously be closely monitored.

Following the planned-progression concept and taking into consideration the student's comfort zone, relating to physical skills/capabilities and personality traits, will provide the safest possible training environment for adults.

Older Adults

Balance becomes an important issue when dealing with older adults. While balance can be learned and improved through practice, it is also affected by the strength levels of the muscle groups involved in providing the stability required for maintaining balance. Muscle strength, and the potential to improve it, does begin to decline after about the third decade of life.

This decline can be slowed through resistance training. Resistance is defined as "anything that opposes movement." Gravity is a resistance to movement, but most people are acclimated to moving against gravity. So, to maintain or improve strength levels, the muscle groups in the body must be forced to work against resistance which is beyond normal levels experienced in daily activities. Weight or resistance training can be a positive factor in slowing the aging process.

The decline in muscle strength will eventually affect the ability to maintain balance. So an important safety consideration to be made about an older adult involved in self-defense training is his ability to maintain balance.

Also, due to the effects of aging on the body, specifically the inability to readily adapt or condition to an activity, an older adult may require a slower degree of planned progression for skill and coordination improvements. He should be made to know that the training and practicing of the various skills should be challenged and measured only by his own potential abilities.

Injuries are more likely to occur when a person tries to work beyond his physical capabilities. Older adults may be inclined to try to keep up with younger classmates, in order to "prove" themselves. Body adaptations required for and resulting from training with equipment must also be considered.

The older adult, due to the effects of aging, may be more fragile in bone structure, muscle and connective-tissue attachment, and flexibility. Reaction times may be slower. Physical movement requirements may be compromised. These facts must be considered in order to maintain a high degree of motivation and safety in a self-defense class involving older adults.

Monitor Class for Safety

The degree to which a class should be monitored depends completely on the students' physical skills/abilities and mental/emotional maturity levels.

For beginner-level training, all movements should be controlled and visually monitored by the instructor. There are many ways to achieve these parameters.

1. Students can perform the techniques only on command by the instructor.
2. Students can be set up into an organized fashion, such as lines. The student then performs the technique/movement upon command of the instructor.
3. Using the planned-progression concept, the instructor could initially break the technique down into components and call out each component, one at a time, to be performed by the student.

As skill level improves, the commands can be for performance of complete techniques, then eventually evolving into the Instructor simply saying, "Go".

In any case, the instructor should always maintain

a vantage point that allows full view of the class at all times. This setup will allow the instructor to easily distinguish an improperly performed technique which could be a potential safety hazard. As skills improve and the instructor "knows" the students' mental, emotional and physical capabilities, a class can be given more freedom in practice and less monitoring is required.

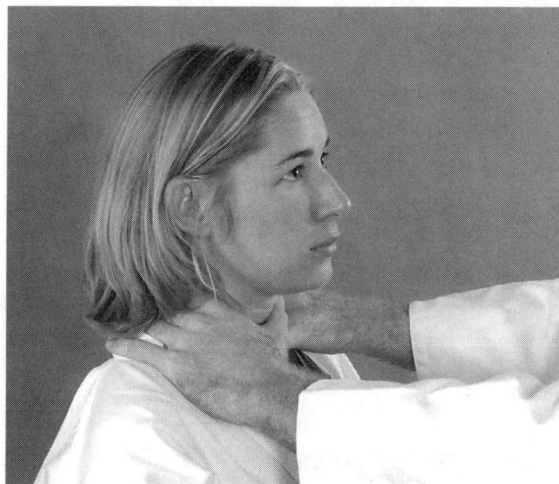

Figure 1a. The student is placed at risk for injury when her partner chokes her with his thumbs on her throat.

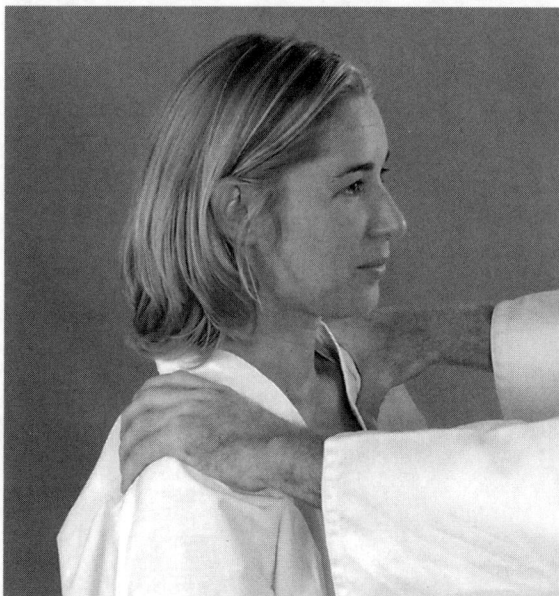

Figure 1b. By grabbing her shoulders and chest-plate, injury risk is reduced while practicing choke escapes.

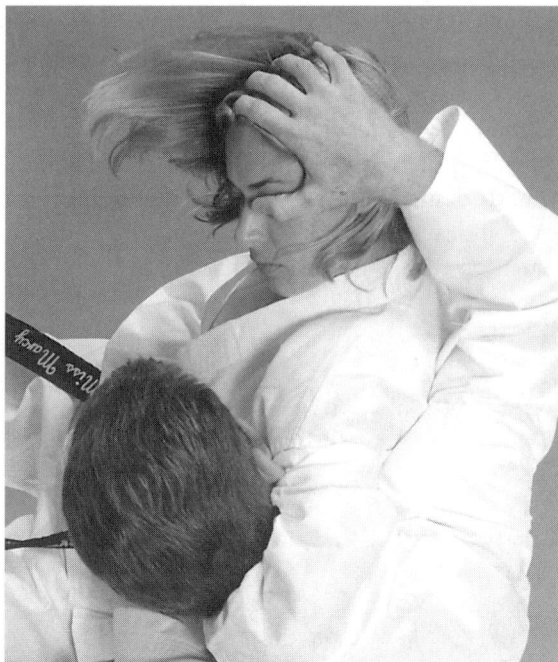

Figure 2a. Defense against a headlock with eye in danger due to thumb.

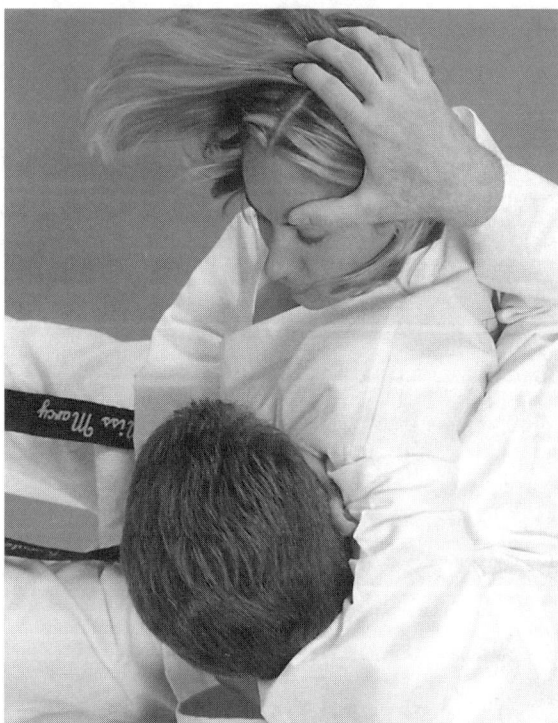

Figure 2b. Danger to eye is reduced by using forehead as alternate target for thumb.

Target Practice

As a student's skill and coordination improve, the speed of the technique and movement performance should increase. This increase in speed, no matter how skilled the student may be, does create a greater risk for injury, especially when engaged in partner practice. To increase safety levels during performance of full-speed and full power techniques, the instructor should have the student use "alternate target areas" which are less prone to injury from incidental contact.

ALTERNATE TARGET AREAS TO REDUCE RISK

1. The Eyes.
Aim at the forehead for a strike or for a pressure technique. Place the fingers or thumb on the cheekbone instead of the eyes.

2. The Throat.
Use the sternum or chest as a target for a strike. To execute a choke, place the thumb or fingers on the manubrium (just above the sternum) instead of the Adam's apple.

3. The Jaw or Chin.
Use the sternum or chest as a target for a strike.

4. The Ears (for the cupped-hand strike).
Strike on the side of the head, above the ears.

5. The Point of the Nose.
Strike to the cheekbone or to the forehead.

6. The Collarbone.
Use the chest or trapezius (the thick muscle group which gradually slopes upward from the shoulder to the neck) muscles as targets.

7. The Floating Ribs.
Use the stomach area (between the left- and right-side ribcages).

8. The Groin.
Strike or grab the inner or front thigh.

9. The Top of the Foot.
Strike the floor next to the foot.

10. The Knee.
Use the mid-thigh as the target.

11. The Elbow

For a strike, aim at a point on the arm between the elbow and the wrist, preferably closer to the elbow since the bones are thicker at that end. This eliminates the potential for hyper-extending the elbow with a strike.

Remember, at this level of training, the student has gained proficiency in focusing techniques on whatever target he is intending to contact. So, defining an alternate target for striking should not lessen the effectiveness of the training because, by this time, the primary targets are well-known to the student.

Anytime there is contact between two people, there is risk of injury. The idea of alternate target areas in self-defense practice is to minimize the potential for injury by minimizing the amount of contact and by using the safest possible target areas for incidental contact.

Equipment

Safety levels can be greatly enhanced or completely compromised through the use of equipment. This article will discuss two types of equipment:

1. Safety Equipment.
2. Training Equipment.

REASONS FOR USING SAFETY EQUIPMENT IN SELF-DEFENSE PRACTICE

1. You never know when an accident will happen.
2. Students are normally required to wear protective equipment during sparring practice, why not during self-defense practice? There is the same risk of excessive contact and subsequent injury.
3. Wearing the equipment tends to relieve the anxiety a student may feel by striking at an "unguarded" partner during practice sessions. The fear of injuring a classmate can affect the concentration levels and the physical performance of a student during technique practice.
4. Wearing the equipment allows the student to relax more when posing as the target for self-defense techniques. There is less fear of being injured, which allows the student to better concentrate on the specific practice objectives.

Safety Equipment

This kind of equipment is intended to be used as protection for the student or instructor. The available equipment ranges anywhere from a mouth guard to a small cloth-covered, foam pad to a full suit of body armor. The amount of equipment to be used in the training is determined by the specific class skill levels and the content of the particular course. Considering the planned-progression model, technique contact should be implemented only after the student is able to properly perform techniques without resistance and normally occurs at a more advanced level of training.

Even full-body suits of armor do not guarantee injury prevention. The student is still susceptible to potential injury if a technique is improperly performed when making contact with the armor. Students may have a false sense of security when striking the armor, not contemplating the possibility of injury risk to themselves. Use the planned-progression model to gradually acclimate the student to striking the armor.

Safety equipment exists for nearly every body part. The instructor should determine the amount of equipment necessary in relation to the risks involved with the specific training that will take place.

Training Equipment

Here, again, the planned-progression model should be used to determine the type of training equipment to be used for a specific class. What are the skill levels involved? Are the students "conditioned" to using the equipment?

Equipment is available in all sizes and density.

Beginner-level students who may not be able to expertly focus or control their strikes should begin their equipment training using larger-size equipment. This will enhance their safety by offering a larger target, since injuries can easily occur when a student expects to make contact with a mass, but completely misses. Joint dislocations and hyper-extensions are common to this scenario. A larger target will also provide the holder (usually another student) with a safer environment.

Also, the equipment for a beginner-level student should probably offer a lower level of resistance and/or abrasion. Students (specifically their bodies) should be allowed to gradually condition to the resistance of striking the equipment. Planned progression for equipment use is the key for a safe and successful training regimen.

The methods for holding training equipment need to be evaluated for safety. How many times has a person holding a kicking pad been sent "flying" across the room from a powerful side kick, because he was not holding the pad in such a manner that the power of the kick was absorbed by the pad instead of the holder's body? Students need instruction on proper holding techniques and methods prior to use. Holding equipment improperly can also put the student practicing the strike at risk of injury.

There are countless practice drills which can be designed for self-defense training. The planned progression model will enhance safety when incorporating equipment into the training. Equipment should be used prior to having "live" opponents involved in the training. As cited earlier, the student should be allowed to acclimate or become conditioned to equipment use, in order to avoid or minimize the risk of injury due to improper contact.

Some examples of how equipment can be used in conjunction with other training "tools" include:

1. Forms are executed against imaginary opponents, executing strikes and blocks into the air. Try having those imaginary opponents become real people who are holding striking pads against which the specific form technique can be performed.

2. Combination practice will progress from strik-

ing "in the air" to striking against equipment. When practicing strikes against equipment, try having the student execute the strikes in various ways, including:

A. Focused and controlled, making light to no contact on the equipment.

B. Focused and controlled, with medium contact to the equipment.

C. Gradually increase the power level of the strikes.

No matter what drill is applied, safety will be enhanced through the use of the planned-progression model. Equipment can be used at any stage of the training, with this in mind.

Prior to the stage of having "live" opponents executing punches, kicks, etc., at the student who is practicing the self-defense techniques and movements, have the opponents hold large striking pads. These are to be used as a target to work on focus/control of strikes and as a padded striking implement against which the student can execute blocking techniques. As the focus/control skills improve, smaller striking pads can be used to further force the students to focus and control their techniques.

Teaching practical, realistic and effective self-defense - in a *safe* manner—almost seems to be contradictory. It is a task that requires much thought and thorough, creative planning. The required preparation is well worth the results and invaluable for the positive long-term success of any martial arts program. ∎

Psychological Issues In Teaching Self-Defense To Women

By Gianine D. Rosenblum, Ph.D.

Women come to self-defense classes for many reasons. Some may wish simply to feel safer in an increasingly threatening world, some may live or work in high-crime areas or feel insecure when home alone. Others may be looking for a way to feel generally stronger and more assertive.

Unfortunately, with violence against women an all-too-common event, many women who seek self-defense training may themselves be survivors of assault and/or rape. Women may seek out martial arts or self-defense training specifically because they have been confronted with assault or abuse in the past or present. For all women, but for assault survivors in particular, participation in a self-defense training program can trigger many emotional reactions that a well-prepared instructor must understand.

Most people don't like to talk or think about assault until it happens to them or someone close to them. Unfortunately, this avoidance prevents people from learning important skills and information that can help keep them safe. The women who have chosen to take a self-defense class have taken the first step toward protecting themselves, by deciding to confront their fears instead of avoiding them.

However, a student may initially react to self-defense training by feeling more vulnerable instead of stronger. Even class discussions or lectures about personal safety, awareness and prevention, and the risk of being assaulted are often frightening to students. When first learning hold-releases, strikes, kicks or blocks, a student may become aware of how difficult and alien these actions are. Most women have never even pretended to hit or kick someone prior to coming to a self-defense class. Years of social training have ingrained the idea that women don't fight back or "get physical."

As she first tries out these new maneuvers, a student may become aware of her small size, how weak and awkward her techniques feel and how vulnerable this makes her. Helping a student cope with these initial feelings is critical to her successful comple-

tion of the first stages of learning. If these initial reactions are not handled properly by the instructor, the student may feel weak, frustrated and frightened instead of empowered and strong.

As the class progresses and the student acquires some basic skills, practice usually involves enacting attack scenarios and having the student practice responses. The more realistic the practice, the better the student will be able to learn responses and the more effective she will be in a real-life situation.

While this type of realistic practice is critical to learning, it is at this point that instructors need to be most aware of the students' emotional reactions. Going through the motions of an attack, even a simple arm-grab, can be a frightening experience. A student may become aware of her tendency to "freeze" instead of responding, or may be unable to remember a technique she practiced just moments ago. She may watch other students' techniques and think self-defeating thoughts like: "I could never do that." Feelings of fear can escalate and destroy a student's motivation, making her feel hopeless about learning to defend herself.

Students who have themselves experienced an assault, rape or mugging may be particularly emotionally sensitive to the "mock attack" part of self-defense training. Memories for significant events can be strongly linked to physical sensations (most of us have strong memories associated with certain smells, for example). When an assault survivor experiences physical sensations similar to those present in the attack (that is, being grabbed, an arm around her neck, falling to the ground, being pinned down, etc.), she may experience some of the same strong emotions associated with the actual attack. These emotions can manifest as terror, paralysis, hopelessness, etc. In the most extreme scenario, an assault survivor may experience a "flashback" in which she feels the emotions and sensations so intensely, it is as if the attack is happening at that moment—similar to "flashbacks" experienced by combat veterans or other survivors of traumatic events.

Consequently, the instructor's response to a student's emotional reactions during training are crucial to maintaining the student's feelings of confidence, self-control and motivation to continue her training.

Another difficulty women students may encounter comes from outside the class itself. Many individuals in our society, particularly men, but some women as well, are not comfortable with the idea of women becoming strong and fighting for themselves. Many individuals still believe that women who are assaulted must have "asked for it," or brought on the attack in some way. Some people believe that women ought to depend upon men to defend them.

Because these attitudes are prevalent, many female self-defense students encounter skepticism, criticism and downright ridicule from others because of their pursuit of self-defense training. A husband or boyfriend may feel threatened by the woman's training, for example. A student may choose to keep her self-defense training secret from a critical spouse. Women in self-defense classes often tell stories about spouses/boyfriends/brothers/male friends challenging them after a class, making derogatory remarks about the class, or making statements like, "I bet I could get you in a hold you couldn't get out of." Such comments reflect efforts by these men to defeat the woman's confidence and elevate their own feelings of power. A well-trained instructor can help students cope with the comments of ignorant outsiders and retain confidence in their self-defense skills.

The following are some types of students who are more likely to experience emotional reactions to self-defense training. Those are:

1. With a history of emotional, physical or sexual abuse in childhood.
2. With a history of assault, rape or domestic violence in adulthood (this includes marital rape and date/acquaintance rape).
3. Currently in a relationship that is abusive.
4. Who are experiencing criticism or ridicule from others.

A well-taught self-defense class, led by an educated, sensitive instructor, can work to reduce a student's sense of fear and vulnerability, and increase her self-confidence and ability to cope successfully with threatening situations. A course that is taught poorly, without sensitivity to the emotional issues that may arise, has the potential to leave a student feeling worse—that is, weaker and more fearful—than she did when she started.

Strategies for Managing Psychological Issues during Self-Defense Training

1. Make the Training Environment Feel "Safe"

A. Recognize that self-defense training is different from other types of martial arts classes. Students of self-defense will probably be more uncomfortable, embarrassed and inhibited at first.

There are several steps that can be taken to enhance students' comfort and feelings of safety in class.

1. Increase Privacy

A. Close the school to other activities during the class.
B. Cover storefront windows and do not allow spectators.
C. Request that other students or staff keep out of the area during the self-defense class time.
D. Discuss confidentiality. Some students may wish to reveal actual threatening situations they have experienced in order to practice skills relevant to that event. Discuss this with students ahead of time and ask for all students to agree that such things will not be discussed with people not attending the class.

2. Prepare Students Ahead of Time for the Emotional Reactions They May Experience

Let students know in advance that the skills they will practice are realistic and may trigger some feelings of fear. Discuss the need to practice the techniques despite unpleasant feelings, in order to overcome the fear.

3. Know Your Students

Many instructors would inquire about a history of physical injury in order to keep students safe during their training. Similarly, give students the opportunity to tell you if they have a history of assault or other threat (being the victim of a stalking, for example). Allow them to indicate this on a confidential registration form.

4. Provide Role Models

Use teaching teams which include a male and female instructor. Allow the female instructor to demonstrate techniques and allow the students to observe the female instructor using each of the skills you wish to teach.

Students will learn better when they are exposed to role models they can identify with and relate to. If you choose your most powerful male and female competition fighters to teach the course, students may be put off by the instructors' level of skill and physical strength. Instead, consider selecting skillful, competent instructors, with good communication skills, who are more in the average range in terms of athleticism and physical fitness.

5. Provide Support

When teaching, provide continuous encouragement and messages of self-worth and empowerment to students. While clear, constructive criticism is important to help students improve their skills, harsh criticism or derogatory comments can be highly psychologically damaging and have no place in these classes. Reassure students that some feelings of anxiety may be experienced during the class and that this is a normal occurrence. Offer the students the opportunity to see you privately to discuss any fears or concerns that may arise prior to or during the course.

Also, choose instructors with good communication skills, who are at ease discussing issues that may arise during classes.

6. Give Students Access to Other Resources

Provide the names and phone numbers of local Women's Resource Centers, Rape Crisis programs or therapists to all students as a matter of course. If you are not comfortable discussing emotional issues with your students, team up with someone who is. Contact a local Women's Resource Center or Rape Crisis program yourself before teaching the course and ask for suggestions on supporting your female students. Consider bringing in a local therapist or counselor to co-lead the class or run discussion groups before or after classes.

Should a student experience powerful emotional reactions during classes, provide ample support during class and encourage the student to seek outside, professional assistance.

Your decision to teach self-defense skills to women is a serious one. As a self-defense instructor, you are in a position not only to teach much needed skills, but to demonstrate to women and girls that they have the right to protect themselves from harm. Do not take this commitment lightly. If you choose to offer self-defense courses, remember that what you teach will affect your students' bodies as well as their minds. ■

How To Teach Sparring Safely

By John Graden

How To Teach Sparring Safely

Few areas of training can define martial arts spirit more clearly than sparring. From 1984 until about 1989, I was training three times a week in a dark, dirty boxing gym with American karate legend Joe Lewis, the retired world heavyweight kickboxing champion. The only reason we would miss the workouts was the scheduling challenges his seminars sometimes presented. The fighting was hard contact, brutal, and as intense as you can imagine it could be climbing into a 12-foot-square ring with the man cited as "the greatest fighter in the history of karate."

Joe taught me that the fighting should be as real as possible. He also confirmed my opinion that point karate had little value in instilling the tenacity or attitudinal conditioning necessary to go three rounds with anybody, which we agreed should be a minimum standard for a professional black belt.

My motivation has always been as a teacher, not a fighter or champion. Even though at the same time I was traveling to Europe regularly to compete with the United States Karate Team, I've never had a compelling drive to be a world champion or trophy collector. I've always competed for the education and experience.

Whenever I'm in a learning environment, such as working with a great teacher or taking a personal development seminar, I am always asking myself, "How can I teach this to my students?" In the case of fighting with Joe Lewis, the question changed to, "How do I teach this to my students without driving them out the door or to the hospital?"

In most schools, sparring is one of the leading causes of drop out among students. Even when the school sticks to the relative stop-and-go safety of point karate, students still drop out. How, then, could I motivate these students to engage in sparring without hurting them or scaring them off?

I learned that the key is in the perspective you keep in working with your students. If your goal is to get your students to black belt, then you must realize that you have three to five years to accomplish that. It's important, then, that you structure your curriculum to gradually introduce the student to sparring. There's no rush.

Some may argue that the sooner students start to spar, the sooner they can learn how to defend themselves. My feeling is that if a student drops out because of sparring too early in his training, then he will never learn to defend himself anyway. Furthermore, he will miss out on all the life-enhancing qualities inherent in the martial arts. A student that drops out of the martial arts because of sparring is a student we have failed.

In the sparring program I developed, white and gold belts are required to learn simple block and counters while wearing pads on their hands and feet. These techniques are executed against the jab and reverse punch—but *without any contact*.

In addition, we will have them work slipping drills, target drills, defensive footwork drills, and set-point movement drills to get them moving and firing techniques. Understand that this represents the first six to eight months of their training. Often, instructors have their students sparring within the first three months. Our students don't even make contact for *eight months*.

When the students graduate into the orange and green belt class, they begin to actually spar following the rules of light-contact continuous karate. That is conventional point fighting without stopping to decide who scored a point. However, there is still no head contact, but body contact is permitted. Of course, the students wear headgear, hand-and-foot protective pads, shin pads, a mouthpiece, rib guards, and a groin cup for the guys.

Limited Sparring Drills

At this point, we begin to devote more and more of each class to "limited sparring drills." A limited sparring drill is a sparring match with a strategy *other than winning* as the goal. For instance, one student might be limited to executing only a jab to the forehead. For these drills we always target the forehead instead of the face, as a safety measure. The student's partner could then be limited to using only positional movement (footwork) and head movement as a defense.

So, in this example, the jabber is working on stepping in and snapping his jab to the forehead, while the defensive fighter is learning to slip and move against an attack. In the following round, we may have the defensive fighter add hand traps to his defensive

Stage One keeps students outside of critical distance practicing only hand strikes, blocks and footwork while wearing hand pads and mouthpieces.

a verbal review of the sparring attitude towards each other, which is, "I'll make sure you don't get hurt."

Also, explain to the students that while control is required and demanded, they are going to get accidentally whacked on occasion just as they are going to whack someone else. Teach them exactly how to inform their partner if the contact is too hard. You can even talk to them about the tone in which they make the request to lighten up. An angry demand may elicit a different response than a respectful but firm request.

Respect and courtesy are the key attitudes. Make sure that the person being requested to lighten up is taught that "Yes ma'am" or "Yes sir" is the *only* acceptable response. *Only the person getting hit can determine the contact level and he cannot be questioned.*

Graduating to Head Contact

After an additional eight months in that class, the students graduate into the blue and red belt level. At this point, they are allowed to make light head contact in addition to moderate body contact to the rib-guard

Stage Two adds kicking drills executed with shin, groin and foot protectors. From this stage, students progress to non-contact or blocking-contact-only sparring.

choices. For round three, we may slow things down slightly and place the defensive fighter with his back against a wall to prevent him from running from his opponent. The final round could allow a counter technique to be thrown.

So, through this structure, we're preventing the fighters from being overwhelmed by trying to figure out on their own what to do. At the same time, they are actively, enjoyably and safely engaged in a sparring-like exercise. The end result is, the defensive fighter gains confidence in avoiding contact.

You can see within this scenario that there is no winner or loser. Instead the students are taught to judge the match by how well they stuck to the strategies of the drill.

While the majority of the classtime devoted to sparring is spent on limited sparring drills, we will allow the students to go a round or two of free-sparring under strict black belt supervision. The matches always begin with the students introducing themselves and shaking hands with their partner and

Stage Three adds a rib guard for body–contact–only sparring.

area. Students are taught to strike the headgear and not the face.

You may think that 12 to 16 months is a long time to wait to spar with head contact. I think many of your students might disagree with you. I would also argue that your students have a lifetime to spar from that point on.

Students must be mentally conditioned and have their confidence and tenacity built to prepare them for actual sparring, which is part of the Phase One Training explained in Chapter 2 in the first section of the book. At that point, mentally they are ready to face the challenges sparring will present. But now, after a year of training, they're ready to meet it head-on with excitement and anticipation instead of anxiety and trepidation.

Eight months later, they graduate into the brown and black belt class, where the intensity and contact level is somewhat more "realistic." But after close to two years of training and preparation, these students are ready for the challenge mentally and physically.

Take good care of your students and nurture them along to ensure they are going to be part of your school and part of our martial arts family for a very long time. When they enroll, they are investing a lot of trust in your leadership and guidance. Few areas of the martial arts can be as confusing or intimidating as sparring. Keep a long-term black belt-oriented perspective on training your students and you will have a much better chance of having them stick around to successfully achieve that goal—and more. ■

The final stage allows full, free–form sparring with light contact wearing full protective gear.

Section III

INTRODUCTION TO PSYCHOLOGY

CHAPTER 12
Teaching Strategies by Age Group

CHAPTER 13
The Power of Instilling Purpose in Teaching Martial Arts

CHAPTER 14
What is a Healthy Martial Arts Hierarchy?

CHAPTER 15
The Power of Motivation and Charisma in the Martial Arts Instructor

CHAPTER 16
The Role of Discipline, Praise and Punishment

CHAPTER 17
Teaching Character Skills Responsibly

CHAPTER 18
How to Teach Students with Attention Deficit Disorder

CHAPTER 19
Working with Parents of Students

The degree of success any martial arts instructor will have in working with today's diverse student body will be in direct proportion to his/her ability to communicate, educate and motivate the students consistently.

Whereas in the past, when martial arts classes consisted of highly motivated adults being pushed to the limit by adult instructors, today's schools have students with a wide variety of ages and athletic abilities.

This section will provide the reader with established methods of effectively teaching in the many different situations that today's martial arts classroom may present. From teaching children with Attention Deficit Disorder to learning how to effectively discipline or even punish students, this section provides the proven tools, techniques and teaching strategies necessary for today's martial arts instructor.

Teaching Strategies By Age Group

BY DERENDA TIMMONS-SCHUBERT, PH. D.

Teaching Strategies By Age Group

Teaching according to developmental levels can make the martial arts learning experience more pleasurable and effective for all students. There are benefits for instructors as well. Specifically, the instructor should create lesson plans designed to meet the needs of students. The better educated martial arts instructors are about the developmental abilities of students, the better the lesson plans can be designed to meet the needs of those students.

The study of martial arts involves thinking, physical conditioning, emotional involvement, and an examination of moral character. For these reasons, this chapter will focus on these aspects of development, and how the martial arts instructor can use the information to design lesson plans which truly meet the needs of students.

This chapter will review the cognitive ("thinking"), communication, physical, emotional and moral developmental patterns of age groups from preschooler to adults. We will explore how these factors influence martial arts training. Furthermore, we will consider special issues such as gender differences, learning styles, and multiple-age ranges training together.

The information presented in this chapter is to serve as a guideline for understanding life-span development. Varying paces of maturation, physical make-up, cultural differences, education, and life experience can affect the pace at which an individual moves through the stages of development. Therefore, consider this chapter your basic guide into child and adult development. To make it easier for the reader to incorporate the information, the chapter has been organized by age groups.

How Children Process Information

One of the most famous theorists in the area of cognitive ("thinking") development is Jean Piaget (pronounced, pee-a-zhay'). His theories focused on how children process information and how that processing changes over time. Piaget demonstrated that children think differently than adults. He was interested in how children acquire and use information about their world and experiences (Papalia & Olds, 1996).

Within the next several sections, Piaget's work will provide the basis for how children, adolescents and adults think. We will use the research about moral development provided by Kohlberg and Gilligan to understand how people develop a sense of conscience. Research has revealed that cognitive and moral development occurs in a predictable sequence of stages, and no stage is skipped.

Specific Age Groups: Preschoolers (Ages 4-6)
1. Thinking (Pre-Operational Stage)

Piaget examined how preschoolers process information and titled this stage the "Pre-Operational Stage."

Children in this stage demonstrate the ability to understand information in concrete, simplistic manners. They exhibit the ability to use intuitive thinking, also known as "doing what feels right." They can engage in pretend play and imitate behaviors that are not being demonstrated in front of them. Since pretend play is such an important element of the preschool age, they exhibit limited ability to separate fantasy from reality.

Furthermore, it's important to note that children in this age range are just understanding at the age that things can be reversed (that is, doors open and close; people can jump up and down). They also have a tendency to attribute human characteristics to inanimate objects. Sophie, a five-year-old martial arts student, told her instructor that her teddy bear wanted to take class to learn how to "do kicks."

Tip: Preschoolers are attracted to animals as characters in their books, stories and movies. A martial arts instructor can take advantage of this interest by incorporating animal images in the teaching. For example, instruct children to "run like cheetahs," "jump like frogs," or "reach tall like giraffes." Children will enjoy the playfulness and think you speak their language.

Preschoolers tend to focus on details of objects, which is why they can get stuck on the color, shape, noise, or fancy move of a new technique, uniform or toy. One child I knew was squirming in class so much the instructor thought he needed a bathroom break. Upon investigation, it was discovered his uniform tag was scratching his back! The instructor gave a sigh of relief, thinking he may have been cleaning up a different kind of a mess.

Additionally, children in this age group have a limited ability to understand the perspective of others. Therefore, the child will *not* understand why the instructor is losing his mind when the five-year-old is running laps (giggling the whole way) around the instructor's legs.

Six-year-old children are typically trial-and-error learners. They attempt a skill, it works, and they do it again. If it doesn't work, they might try the skill in a different way. Six-year-old children can state their age, print simple words, and know the difference between day and night.

2. Physical

A four-year-old child can run as well as control stops and turns. The four-year-old can jump 24-33 inches. They can hop four-to-six steps on one foot and descend a staircase alternating feet. Four-year-olds can jump, run and throw a ball. Four-year-olds are beginning to learn how to skip (Papalia & Olds, 1996).

A five-year-old is able to run with skill and hop and jump rope. While playing a game, five-year-olds are able to start and stop. They can easily hop a distance of 16 feet and use alternating feet without help to descend a staircase (Papalia & Olds, 1996).

A six-year-old child can jump rope, trot, climb, hop and gallop around the training floor. Six-year-old children begin to use their hands as tools, as seen in their ability to tie shoelaces. They can skip on both feet alternately and hop on one foot for ten feet. They are able to walk heel-to-toe in a straight line and catch a bounced ball (Papalia & Olds, 1996).

Tip: Energetic preschoolers love to run, jump and hop around a training floor. Take advantage of this energy by incorporating these skills into warm-ups and skill-training exercises.

Tip: The game "Alligator Pits" is a fun way to incorporate physical and cognitive skills. Place five or six shields on the floor in a straight line approximately five feet apart or in a random pattern. Instruct the children to jump/hop over the shields (alligator pits) with feet together. For a variation, ask the children to hop on one foot or jump side-to-side over the shields.

If the student lands in the alligator pit, he or she does two-to-five "fun-ups" (push-ups).

Tip: Each instructor holds a foam-padded "blocker" and the children form lines in front of the instructors. The instructor moves the blocker left and right, low to the ground, and the student is expected to jump over and out of the way. The instructor also moves the blocker vertically and then horizontally at the student's head. The child is instructed to duck a horizontal blocker move and move side-to-side for a vertical blocker move. As the children become more familiar with the activity, the instructor can speed up and vary his blocker moves.

3. Social/Language

Preschoolers are a talkative group of people. One mother commented that on a stressful day, she felt her preschooler's incessant talking was comparable to Chinese water torture!

Preschoolers begin to explode with language abilities and the excitement that they can communicate and express themselves in a way that is understood by others. Plus, their growing awareness and curiosity about the world around them gives them much to talk about. They can express themselves, but they may not understand complex questions.

As an example of the difference just one year makes at this stage, by the age of five, children have a vocabulary of over 2,000 words; they can repeat sentences of ten syllables or more. Six-year-olds can understand 2,500 words. Preschoolers can answer questions beginning with the phrase, "What do you do when you are scared, cold, happy…? Six-year-olds use all types of sentence structures and use pronouns (for example, I, you and we) correctly (Papalia & Olds, 1996).

Preschoolers can dress with little supervision. They can separate from parents fairly well. Preschoolers like to succeed at all they attempt. When frustrated, the child may exhibit a temper tantrum or cry when things do not go his or her way.

Preschoolers respond well to praise and encouragement. The use of external rewards, such as stickers, can have a positive impact on the children. Stickers and patches may serve as concrete symbols of accomplishment.

They are able to play cooperatively with others in

imaginative or pretend play. Also, they are able to develop relationships with relatives and believe that death is reversible.

Tip: Preschoolers enjoy playing with other preschoolers. The martial arts school is a natural place for positive preschool interactions to occur. They are talkative and curious. Consider asking them questions about their strengths (things they are "good at") and weaknesses (things they wish they could "do better").

Incorporate how rules of respect and self-control they learn at the school can happen at home, too. They will try their best to impress you with their skills, and their parents will appreciate the teaching of important life skills.

Tip: Team Work Drills are popular ways to incorporate cooperation and interaction between children. The drill, "Pass the Ball," requires the children to stand in a straight line all facing the same way. The instructor gives the first student a ball and the child passes the ball over his head. The ball is passed down the line in this manner. As the ball returns to the first person, it is passed between the students' legs. To increase the difficulty and challenge, incorporate two or more balls into the game.

Tip: "Kick the Balloon" is another Team Work Drill. Break children into smaller groups of three or four. Each group is given an inflated balloon. The children are in a circle. The instructor throws the balloon into the middle of the circle, and the children are instructed to keep the balloon in the air by using a specified kick. This is a popular and fun activity. It gets rave reviews from the kids!

School Age (Ages 7-12)

1. Thinking (Concrete Operational, 7-12 Years Old)

Piaget studied elementary school-aged children to understand how they gather and make sense of information. He called this stage "Concrete Operational."

He discovered that children in this age range take in information, transform it, and manipulate it so that it makes sense to them. They can classify information putting ideas and facts into categories and sets (Papalia & Olds, 1996). Instructors can teach martial arts in sets by grouping skills. For example, the instructor might teach all of the blocks one week and all the kicks that move forward the next week.

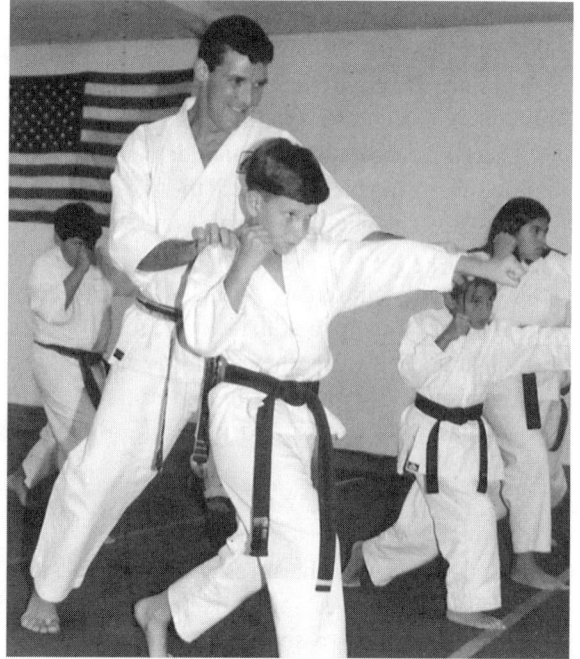

Tip: Elementary-school kids (ages 7 to 11) organize information in categories and sets. Organize your lesson plans by focusing on one skill area for each class. Too many different, disconnected skills will confuse and frustrate a school-age student.

For example, cover blocks by teaching the specific block, then explain the purpose of the block. After you teach the block, have the children pair up with partners and practice the block. Have the children take turns defending against the block and then, exhibiting the block.

Children within this stage can understand sequencing (Papalia & Olds, 1996). More specifically, they know how to think of things in the following logical manner: first step, second step, third step, etc. Martial arts training is often sequenced-based, from forms to sparring. Thus, children in this age range can thrive in the martial arts-training experience.

Children in this age range also understand comparisons of size, such as big and small or big and bigger, or kick high, medium and low. During this stage, the growth and development of intellectual skills supersedes physical development.

2. Physical

Seven-year-old children enjoy high-energy

sports as well as sitdown games. Because of their more developed physical abilities, these children begin to display the ability to execute accurate jumping jacks. Their gross motor abilities are so well-developed they are able to ride a two-wheel bike successfully.

Eight-year-old children further develop their bike-riding, running, skipping, jumping and climbing skills. An eight-year-old child's movements are more graceful than younger peers. They exhibit skill in using their eye-hand coordination. Thus, children are often taught cursive writing (handwriting) at this age.

Nine-year-old children become skilled in active physical play. They experience well-developed hand-eye coordination. During this stage of development, the children reach a growth plateau.

Ten to 12-year-old children possess good muscle control. Their manipulation skills are almost equal to those of adults. Manipulation skills refer to the use of hands, arms and legs to move or control an object. Dribbling a basketball or using nunchaku are examples of manipulation skills.

Between the ages of ten and 12, gender differences become more pronounced. Girls have a tendency to lag behind in physical strength. Children within this age range experience a growth spurt. This growth spurt is observed in girls sooner than in boys (Papalia & Olds, 1996).

Tip: School-age children possess physical abilities, which allow them to be successful in the martial arts. They are able to demonstrate good eye-hand coordination and an interest in physical sports.

Incorporate multi-skilled activities into warm-ups, such as running to one wall, jumping over shields, and punching a heavy bag in an obstacle course type configuration. The kids will enjoy the variety and physical requirements of such a drill.

3. Social/Language

Seven-year-old children use language to share their experiences with others. Eight-year-old children use many words and sentences and adjectives appropriately. By the age of nine, children demonstrate well-developed use of language and sentence structure.

Seven to nine-year-old children are increasingly self-sufficient, as evidenced by their ability to dress and undress themselves. They begin to utilize social skills, such as manners, on a more frequent, independent basis. Seven-year-olds begin to enjoy some time alone. They will typically have a best friend.

Eight-year-old children begin to develop a variety of friendships. Seven-year-olds begin to note differences between themselves and others. Eight-year-old children are concerned with others' opinions of them. Nine-year-old children become less influenced by their parents and begin the journey of defining their own values. They also start to become more friendly and engaged with others.

For ten to 12-year-old children, their peer group is extremely important. They prefer to play with their own gender. Children in this age range make comparisons about others based on psychological characteristics, such as nicer, smarter and funnier.

The most important social influences are people in the neighborhood and school. The children monitor their behavior to avoid feelings of inferiority. The developmental social task of children within this age range is to master social and academic skills (Papalia & Olds, 1996).

Tip: When talking to children, consider the language you use. The younger the child, the shorter the sentences and the more simple the language. The older the person, the longer the sentences and the more abstract, philosophical you can be. Also, look the children in the eye, by kneeling down to speak to them. Convey respect, model positive social skills, and you will increase the probability of attention and self-respect.

Adolescent (Ages 13-17)
1. Thinking (Formal Operational, 13-18+ Years Old)

Piaget identified the final stage of cognitive development as the "Formal Operational Stage."

The Formal Operational Stage extends into adulthood. During this stage, people develop the ability to think abstractly and consider hypothetical situations. When given a premise or issue, they can logically

develop a conclusion. Thus, they have the capability of debating and considering philosophical issues. Because of this newfound way of analyzing information, adolescents can appear indecisive and hypocritical.

The skills of the Formal Operational Stage allow people to consider alternate explanations for observed events. Also, individuals develop an awareness that one must anticipate, formulate and develop strategies for dealing with problems (Flavell, 1977). Cognitive ("thinking") maturity occurs because of the internal and external changes in the adolescent's life. They are being exposed to more experiences, and the brain matures.

Tip: The "Tunnel of Doom" exercise can promote thinking development. The Tunnel of Doom requires the students to stand in two lines facing each other. One student is asked to close his eyes. Then, the instructor chooses several students to grab the identified student. The child opens his eyes and walks down the Tunnel of Doom. The identified attackers grab the student, and he or she must react with a self-defense technique. This activity can also be used with adults.

It is estimated that half of the adult population reaches the Formal Operational Stage of development (Papalia & Olds, 1996). Many people do not reach the Formal Operational Stage of development because of limited exposure to advanced educational challenges (that is, college, graduate school, traveling to different countries/cultures). Therefore, most students will be operating in the Concrete Operational Stage of development. Presenting information in a straightforward, concrete manner will be a successful teaching approach. With further cultural and educational challenges, the adolescent and adult can promote advanced formal reasoning.

2. Physical

Adolescents experience rapid maturation and physical development. In both genders, the growth spurt impacts all skeletal and muscle groups (Papalia & Olds, 1996). The changes occur at their own rate, which means parts of the body may be out of proportion. Thus, adolescents experience awkwardness and clumsiness. Agility, strength and flexibility eventually return. Additionally, adolescents experience the development of sexual characteristics, which leave the adolescent feeling self-conscious.

Tip: Instructors can promote positive self-esteem during this awkward time of life by complimenting the student on skill development and offering the adolescent age-appropriate leadership responsibilities (that is, assisting in the younger children's classes, performing on the demonstration team).

3. Social/Language.

The language abilities of adolescents are comparable to those of adults. With the exposure of education and culture, the adolescent's vocabulary and eloquent use of language expand.

During adolescence individuals develop a renewed self-centeredness, characterized by self-consciousness and self-criticism, because they're in search of an identity. It is as though they imagine an audience watching their every move.

Adolescents are susceptible to peer pressure. Most of the conformity to peers is usually restricted to fashion, music and social activities. Family attitudes about careers, politics and morality typically influence the teen. (Sebald, 1986; Wilks, 1986).

More specifically, 13-year-olds struggle with independence versus dependence. Fourteen-year-olds challenge authority, and vacillate between being reasonable and competent to rebellious. Fifteen-year-olds present a range of behavior described as that of admiring adults alternated with arguing with adults about unimportant details. 16 to 19-year-olds adopt adult responsibilities with sudden, short episodes of regression to typically younger behavior.

Tip: At times, the attitudes of adolescents can appear less than respectful of adults. It would be natural to respond to this disrespect by harshly punishing or speaking to the student. However, a more beneficial response, which addresses his developmental level, would be to clearly and firmly state a more appropriate way for the teen to speak to you or other members of the school. Give the teen a chance to correct the mistake. If the teen continues to be defiant, request that he or she "cool off" and return to class on another day. Speak to the teen in private. Confronting the teen in front of peers will promote humiliation and continued disrespect.

For Your Information

Anorexia nervosa is an eating disorder involving self-starvation. *Bulimia nervosa* is an eating disorder in which the individual eats a lot of food and then vomits to rid oneself of the food. *Obesity* is an eating disorder which involves overeating (Papalia & Olds, 1996).

These eating disorders commonly occur during adolescence and have life threatening consequences. Anorexia and bulimia are more commonly seen in females, but males can also be affected. If you suspect a martial arts student suffers from one of these disorders, discuss the matter with the student and parents. You could save a life.

Adults (Ages 18+)
1. Thinking (Formal Operational)

As indicated in the previous section, it is estimated that one-half of all adults reach Formal Operational Stage of cognitive development. With more cultural experiences, opportunities for experimentation, and educational experiences, one can expand knowledge and wisdom. In general, adults have the capacity to understand abstract information, incorporate various pieces of data to form conclusions, and consider alternative resolutions.

Tip: The "Tunnel of Doom" exercise described in the adolescent section can be modified for adults to promote thinking development. This activity is called "The Box". The Box exercise for adults requires the students to stand in groups of five. Four students form a box, and one student stands in the middle of the box. The box is formed by having two students stand on the side, one student stands in front of, and the other student stands behind the person in the box. The identified attackers randomly grab the student, and he or she must react with a self-defense technique.

2. Physical

Physicians and mental-health professionals recommend exercise as an adjunct to medical treatment and the overall health benefits for a variety of medical, physical and mental-health reasons. Research has indicated that health is an important predictor of life satisfaction as people age (Chappell & Badger, 1989; Willits & Crider, 1988). Therefore, martial arts instruction can become an integral part of an adult's health regime.

Studies have indicated the physiological benefits of exercise for pulmonary, cardiac, and flexibility and strength (Kastenbaum, 1993). Research has also indicated exercise has a positive benefit for the mental health of adults (Kastenbaum, 1993).

The mode of exercise most commonly prescribed for adults is a low-intensity, rhythmic activity which uses all the muscle groups (Kastenbaum, 1993). Walking and jogging are commonly-prescribed activities. Martial arts provide the added benefit of mental exercise by focusing on the use of concentration and meditation.

The physical abilities of an adult are most dependent on how that individual has cared for himself or herself. The martial arts instructor needs to consider the adult's overall health and encourage the adult to work consistently at his own pace. This attitude is likely to reduce the incidence of injury and keep the adult engaged in the martial arts experience.

3. Social/Language

Language skills are well-developed. Adults are able to use language to communicate and entertain.

In general, an adult has typically developed the ability to engage in meaningful interpersonal relationships, read social cues, and display appropriate manners.

In Early Adulthood, the establishment of intimate emotional bonds is the main developmental task. During Middle Adulthood, the focus for adults is to be committed to future generations. During the later years of adulthood, one begins to focus on a sense of integrity and coming to terms with one's own limitations (Papalia & Olds, 1996).

PIAGET'S STAGES OF COGNITIVE DEVELOPMENT

Pre-Operational (Ages 4-6)
Concrete, simplistic thinking
Concrete Operational (Ages 7-12)
Transforms and manipulates information
Formal Operational (Ages 13-Adult)
Abstract thinking, logical problem solving

Moral Development

Since much of martial arts training emphasizes character development, a discussion of moral development will be presented here (see also Chapter 17: Teaching Character Skills Responsibly).

Lawrence Kohlberg created a system for understanding the stages of moral development, or how people determine exhibiting appropriate behavior.

Criticism has followed Kohlberg's system because he based his ideas only on Caucasian males. Therefore, disagreement exists as to how the information applies to other cultures and to women.

KOHLBERG'S STAGES OF MORAL DEVELOPMENT

Preconventional Morality (Ages 4-10)

Stage 1: Punishment and Obedience Orientation. Focus on avoiding punishment.

Stage 2: Instrumental Hedonism
Obtain rewards and satisfy personal needs.

Conventional Morality (Ages 10-13)

Stage 3: Good Boy/Good Girl
Behavior is linked to acting how others approve or like.

Stage 4: Law and Order
Follow rules set by legitimate authority.

Post-Conventional Morality (Ages 13, Young Adulthood, or Never)

Stage 5: Morality of Contract, Individual Rights, and Democratically-Accepted Laws. The right action is the one that is consistent with democratically determined law.

Stage 6: Morality of Individual Principles of Conscience
Right and wrong are determined by self-chosen universal principles.

Gilligan (1982) stated that women are more likely to define morality based on their relationships to others and their sense of caring and responsibility within relationships. Both Kohlberg's and Gilligan's theories are presented in chart form in this chapter.

As Kohlberg's system suggests, preschoolers and early elementary-school students are motivated to behave by avoiding punishment. Therefore, when teaching martial arts to this age group, focus on clearly defining the consequences of misbehavior, such as time out. (See also Chapter 16: The Role of Discipline, Praise and Punishment).

As indicated by Kohlberg's system, older elementary-school students will likely be influenced by their concern to please others and obey authority. Therefore, an instructor can focus on the use of the relationship with a child as a way to manage behavior in the martial arts school.

Adolescents and adults make moral decisions based on laws or their own principles. To facilitate a positive experience, clearly display and define the "laws" of the martial arts school.

GILLIGAN'S ETHIC OF CARE: MORAL DEVELOPMENT

Survival
Caring for self with the aim of ensuring one's happiness and avoiding suffering or being hurt.

Survival to Responsibility
Understanding connection between self and others; aware of others' needs, but care of self is most important.

Goodness
Caring for others; elaborating the concept of responsibility; conflict arises over hurting someone.

Goodness to Truth in Relationships
Flexible, thoughtfulness; struggle with dilemmas; reconsider relationship between self and others.

Caring for Both Self and Others
Focus on dynamics of relationship through an understanding of the connection between others and self; condemns hurt and exploitation.

Within any relationship, issues of trust and caring emerge. Martial arts instructors will have such issues emerge with his or her students. As Gilligan depicted, our relationships to others can significantly impact our moral behavior. Interactions with others may be influenced by how much caring we feel toward the person. This theory of moral development may provide an explanation to male instructors and students on what appears to be "peculiar" behavior displayed by female students.

For instance, I witnessed examples of the role of caring influencing behavior while watching adult women spar. After a good point is scored, it is not uncommon to hear the scoring woman say to her opponent, "I'm sorry."

Memory

Memory capabilities are different for the various age groups.

Tip: When asking a preschool student or early elementary school student (7-8 year olds) to remember a move, display the move and then ask the child what it is you are demonstrating.

At all ages, recognition memory (recognizing a familiar concept, word or movement) is better than recall (pulling it from the recesses of one's mind), but the difference is more pronounced in younger than in older children.

With development, children's memory relies more on symbolic concepts. Their ability to remember information and access their strategies for remembering information improves with age. Problem-solving strategies become more efficient and flexible as children age. (Mussen, Conger, Kagan, and Huston, 1986).

Children do not use rehearsal and memory strategies until age nine or ten. Thus, a child under the age of nine will not utilize special ways to remember information. Singing a song or stating the information in a rhythm can facilitate remembering for younger children. Under age seven, children overestimate their ability to remember information, but by the ages of nine and ten, they remember as accurately as adults (Flavell, 1986).

Tip: Use memory aids such as acronyms, which are defined as using the first letter of each phrase or word to make a word that reminds the student of the concept. For example, when teaching the five tenets of tae kwon do, which are Courtesy, Integrity, Perseverance, Self-Control and Indomitable Spirit, the instructor tells the students to think of "CIPSI," which sounds like Pepsi.

The children are now given an acronym to help them remember a large chunk of information.

Learning Styles

When teaching the student, not only does the martial arts instructor need to consider developmental level, one needs to address Learning Styles as well.

The title, Learning Styles, refers to how a person receives information and the mode in which the information is perceived and organized internally (Gittins, 1995).

The different styles of intaking information include:

1. Hearing (auditory).
2. Seeing (visual)
3. Doing (kinesthetic)

We all have preferences for how we incorporate and learn information. It is likely that we all use these senses in some combination with a preference of one of the senses.

The two styles of perceiving and organizing information are referred to as:

1. Global
2. Analytic

As you read this chapter, consider your own style of learning. The more you understand about your Learning Style, the better prepared you will be to teach.

1. Auditory

Auditory learners understand best by hearing information presented to him or her. The use of clearly-spoken, specific directions allows the auditory learner to be successful. Instructors need to provide such details as left, right, high, low, foot, hand, forward, back, and the name of the stance (Gittins, 1995).

Auditory learners tend to talk to their instructors, to their neighbors, to the audience members, etc. While this may appear disrespectful, an instructor needs to consider that the student is attempting to process the information.

One way to minimize disruptive behavior is to have the learner participate in a question-and-answer time. Other ideas include having the auditory learner count during training or explain a technique (Gittins, 1995).

2. Visual

Visual learners need information presented in clearly observable methods. Watching how a technique is executed by a role model is the easiest way to teach visual learners. Gittin (1995) suggests staggering lines to allow visual learners to take advantage of role models. The use of assistant instructors as role models (see Chapter 23: Proper Use of Student Instructors) can be immensely helpful to a visual learner.

3. Kinesthetic

Kinesthetic learners acquire information by participating in the activity. To effectively teach a kinesthetic learner, demonstrate the technique and have the student practice the skill. Once the student starts to "get the feel" of the technique, the instructor needs to explain the concept behind the technique and make corrections (Gittins, 1995).

This teaching sequence is important to ensure that the information is fully comprehended by the kinesthetic learner. It is suggested that the kinesthetic learner needs to gain a little competence or, again, "get the feel" of a task before verbal information is meaningful (Gittins, 1995).

Kinesthetic learners need a variety of activities to maintain their interest. Pairing a kinesthetic learner with an advanced martial arts student is a winning combination because the kinesthetic learner will acquire new skills (Gittins, 1995).

Kinesthetic learners are active people. Standing still is not part of their nature. They are not exhibiting disrespectful behavior, just attempting to learn. Therefore, you will want to keep lectures relatively short and include numerous opportunities for movement and practice.

4. Global

Global learners take in and organize information in an overall manner. They observe connections between concepts and try to understand the "big picture". Global learners prefer an overview of the information.

While they take in all of the information, global learners have difficulty organizing and structuring the data. Therefore, the instructor will need to provide the structure and organization. Setting and meeting goals along their martial arts training can provide the necessary structure. Furthermore, global learners comprehend information best if the instructor can explain how the technique or philosophy can be applied to the student's life outside of the school.

Analytic learners take apart a skill to understand precisely where an arm is placed in, for example, a high block and the exact angle one should have the base foot in a roundhouse kick. The instructor will need to encourage the student to understand that while there are some precise expectations, individual differences may result in a wide range of correct techniques.

Analytic learners may become overwhelmed learning a martial arts form all at once. Therefore, an instructor needs to break down the task into smaller parts. Analytic learners will feel most comfortable with time to work on the technique alone. This makes them faithful, hard-working students.

Tips for Teaching

First and foremost, discover your learning and processing styles. Such awareness will provide you with valuable information. When teaching class, you will have a variety of learning styles and processing styles present among your students. Adopt a style of using a variety of techniques and modes of information delivery (visual, auditory and kinesthetic) to convey martial arts concepts. By using a multi-modal approach, you will likely appease most of your students.

1. Just for Fun

The next time you are learning to play a game—any game—with a group of friends, listen to how each player wants to learn the rules.

You will likely hear someone say, "Tell me how to play." This person is probably an auditory learner. Someone else may say, "Let me read the rules." You probably have a visual learner in the crowd. Another friend may say, "Let's just play a round and see how it goes." This person is likely a kinesthetic learner. Have fun with the investigation!

2. Gender Differences

When teaching martial arts, gender differences are an important consideration. This does not mean that males or females are superior to one another, but an instructor needs to acknowledge the differences and strengths of each gender.

Research indicates that males and females

Global learners can work well in groups and with partners because the interactions further assist their learning. Global learners respond well to external rewards, such as praise and promotion.

5. Analytic

Analytic learners examine the parts or details of a situation and then make their decisions. They prefer accurate, detailed, organized information (Gittins, 1995). They prefer to work alone and require time to perfect their skills.

This emphasis on the details of a technique can impede progress. The instructor will need to monitor the pace and find ways to encourage the student to move on to another detail.

differ little with regard to cognitive ability. When gender differences are noted, they generally do not appear until preadolescence. However, males score higher on tests of visual-spatial abilities and, at age 12, on measures of math (Maccoby & Jacklin, 1974).

Between the ages of ten and 11, females tend to score higher on verbal ability tasks (Maccoby & Jacklin, 1974). During adulthood, females display superiority in verbal reasoning and word fluency while males continue to excel in tasks involving numbers and spatial relationships (Maccoby & Jacklin, 1974).

Hyde and Lin (1988) report that gender differences have declined in the last decade or two. Much of the difference between the motor abilities between boys and girls has been the expectations and level of coaching and the rates of participation (Hall & Lee, 1984).

Summary

As this chapter has presented, there exists a vast amount of information regarding cognitive, physical, social, language and moral development.

Young children are more simplistic in their understanding and processing of information. They look to their family for comfort and values. Preschoolers are talkative and active. Elementary-school-aged children begin to internally manipulate and transform the information they receive. Socially, they begin to notice differences between themselves and others. They tend to spend some time alone and develop a best friendship.

Adolescents experience a growth spurt, which assists in the development of more abstract reasoning and physical maturation. Such bodily changes can create self-consciousness. Adolescents may test the authority of teachers and parents. It is their avenue for defining themselves by rejecting or challenging the values presented to them.

Adults have the ability to think abstractly and problem-solve. Generally, they have well-developed social skills and tend to establish relationships with others.

Moral development spans from behaving to avoid punishment to making decisions based on one's own principles. Furthermore, learning styles and different ways to perceive information challenge the martial arts instructor's lesson planning.

Given all of these differences between the age groups, it would be quite a challenge to teach a martial arts class that met all of the learning needs of various-aged students. When a class is taught at a level beyond or below the capabilities of the student, he or she may become frustrated or discouraged. The instructor is then at risk for losing a student.

There may be types of classes in which it would be enjoyable and appropriate for a mixture of age groups. The age groups designated in this chapter serve as guidelines for instructors to implement in their schools. At times, because of a student's level of physical and social maturity, an instructor may decide to place the student in a class different from his or her same-age peers.

> For example, Joshua was a 13-year-old male who was 5'8" and 160 pounds. He towered over his same-age peers and certainly intimidated a few of his fellow students! Due to his size and level of maturity, his instructor decided to place him in the adult classes.

Understanding the various developmental tasks of the different age groups will assist instructors in creating lesson plans that truly meet the needs of their students. When you meet the learning needs of your students, you will likely retain happy, well-trained, devoted students. Consider all of the developmental aspects presented in this chapter, and you will increase the probability of effective, well-designed lesson plans. ∎

Bibliography

Chappell, N. L. & Badger, M. (1989). Social isolation and well–being. Journal of Gerontology, 44, 169–176

Flavell, J. H. (1986). The development of children's knowledge about the appearance–reality distinction. American Psychologist, 41, 418–425

Flavell, J. H. (1977). Cognitive development. Englewood Cliffs, N.J.: Prentice–Hall

Gilligan, C. (1982). In a different voice: Women's conceptions of self and morality. Harvard Educational Review, 47, 481–517

Gittins, C. J. (1995). Adapting karate instruction for learning styles. In martial arts teachers on teaching. Carol A. Wiley (Ed.). Berkeley, CA: Frog, Ltd

Hall E.G. & Lee, A. M. (1984). Sex differences in motor performance of young children: Fact or fiction. Sex Roles, 10, 217–230

Hyde, J. S. & Linn, M. C. (1988). Gender differences in verbal ability: A meta–analysis. Psychology Bulletin, 104, 53–69

Kastenbaum, R. (Ed.) (1993). The encyclopedia of adult development. Phoenix, AZ: Oryx Press

Kohlberg, L. (1976). Moral stages and moralization: The cognitivedevelopmental approach. In T. Likona (Ed.), Moral Development and behavior: Theory, research, and social issues. New York: Norton

Maccoby, E. E. & Jacklin, C. N. (1974). What we know and what we don't know about sex differences. Psychology Today, 109–112

Mussen, P. H., Conger, J. J., Kagan, J. & Huston, A. C. (1984). Child development and personality. New York: Harper & Row

Papalia, D. & Olds, S.W. (1996). A child's world: Infancy through adolescence. New York: McGraw–Hill, Inc

Sebald, H. (1986). Adolescents' shifting orientation toward parents and peers: A curvilinear trend over recent decades. Journal of Marriage and Family, 48, 5–13

Wilks, J. (1986). The relative importance of parents and friends in adolescent decision–making. Journal of Youth and Adolescence, 15, 323–334.

Willits, F. K. & Crider, D. M. (1988). Health rating and life satisfaction in later years

The Power of Instilling Purpose In Teaching Martial Arts

By Joe Lewis

The Power Of Instilling Purpose In Teaching Martial Arts

Martial arts students vary as widely, in both physical and psychological attributes, as do the teaching styles of various instructors. Whereas our first impulse as instructors may be to teach in the way that we ourselves were taught, it is important that we consciously develop a teaching style that can effectively address the needs of *each* student in our classes.

This chapter will convey, in abbreviated form, the basic lessons I have learned through my 30 plus years regarding:

1) The importance of recognizing and honoring each student's individuality.
2) Teaching methods that I have found to be particularly effective with a wide variety of students.

Individual Goals, Individual Needs

One of the greatest ongoing challenges in teaching a group class is to provide each student with the sense of being "seen" by his teacher. To be recognized as an individual with individual goals and abilities, a martial artist whose specific needs are respected and addressed. This is a challenge that must be met daily, even hourly, if we are to be responsible and effective teachers of the martial arts.

But how do we go about helping promote a student's individuality in the typical group-class teaching situation? Students like a good challenge, but how do we avoid making the class experience too easy for some and impossible for others?

Cultivating the following personal qualities will go a long way toward addressing these issues:

1. Awareness. The teacher must be familiar with each student's desires and needs as they relate to the martial arts. While not all students are interested in combat, all students do need to have a sense of steady accomplishment. For some, this means executing their skills in a sparring context; others are content with simply knowing what to do and how to do it.

2. Acceptance. The instructor must understand and be willing to accept the starting point of each student. For instance, one student may be very assertive and eager, even overly aggres-

sive, while another may have a low pain tolerance and be more reserved about engaging wholeheartedly in any combative physical activity. While your natural inclination might be to favor the combative aspect of the martial arts, an educated teacher must accept and understand the more reserved individual as well. Consequently, instructors must formulate a program to assist both of the above students equally despite their differences. (Indeed, by many standards it is the reserved student that can actually benefit more from the martial arts.)

In other words, the instructor must create a level playing field on which all students are equally important and recognized. Even though one may need more time to learn than the other, that extra time does not mean that you are favoring one student over the other. The playing field always remains level.

Responsibility

The instructor must assume personal responsibility, through his behavior, for maintaining that level playing field; that is, to teach by example. Act out the attitude that respect is not rank-oriented but mutual and universal. Recruit your senior students to assist in creating an atmosphere of acceptance and encouragement for *all* students regardless of rank, size, strength or aptitude.

Self-Implementation

How do we provide individual students with a sense of purpose and the experience of steady progress? This is where thoughtful and effective teaching methods come in, as described in the following sections.

Effective Teaching Strategies for Instilling Purpose in Training

Often, schools fall into the trap of teaching what could be described as clinical, sterile, technical execution. In these situations, there is an overemphasis on "correctness" of execution rather than on the technique's *purpose.* Good execution is important, of course, but without purpose behind it the result can be a seemingly heartless, clone-like, rote performance.

It is my conviction that the most effective way to teach martial arts is by a three-level approach.

1. Level One

Level One involves, yes, a focus on execution. For example, the instructor holds in his hand a focus pad and directs the student to fire a strike such as a side kick against the pad. The instructor first goes about correcting the student's form, commenting on how to achieve good balance, good torque in the hips, good extension on the strike, etc. But he doesn't stop there.

2. Level Two

Here, the instructor attaches a purpose or strategy to the specific technique being taught. For example, after spending time on the correct mechanics of the kick in Level One, you might move on to the application of the kick defensively. In this drill, you might tell the student that every time you step toward him he is to adjust his distance backward and fire a defensive side kick to stop you in your tracks.

Now the kick has a purpose and you are ready to move on to Level Three.

3. Level Three.

The third and very critical phase of instruction has to do with helping a student improve his overall attitude or demeanor of execution. In addition to: 1) executing correctly; and 2) combining the execution with appropriate strategic principles, the student must also put *emotional intent* behind his efforts.

Every technique execution needs to have an emotional intent behind it. For example, in executing a strike, one can fire with the intention of just locating a target, or with the intent to stun or damage your opponent upon contact. Coaches refer to this as putting emotional definition, "teeth" or "backbone" into executions. When a student learns to put his body weight (using the correct mechanics) together with an emotional intention, it equals what we in the martial arts refer to as "substance." If a student has substance, he will move with a conviction of purpose; when the student moves with this conviction, he is more apt to convince the opponent who is in charge.

Applying What You Know: Resolving Specific Teaching Challenges

The following are some examples of how various aspects of the three-level approach can be applied to everyday situations all of us are likely to encounter in teaching martial arts.

Working Through Fear of Sparring

How does an instructor help a child overcome his fear of sparring? The first step is to get the young student to accept his fear. Explain that fear is *not* something you run from. It is *not* a sign of weakness, nor does it make you a bad person. All people, all students, and certainly *all* great martial artists feel fear. You should be afraid when you spar; otherwise, you are not going to do well and definitely will not do your best.

So, fear is something you recognize and learn to embrace. Teach that being afraid is not the barometer we use to judge one's lack of courage, but rather how a student chooses to deal with it. Then run a drill such as the following to demonstrate how to use fear as a tool to give your technique executions more energy.

Set up two young students to begin an academic limited-sparring drill. Do not call it "sparring" or a "combat". No score will be kept, no winner declared. The only goal is to follow the strategy you assign to each student.

Inform the child you will work with, that it is not important why he is afraid. It may be fear of getting hit, of not looking good, of feeling helpless or inadequate, etc. Tell the student that the instant he feels fear, he should just fire off his favorite technique, whatever it may be. He must not use any other techniques at that point.

The purpose here is to keep the student's focus simple: Feel the fear and instantly fire the favored technique. For this drill, the student's performance is based solely on how well he follows the prescribed instructions. This relieves the pressure and tends to make the child more assertive. He need no longer worry about deciding what technique to use, but simply fires at the impulse of fear.

Now the student is on the way to accepting his true feelings and integrating them with technique executions. The normally paralyzing aspects of fear should now be replaced with—or at the very least, balanced by—a newly-discovered power to counteract the fear. The student is very likely to repeat his actions, thereby also repeating the lesson and building a pattern of success.

Teaching through Visualization

Great forms performers, like great fighters, share a common trait—an identifiable one that often elevates them above their peers. They project a powerful "emotional energy" during the execution of their form (kata, poomse, etc.). This energy is what Japanese martial artists call "indomitable spirit," but it's not a trait exclusive to any single art or style. Members of the famed wushu troupes of China masterfully display this quality too, part of the reason they generate standing ovations from audiences wherever they perform.

Forms are almost a universal element of today's martial arts curriculum, and are usually a standard part of belt-rank exams. Despite the importance attached to forms, students' attitudes toward learning them are mixed. Some feel awkward, others lackadaisical, and others, especially those predisposed to fighting/sparring, totally bored.

A student's enthusiasm (or lack of it) toward learning forms starts with the instructor and how he teaches them. Then it has to do with the degree of skill and enjoyment each student feels when practicing forms. Teaching students how to identify and then integrate their emotional energy into a form is a means of instilling enthusiasm and even passion into this learning experience.

Students who lack emotional energy while doing a form appear lifeless when executing the moves—to draw an analogy, as if they are "shooting blanks" instead of live ammo. You can exhort these kinds of students over and over— "Move faster! Strike harder!"—without achieving the desired result. This may be because they do not yet understand the kind of emotional energy that will enable them to reach the desired result. Nor do they understand how to connect with it.

One way to facilitate understanding and instill some "fire" or spirit into this kind of situation is to use a visualization exercise. It is the key to opening up the student's emotional energy.

Direct the student to think about some particularly traumatic time in his early life. Perhaps in grade school he was teased or rejected from a group; perhaps in the case of a male student, he was the target of a bully, etc. Such treatment angered the student, hurt his feelings; he felt he deserved better.

This mental exercise ideally gets the student to tap into his emotions. The goal is to get them to express that emotion physically.

Now have the student think about that unpleasant incident while doing the form, but using *only* body language. Tell him to put their emotions behind each move. As they do the form exhort them further, "Now that the strikes look pretty, fire them as if *you really mean it.*"

You should see a big improvement in the "life" or "passion" the student injects into his execution of the form. Having summoned a strong emotional energy, he is much more likely now to know what you mean and to make real, lasting improvements in the performance of the form.

Instilling Purpose in Forms

A teacher needs to explain not only what a student should practice in a form, but also cite the reasons. These three questions should always be answered, and none should be neglected:

1. What?
2. How?
3. Why?

Suppose, for example, that a student executes a kick in a form. The kick is the *what*. Then explain the *how* and the *why*. That is, that folding the knee high keeps the opponent from jamming or smothering your kicking leg. Locking out the kick teaches one that the maximum power is on the end of the strike, the last three or four inches. Defensively, full extension helps keep the smaller, tougher opponent from getting too close and smothering your fire power.

Overcoming Odds

Another challenge instructors face is dealing with students who always experience being at a disadvantage. These individuals constantly find themselves facing off against partners who are much taller or much faster. It is the teacher's task to make sure that these students keep a positive attitude; that they believe they *can* make martial arts work for them.

A typical example would be having a shorter student attempt to control a taller one who is an excellent kicker. The shorter student prefers punching. Watch how focusing plays a part in the following exercise.

The instructor has the students paired together in a drill format. The taller student chooses one kick, the shorter chooses a particular punch. Each is limited to that technique only. Each is to do everything in his power to score with his chosen technique.

There are several ways the instructor can assist the shorter student. (See sidebar for specific drills.) He can have him practice specific footwork strategies to avoid the tall student's kick. He can put the pair through an exercise designed to improve timing skills and sharpen awareness of the opponent's initial move. He can explain to the shorter student that the only way you can be hit by a kick is to

be caught in the "trap" between the end of the kicker's foot and his knee, and then initiate a drill to illustrate.

The last step is to have the two students attempt a limited sparring-type drill. Each will move back and forth trying to score with the kick or the punch. What each will discover is that it is not the tall kicker who has the advantage over the short puncher, but rather the one who focuses best on using his footwork to maintain the correct distance.

The teacher has thus demonstrated to both students the power of using their thinking skills. He has shown both how to gain better control by focusing solely on an effective tactic, instead of worrying about the opponent's technique or physical advantage.

Improving Students' Transitions And Follow-through

Many students have a difficult time landing their first attempt at a favorite technique against their partner. One student may have a great side kick, but inevitably it will sometimes simply not work. In these cases, instructors can show them how to focus on using their technique (in this case, a side kick) not as a striking tool but as a distraction—to collapse their partner's defense or perhaps enable them to bridge the gap. In this way, a primary weapon or favorite technique can also be used as a transition maneuver to help create an opening for a follow-up technique.

The instructor's job is to help the student focus and work on making the transition and executing the follow-through. But you must be careful here: If the student focuses too far ahead he may fail anyway due to a weakened initial move.

To create a drill for a student with a good side kick or a takedown, pick a follow-up punch and have him work on the transition between the finish of the side kick and the beginning of the punch. Make sure there is no time gap between the two. When the student practices the drill with a partner, explain that the focus should not be on the side kick itself, but on how well he makes the transition immediately after firing the kick.

In the course of the drill, the instructor's role is to help the student focus on the transition by commenting repeatedly about how well he is executing the transition. The idea is to encourage the student to move ahead when his favorite move does not work, rather than think about *why* it didn't work this particular time.

Taking It a Step Further

Any instructor can teach students technique, striking skills and grappling strategies. The ACMA instructor should have the skills to go beyond these basics and teach students how to focus properly, and to maximum effect.

First, we need to help our students understand the three aspects of the concept "focus" as it applies to the martial arts:

1. Direct your attention toward your partner.
2. Specifically target your attention on the initiator's shoulder or hip movement.
3. Stay in the present tense.

Here's a drill to help illustrate focus in this context.

In a classroom setting, ask your students to draw their attention away from you and look in the direction of the school's entrance. Then have them look back at you. Explain that this is the first aspect of focusing: to direct your attention toward something.

Next, have them shift their attention back to the entrance and specifically identify the color of the door. As they shift their attention back to you, explain that this is the second aspect of focusing: One must not only direct his attention, but also specifically target that attention, placing it on something he can identify.

Example: When doing drills in class, how does a student focus against his partner? First, of course, he looks in the direction of his partner. This should include looking not only at his body but *beyond* the body, almost as if he is monitoring the opponent's torso out of the corner of the eye. He can see what is behind where the opponent is standing.

Now explain to the class that for any moment the partner attempts to trigger a strike or a shooting movement for a takedown, *either the shoulder or the hips will move first.* (No need to watch the eyes; you will not find useful information there.)

The third aspect of focusing is to stay in the present tense. This is the way I like to think about it: When you try to anticipate your partner's initial move, thereby operating in the "future" tense, you are practicing what I call "ego leadership," which distracts from your ability to deal with the present. On the other hand, if you find yourself judging a "past" mistake, such as missing a block and getting hit, your thinking is in the past tense where fear is in control.

In sparring, it is essential that the mind learn to trust itself in the present, moment by moment, at ease in the knowledge that it will know not only *what* to do but *when* to do it. This inner faith in one's thinking skills keeps the student focused and ready to deal with the actual, present-tense situation.

Teaching a student to trust himself and stay in the present is the most difficult aspect of teaching him to focus, but there are physical drills that can help. For example, have two students face off against each other. One will attempt to throw a forward-hand strike at the head and the other will try to block it. The striker places himself about a half-step out of range against his partner. He must take a quick half-step as he executes the punching strike. The striker's goal is to get his hand within inches of his partner's face and quickly retract it before his striking hand is touched by the receiver.

The receiver does not have to literally block the strike, but simply touch the incoming arm or fist. As a result, he keeps his hand very limp and fans his hand up and down in a pendulum-like or windshield-wiper motion. It is not a tense, hard block.

The striker takes his time—a good four to five seconds between each attempt—so that his partner can practice proper focusing. He must visualize seeing his hand already at the point of contact before he squeezes the trigger. He must also make sure that his hand moves before he steps or rolls his shoulder, otherwise he will telegraph his movement or trigger-squeeze.

The receiver's job is to stay in the present, simply watching his partner. If he starts anticipating, you will see his defensive hand attempting to block before the striker triggers his initial move. If the receiver does make a false move, either by prematurely blocking or by missing a block, he may catch himself making a brief, silent reproach of his mistake. At the moment of the reproach he is in the past tense, judging something that just happened rather than watching his partner in the present.

After awhile both partners have a tendency to drift into that mental state that many martial artists call the "Zen state" or the "alpha state" of consciousness. What this means (to martial artists) is that the opponents are no longer inhibited by logical thinking, they are simply watching each other and acting/reacting. This is a state of pure focus, of undiluted concentration, in which the usual action sequence of sense/conceptualize/react is short-circuited and replaced by a primal (and faster) sense/react sequence.

Here's another effective focusing drill: Two students square off. One will attempt to execute a lead-leg round kick, targeting his partner's belt just around the navel area. Again, the striker takes his time—five to six seconds between attempts, with no regular rhythm. The defensive partner positions himself a half-step beyond the extended kick. (If both are new at this, they can begin a little closer until their confi-

dence builds and then extend the gap an additional half-step.)

The kicker's foot must move before he cocks the hip, to avoid telegraphing the initial move. The defensive partner practices reading the kicker's trigger-squeeze. The moment he detects the initial move, he quickly takes a half-step back, making no attempt to block.

Drills like these are instructional as well as fun. They are powerful aids in developing a student's sense of timing and demonstrating how important timing is to accuracy. Being successful at the drills is not dependent upon physical attributes and so gives the instructor one more way to create a level playing field for all students. And, as students increasingly understand the importance of thinking and mental preparation, they progress to a higher level as martial artists.

In the Final Analysis

Instructors must realize that constantly pushing students to increase their speed, power and conditioning has its limits as a way to improve them as martial artists. Experience has convinced me that the blueprint to success as an instructor involves giving your students the tools they need to grow in all three levels discussed in this chapter—the execution using proper mechanics, the technical application (which involves learning tactical principles), and the psychological level (using focusing skills, attitude strategies and mindsets).

And do not forget your instincts; trust them. They will enable you to apply the method, along with all the other instruction in this manual, in a way that works uniquely well for you and your students. ∎

Sample Drills To "Even The Odds" For A Short Puncher Versus A Tall Kicker

1. Develop Explosive Footwork.

The kicker practices firing his kick as the shorter student practices backward footwork to avoid the kick, doing everything he can to stay just beyond the kicker's foot.

2. Improve Timing Skills.

Have the kicker just trigger his initial move by exploding and cocking the hip to see how quickly he can get the initial jump on the shorter student. As soon as the defensive student detects his partner's initial move, he makes a quick, verbal sound and immediately shuffles away to avoid the initial move, trying to maintain the beginning distance.

3. Repeat the Drill.

Only this time have the kicker add the kick, as the shorter student practices his detection skills and times his footwork to avoid the kick.

4. Avoid the "Trap".

Have the kicker do all he can to catch his partner in the trap. As the kicker begins to execute, the shorter student focuses on using footwork to time the kick and be just beyond the foot or inside the knee at his opponent's intended contact time. The defensive student can use his hands to block only as a last resort (should his timing be a little off).

What is a Healthy Martial Arts Hierarchy?

By John Donohue, Ph.d.

What Is A Healthy Martial Arts Hierarchy?

We can think of the martial arts school as a small society, an organized group of people devoted to a particular end. And it seems that, more often than not, this martial society is organized along hierarchical principles. "Hierarchy " refers to a way of classifying or dividing groups into units of higher and lower status.

Every society uses slightly different characteristics to make this division. In the martial arts world, we typically use criteria such as skill and experience. We divide this society into "teachers" and "students," black belt ranks and non-black belt ranks, "masters" and "disciples," etc. Some may ask, "How is a disciple different from a student?" There is an emotional and personal commitment in discipleship that may differ from a consumer-oriented relationship.

We often identify different groups by special articles of clothing, in most cases, the rank belt. Many schools require certain types of behavior from these groups. And this, many people assume, is an integral part of martial arts training.

But assumptions can be dangerous and misleading. Every professional martial arts instructor needs to examine the way in which his or her school is run and examine the assumptions.

Pitfalls and Abuses

There are a number of potential problems with hierarchy:

1. Too much rigidity

By stressing this type of organization too much, the teacher lets method obscure the objectives of teaching. In other words, how the instructor teaches limits what the student learns. It introduces a lack of flexibility on the part of the instructor that inhibits a more individual, customized approach to teaching. As a result, students may be turned off. In other words, how the instructor teaches limits what the student learns.

2. Arrogance

A "take-it-or-leave-it" attitude is a type of negative marketing. If part of the American genius is innovation, maintaining the old ways may suggest that a school is less progressive (and hence, less competitive). In addition, it suggests an uncritical acceptance of tradition. This may lead to the appearance of a type of surface mastery on the part of the teacher, but surely implies that what is taking place here is mimicry, not mastery.

3. Inequality

Too much respect for some can mean too little for others. Part of professional teaching is presenting students with both support and constructive guidance. Couching your lessons in an "I-teach, you-learn" form can mean that the emotions involved in questions of dominance and submission obscure the lessons you are trying to impart.

We are all familiar with schools where the instructor struts across the room and barks orders to a class of robots, programmed to obey without thought. There are other schools where this military flavor is absent and the arts seem to be learned nonetheless. These two types of sites seem, however, to be at opposite ends of the school spectrum. The hierarchical model replete with uniforms and uniformity, obedience and submission, and all the psychic abuse possible in such an environment, seems almost to be inseparable from the martial arts tradition itself.

But is it? Where did this hierarchical tradition come from? For many American servicemen (among the first Westerners to seriously study the martial arts), it was part and parcel of the experience of training many of them received overseas. In the decades since many of these martial arts pioneers returned from Asian duty stations, the whole "master complex" has become an integral part of martial arts lore as well as a significant theme in countless B movies.

It seems every celluloid dojo drama features a good sensei/bad sensei scenario. The bad sensei inevitably dresses in the predictable black outfit of evildoers everywhere, and is a relentlessly rigid and hierarchical character. The good sensei is inevitably wise and laid back, played by a series of slightly overweight, graying actors who are decidedly unthreatening. Like

Today, instructors seek to find a healthy balance between the rigid, military mindset of "Absolute subordination" and the modern and mature approach of mutual respect.

most things theatrical, these characters are usually exaggerated. But, as is usual with movies, their themes often hint at something significant.

Many instructors believe that there is a role for some type of structure in the teaching of the martial arts. Others feel that there is a possibility that too much emphasis on dominance and submission, superiors and inferiors, may be problematical. For professional martial arts instructors, these ideas reflect a growing maturity in the way we approach the art. In short, as we grow more confident ourselves in passing on the essence of the martial arts, the whole question of determining what is a healthy martial arts school hierarchy is bound to arise.

Evaluating the Reasons for Hierarchy

For Americans, the whole idea of hierarchy is one fraught with difficulties. If nothing else, we believe in the American ideal of equality. We are extremely sensitive to any sort of system that prejudges individuals. We feel that each of us is as good as the other and want to be free to act that way.

The Asian martial arts, on the other hand, developed in societies that were relentlessly hierarchical. The ancient Chinese created a social model with four classes that were graded in terms of worth and esteem. In addition, they placed a high value on personal cultivation and development, usually achieved through systems that demanded years of onerous work. Confucian scholars, who effectively dominated

the social world of pre-modern China, labored for years to master calligraphy and the orthodox texts of their philosophy. As a result, this culture also placed a status value on age, since it usually took quite a few years to attain skill in the Confucian arts.

In Japan, we see much the same pattern: rigid social categories, a hierarchy of social classes, and an emphasis on a tradition of cultivation that accorded the elderly and the skilled greater status than other people. The linkage between such hierarchical systems and martial arts was further strengthened, of course, by the fact that the samurai, the warrior class of feudal Japan, were at the top of the social and political ladder. Since effective fighters were those who survived, the grizzled martial arts master was a living embodiment of the Asian linkage between rank, status, achievement and age.

The East Asian cauldron in which the martial arts were developed was a cultural environment where status was assigned to you according to broad characteristics. These statuses served as a guide to proper behavior: People in lower status positions were required to acknowledge their inferiority before individuals higher up the social ladder. It didn't matter whether you were faster or smarter than your seniors (or at least suspected you were); what mattered was that you were expected to behave in a certain way toward them. To many, this emphasis on status offends the American democratic sensibility.

Methods of teaching martial arts, then, were developed in a cultural environment where status and rank were very important. As a result, ways of designating rank within martial systems were developed and certain codes of conduct were established that fostered and passed on a tradition of hierarchy in martial arts training. Like many aspects of the martial arts, parts of this tradition can be useful. An unthinking fidelity to old patterns of training and teaching, however, may not necessarily be the best strategy for the professional.

Bruce Lee exhorted us to "absorb what is useful" in the Asian tradition. An even older American tradition encourages us to look carefully at what and why we do things before rejecting old ways. In short, when we critically evaluate hierarchy, we need to be sure we don't throw the baby out with the bathwater.

Why Hierarchy?

The best way to evaluate the role of hierarchy in professional martial arts training is to begin asking questions. It is quite common in schools to observe various displays of rank and behaviors associated with them: belts of varying colors, special clothing like the hakama ("pleated skirt"), bowing, honorific titles (sifu, shihan, sensei, sempai, elder brother, etc.), as well as a variety of ritual performances that draw attention to them.

Specific characteristics vary from art to art and school to school. There also seems to be considerable difference between schools on the emphasis placed on hierarchy. But the *basic principle* seems almost universal. This leads us to the logical, but often un-asked question, "Why?"

There are a variety of reasons that can be supplied to explain why some type of hierarchical organization is needed in martial arts training. Not all of them are good ones, or, at the very least, they are not the types of answers you would expect from a professional instructor. All answers, however, fall into three broad categories. Those relating to:

1. Tradition
2. Accomplishment
3. Functionality

The tradition argument is a common rationalization for martial arts hierarchy: "This is the way the masters have passed the art on." This kind of response is a statement, however, not an explanation.

Given what we have learned about Asian culture in general, it can be argued that hierarchy did form an essential part in the ways martial arts schools organized themselves. We have very well-documented studies of Japanese martial training going back hundreds of years that demonstrate this. It may also be that there is something about teaching this way that is beneficial. But to say, "We have a hierarchical system because we have always had one" implies that the instructor is blindly and uncritically passing on an art without really attempting to understand it at all. Again, mimicry instead of mastery.

Another seriously flawed explanation is one that focuses solely on the instructor and the respect due him. I like to characterize such scenarios as arising in "Darwin's Dojo." Here, the head instructor is obeyed (if not feared) due to the fact that he dominates the school physically in a scenario that illustrates the whole notion of "survival of the fittest."

Now, in arts that are concerned in part with physical questions of offense and defense, it would be absurd to contend that skill in the art in question has nothing to do with the elevated status of an instructor. But to say that someone is the master simply because he is the meanest, strongest or most skilled practitioner of the art, is juvenile and could have a negative impact on a professional's livelihood or, for that matter, the martial arts image as a whole.

A martial arts School of Hard Knocks may create some tough students, but it will also "wash out" large numbers of others. Besides, we respect people in the martial arts for a variety of reasons. Physical skill is one reason among many, which is why we teach martial "arts"—the term suggests that there are many dimensions to these systems that include, but is not limited to, physical prowess alone. To create hierarchies founded on simplistic (and short-lived) criteria is to suggest a lack of maturity on the part of the instructor.

Of course, we can also assert that a hierarchical organization is one that makes managing people easier. To a certain extent, this functional explanation is true and is the one that is least objectionable. In a training situation, with a great many bodies flailing or flying around, executing techniques that could inflict damage to the self or others, it helps to have someone in charge. Particularly in situations where students are using weapons, which multiply the potential for injury exponentially, a clear chain of command assists in creating a safe training environment.

In addition, since there is an emotional dimension to fighting, it also helps to create a dynamic where trainees respond even in the heat of a match to commands from their teachers. Particularly with younger students, instructors must maintain a certain control over their charges. Inculcating a type of habit of obedience, then, can be helpful.

The Problem with Superficial Responses

The problem with the three categories of responses listed above—tradition, accomplishment and functionality—is not that they are irrational, but rather that they are too simple. They suggest that the instructor's command of the topic is so superficial as to call into serious question his mastery of both his art and his educational technique. To be able to establish an appropriate teaching environment in martial arts training, the instructor needs to think clearly and deeply about the implications of instructional methods.

The martial arts are a vastly complex human endeavor. This complexity extends to the psychological dynamics of teaching and learning. In other words, one thing in the martial arts often has many applications or implications. A professional instructor needs to be familiar with as much of the theory of the art as possible. This extends to the theory of instruction as well. Indeed, this is the core of the ACMA certification program.

As a teacher reviews how lessons are structured and how students acquire skills, he needs to evaluate his instructional effectiveness. Because a teacher was taught a certain way in the past is *not* a professional rationale for current teaching methods. If you can't integrate various rationales for hierarchical organization into your instructional theory, and adjust your methods and preferences accordingly, then you may end up with a school shaped by whims created by your personal psychological makeup, but you certainly don't end up with a *professional* school.

Tradition, Accomplishment and Functionality Revisited

Let's look at these common explanatory themes again, and attempt to relate them more systematically to the instructional dimensions of the martial arts.

The common assertion that hierarchy has been part of martial arts training for centuries is, of course, accurate. But like most phenomena relating to these arts, there are often multiple layers of significance that need to be explored. It is not enough to merely establish the fact that there is a cultural heritage that shapes martial arts training. We need instead to reflect on its significance.

We briefly explored the cultural influences that helped shape the hierarchy of martial arts schools. Today, we may look upon some of the "traditional" ritual and organization involved in learning the mar-

Instructors must carefully evaluate "traditional" practices to determine if they enhance or inhibit learning.

tial arts as dead customs from the past, customs that make learning the arts inefficient from modern standards. Yet we need to be open to the possibility that this approach developed centuries ago for reasons that actually had to do with efficiency. The arts developed, after all, from combat systems, and fighters have little interest in practices that are not going to yield them results.

What is needed for professional instructors today is to carefully evaluate "traditional" practices to see what possible use they may hold on the one hand, or how they inhibit learning in a contemporary situation on the other hand. In this regard, simply because something is "traditional" does not mean that it should be discarded, any more than everything that is "contemporary" is worthwhile.

For contemporary martial arts instructors, mindlessly mimicking Asian traditions that emphasize extremely hierarchical behavioral codes is both silly and dysfunctional. We need to remain open to the suggestion that some sort of hierarchical structure may serve a positive educational purpose for a number of reasons.

If fighters (never a particularly submissive set of people) accepted the dominance implied with hierarchical systems, then it must have been because such systems brought with them a type of benefit. That benefit may have been linked to the practical interest fighters had in enhancing their skills. In this climate, instructors were individuals who, simply by virtue of survival, had something valuable to impart to trainees. By submitting to their tutelage, by obeying their commands, these trainees were voluntarily accepting inferior status in the hopes of eventually achieving the practical efficacy of their teachers.

Of course, not all fighters were willing to submit without a challenge. The number of martial arts stories that relate the adventures of young champions wandering the countryside and taking on the masters of the various schools they encountered are legion. In feudal Japan, such "knight errantry" was known as *mushashugyo*; "austere training in warriorship" is a literal translation, but this process usually entailed warriors visiting new locations and challenging local masters to duels. It was one way to learn. It also had a down side, however. Challengers who had not learned well were often maimed and sometimes killed.

Today, of course, we practice the martial arts for a variety of reasons. One is the acquisition of skill. And, by voluntarily entering training, students signal a willingness to believe that the system and the teacher they've chosen have something significant to teach them.

In the martial arts school, the instructor does not merely represent personal individual accomplishment, but the embodiment of hard lessons learned by generations of teachers. If we create an awareness of this through special honorific terms (like sensei) and ritual behaviors (bowing, etc.), it is to create an atmosphere where teachers (and students) are respected for their roles, not as individuals, but as links in a chain of martial tradition.

So, in the final analysis, the hierarchy of tradition is *not* something that is intended to elevate the teacher over the student. It is certainly not meant to make the student feel inferior. It is rather to create a mindset that places trainees in a unique world—a world that attempts to preserve its linkages with an ancient heritage and create an awareness among all students that they are involved in something larger than themselves. In this sense, hierarchy serves to link martial artists, teachers and students together, not separate them.

A Healthy Hierarchy

We can examine a few hypothetical situations for some initial illustrations of healthy and unhealthy hierarchy. There is an embarrassing wealth of grand masters out there in the martial arts schools of America. An egotistical insistence on wildly exaggerated titles and a practice of making students use them is a sure sign of an unhealthy hierarchy.

Part of the important message that needs to be communicated in the martial arts is that all of us, teachers and students, are constantly learning and striving for greater skill. The smug self-satisfaction of a "master" is an indication that this individual's use of hierarchy has nothing to do with teaching and everything to do with self-gratification.

Healthy hierarchy stems from an *attitude*, not a title. If students respect their teacher, it really matters very little whether they call that individual "sensei" or "sifu," or Bob. For younger students, it sometimes helps to use formal titles in order to communicate a

The bow can be thought of as a ritual behavior demonstrating respect not for the instructor as an individual, but as a link in a chain of martial tradition.

sense of distinction between seniors and juniors—in a way that is common in adult/child relationships in this country—but is clearly not necessary for maturer students.

A related issue is bowing. Various schools may use this as a mechanism for reinforcing a notion of hierarchy and as a special (as in, out of the ordinary) way of demonstrating respect. To insist, however, that students bow to the teacher out of the school (in a KMart, for instance) is ludicrous and, once again, demonstrates just how poorly the instructor in question understands the educational rationale of hierarchy.

It may be, for some schools, that items of etiquette like bowing are used in training to indicate the unique experience of learning the martial arts. The message here might be summarized as "special activities have special customs." But, in America, we don't do much bowing. As a matter of fact, one of the things we prize most is independence. It seems silly (and pretentious) for an instructor to insist that students bow to him or her on the street.

A healthy approach to bowing or to other customs that smack of hierarchy, is one that presents students with a clear rationale for the action. Students shouldn't be *forced* to bow. It is much better to explain that, in this particular school, a bow is used as a signal of mutual respect and is a ritual action specially used in the school. Period. And if you make students bow to you, you better be bowing back!

A final example of unhealthy and healthy hierarchy is the way in which the instructor approaches the questions generated by the class skeptic. Traditional instruction in some martial arts styles featured almost no explanation or commentary. We know, however, that some verbal reinforcement assists in mastering various tasks. It may be that a student question—the inevitable, "How come. . .?"—can serve a good purpose in a class. If one individual has this question, then others may, too. Yet, sometimes, the persistent questioner may ask so many questions that it gets in the way of actually learning. (When I was in grammar school, this was a favorite tactic used on substitute teachers).

An instructor with an unhealthy concept of hierarchy will, in this situation, respond with the "Because-I-said-so" response. It is a clear indicator of school hierarchy—*I teach, you learn*—but not a brilliant teaching technique. Healthy hierarchy is one that fosters learning, maintains structure, and builds mutual respect. In this situation, rather than an abrupt reply, the instructor can say something like, "That's a good question, but I'm a bit worried too much talk right now might interfere with everyone's having a chance to practice this technique as much as they would like. After class, why don't you stick around and I can explain this to you a bit more."

This way, the questioner is treated with respect, the instructor keeps the class on track, and everyone is gently reminded of the dynamics of the teacher/student relationship.

Ultimately, the most persuasive argument for attaching any type of hierarchical structure to training is one that relates directly to its role in assisting us to teach others. In fact, *all* our actions in the school should have a functional rationale. Notice that when we looked a bit closer at the "tradition" and "accomplishment" arguments, what we ended up with were explanations that showed how hierarchy could play a part in creating a healthy dynamic that assists students in learning their art in a truly comprehensive sense.

When we look at teaching the arts to others, we have to examine just how a hierarchical organization can help us become more effective instructors.

1. Order and Safety

A well-established command structure can assist in creating a school atmosphere that exposes students to a minimum of risks. The potential for injury, and consequent questions of liability, are a major concern to school owners. An instructor-imposed structure in training, which includes tailoring exercises and activities to the capacity of trainees, is a must. It is also a well-established tradition.

Most people think of systems of colored belts as being a way to identify students according to their rank, and understand this as a practice that is symptomatic of an unhealthy emphasis on status. In point of fact, when Jigoro Kano, the founder of judo, became the first martial arts instructor to use a colored-belt system to indicate rank, it was so that he would be able to quickly identify the skill level of judo students from all over Japan. Kano was known to be an excellent teacher, and he was vitally concerned with creating training sessions that were challenging and safe for all his students.

In addition, as we have discussed before, there is an art in managing groups of active, often young people. According to the National Association of Professional Martial Artists' 1997 Industry Survey, children under age 12 comprise a massive 50% of American martial arts classes. Creating a school etiquette that dictates methods of entering and leaving the training area, of approaching sparring partners, etc., is not necessarily a symptom of an overbearing instructor, but rather a way of creating a smooth flow of people with a minimum of problems.

2. Keeping Cool

Much of the healthy hierarchy in the school revolves around "respect" and the ways in which students express it. The almost universal practice of bowing between seniors and juniors, as well as opponents, should not be an exercise in domination and subordination.

I once had a college professor begin studying with me. He later confessed that at the beginning he could not stand the etiquette that involved bowing. He was used, in many ways, to having students bow to him in the classroom. The whole experience of now being the one who bowed was repugnant to him.

With this student, who clearly placed great emphasis on his self-worth and who was used to having things explained rationally, a "take-it-or-leave-it" attitude was clearly inappropriate. By taking the time to explain the rationale behind the custom and letting him experience the fact that everyone bowed to everyone at this school, he eventually came to realize what all that bowing was about.

Most martial arts involve conflict in the form of physical confrontations. As such, there is the very real likelihood of individuals getting excited, or frightened, or angry, or contemptuous, depending on the situation. There is an emotional dimension to sparring. And while this is an inevitable part of human nature, the whole purpose of martial arts is to assist in refining this nature.

By insisting on etiquette that stresses mutual respect between seniors and juniors, winners and losers, we do two very important things. In the first place, ritual etiquette serves to cool tempers and reduce emotional extremes. In the second, it creates a psychological environment where students are required to physically express mutual respect.

3. Remaining Open

In the same way, the creation of a hierarchy of status based upon skill is not about setting the instructor up on a pedestal. It is really about creating a situation where students remain open to what a teacher has to teach them.

It is often the case that students come to a school with some preconceptions about what the art is like, what they know about it, and what they want to know about it. In other words, people often want to learn a martial art, but they sometimes want to learn it *their* way. And as professionals, we have to gently yet firmly get them to see that the correct way, which is not always the hoped-for way, is the only real path to learning the art.

Convincing individuals of this is made much easier by creating an atmosphere in the school that stresses the authority of the instructor and sets up a dynamic where students are willing to cooperate in the educational process that the teacher charts. This is, of course, an expression of trust on the part of students.

To create this trust, an instructor needs to demonstrate a mastery of the art that is totally convincing. This means that the professional must be prepared for each training session with a well thought-out class.

4. Pushing the Limit

I know many instructors who feel that it is possible to create a productive learning experience without hierarchy. This is, of course, a big and contentious discussion in *all* educational fields. Professionals from various fields are continually reexamining this issue. Martial artists should too.

Part of what we do as martial arts instructors is to help students achieve skills they never thought possible. All students are different and some individuals learn some techniques more quickly than others. If they sincerely pursue their training however, (and if we are doing our jobs correctly) they will eventually come up against something that is truly difficult, or elusive, or frightening.

In these sorts of situations, there is a strong human instinct for avoidance. As teachers, we have to take our students farther than they thought possible within the parameters of common sense and safety.

Most martial artists are not going to be great competitors or famous champions. Most validation takes place on a personal level. To create an environment that encourages challenging activity for individuals and which can present them with social support for this struggle, it is often the case that the development of common symbols, rituals, and special statuses creates a small social universe. This lends psychological support to students. The military is an excellent, although extreme, example—a segregated universe outside the mainstream, with little financial reward, great discomfort, but elaborate hierarchy and symbols.

The process of students being pushed farther than they thought possible is very often unpleasant, or painful, or downright scary for our students. The only way we can get them to do it is by creating an instructional dynamic that fosters students' sense of respect and trust for the instructor, as well as a tradition of doing what is asked of them. In addition, in a consumer-oriented society, students may want to learn only what they want to learn. This is problematic if we are intent in passing on a "martial art" in its most comprehensive sense. Students may also want to run before they can walk, leading to potential injury and other problems. A measure of trust for the instructor, generated by respect that can be fostered through a healthy hierarchical structure, can pave the way for this.

Tips For the Instructor

A healthy hierarchy has the following characteristics:

1. Organization and structure is a means to an end, not an end in itself.
2. Respect due to instructors is a result of their demonstration of mastery in an instructional situation.
3. Your school's system and organization creates an effective teaching dynamic that:
   A) encourages the willing acceptance of appropriate guidance;
   B) develops trust between all participants; and
   C) creates an environment of mutual respect.
4. The teaching and learning environment is made physically and psychologically safe.
5. The school atmosphere and how students perceive the training environment. The school atmosphere is built on overt and subliminal actions: What is said and how it is said; what isn't said; how individuals are treated by teachers; and how students treat the teacher and other students. Even visual cues contribute toward this feature, such as the cleanliness and physical organization of a school, the appearance of students, their uniforms, etc.

In assessing what level of hierarchy you should use in your school, here are some things to remember:

1. Hierarchy is a means to an end, not an end in itself. Getting students to conform to your school's etiquette is not a psychic battle of wills, it's an educational technique. Different techniques work with different people at different points in their lives, so a little flexibility in this regard may be needed, particularly if your school has many different types of students.

2. Let prospective students know in advance what type of behaviors you will expect of them. Professionals plan ahead. They make their expectations clear. By telling people how you run things, you can let them decide whether they wish to abide by the practices you have set in place. This can help you avoid an embarrassing and often counterproductive battle of wills with a nonconforming student.

Printed material should always contain mention of your instructional philosophy and how it influences the way your school is run. If you or your staff routinely give orientation sessions to prospective students, make sure this area is covered.

3. Be willing to explain things to students, including the reasons for your school's etiquette.

We often take it for granted that people know what we know. Yet instructors, many with decades of martial arts experience behind them, are vastly more knowledgeable than their students in these areas. This knowledge needs to be shared. Especially in the West, people like to be presented with rational explanations of why they have to do things. Taking the time to explain the benefits behind things is a minor investment that yields solid results.

This runs counter to some "traditional" schools, where students learn by trial and error over a long period of time. Such "take-it-or-leave-it" environments may have worked in feudal Japan; for the martial arts instructor today, however, they have a decided downside: Some people *do* leave.

4. Gear your demands to the abilities of your students. Hierarchy is built on respect and trust. As an instructor, your role is to challenge and guide your students, but to do so in a way that is safe, appropriate, and created by a respect for student capabilities. To force students into activities that is beyond them is unprofessional and unethical and may be unsafe.

A suburban school with adolescent students should not resemble Navy SEAL training. Middle-aged ex-

ecutives may be attracted to the warrior mentality, but most are samurai with briefcases. You may believe that meditation is an essential part of martial training, but to many individuals it may have religious connotations they may feel conflict with their beliefs.

In short, part of being a professional instructor is to be aware not only of what you have to give students, but to also know how much your students are capable of absorbing. To continue to pour tea into a cup already full does nothing to expand the holding capacity of that vessel; it merely creates a big mess.

Conclusion

A good martial arts school is one where *all* members are respected. The school should challenge students mentally and physically, but do so in a way that is age- and skill-appropriate. Above all, everyone—teachers and students alike—should be united in a common purpose that transcends questions of individual merit and status.

A healthy hierarchy can help in achieving this. Those of us who have been studying these arts for any length of time know just how seemingly contradictory they are. Through the study of violent arts, we seek peace. In strict adherence to form, we discover freedom. By creating calm minds, we create the potential for vigorous action.

So it is with hierarchy. In submission, we gain the respect of others. In the artificial structures of a system, we discover new ways of being natural. And in accepting a place in a specific school, we become one with seekers of the way everywhere. ∎

.

The Power of Motivation and Charisma in the Martial Arts Instructor

By Brian Tracy

The Power Of Motivation And Charisma In The Martial Arts Instructor

The Webster's Dictionary defines *charisma* as "A personal magic of leadership arousing special popular loyalty or enthusiasm for a public figure." Charisma is also that special quality of magnetism that each person has and uses to a certain degree. You have a special charisma to the students who look up to you, who respect and admire you: the members of your family and your friends and peers. Whenever and wherever a person feels a positive emotion toward another, he or she imbues that person with charisma.

In trying to explain charisma, some people speak of an "aura." This aura radiates out from a person and affects the people around him or her in a positive or negative way. The halo around the heads of saints and mystics in many religious paintings was the artist's attempt to depict the light that people reported seeing or sensing around the heads of these men and women when they were speaking, praying, or in an intense emotional state.

As a martial arts instructor, your charisma can have a major impact on the way your students treat you and deal with you. Top instructors seem to be far more successful than the average instructors in getting along with their students. They're always more respected, more positively received, and more trusted than the others. They make a better living, and they build better lives. Instructors with charisma get far more pleasure out of their work and suffer far less from stress.

Few professions are as personality or charismatically driven as the professional martial arts instructor or leader. Charisma is often the X factor that will determine the success of one instructor over another.

As a martial arts instructor, developing greater charisma can help you tremendously in working with and motivating your staff, your students, your family, your student's family and everyone else upon whom you depend for your success. People seem naturally motivated by those who possess charisma. They want to help them and support them. When you have charisma, people will open doors for you and bring you opportunities that otherwise would not have been available to you.

The Law of Attraction

There is a close association between personal charisma and success in life. Probably 85 percent of your success and happiness will come from your relationships and interactions with others. The more positively others respond to you, the easier it will be for you to get the things you want. In essence, when we discuss charisma, we are talking about the Law of Attraction. This law has been stated in many different ways through the centuries, but it basically says that you inevitably attract into your life the people and circumstances that harmonize with your dominant thoughts.

The critical thing to remember about charisma is that it is largely based on *perception*. It is based on what people think about you. It is not so much reality as it is what people perceive you to be.

For example, one person can create charisma in another person by speaking in glowing terms about that person to a third party. If you believe that you are about to meet an outstanding and important person, that person will tend to have charisma in your eyes. If someone told you that he was going to introduce you to a brilliant, highly accomplished martial arts instructor who was very quiet and unassuming about his success, you would almost naturally imbue that person with charisma, and in his or her presence, you would not act the same as you would if you had been told nothing at all.

Charisma begins largely in the mind of the beholder. *Lasting* charisma depends more upon the person you really are than upon the things you do. Nevertheless, you can increase the perception of charisma by utilizing the 10 great powers of personality that have a major impact on the way that people think and feel about others.

The Power of Purpose

Men and women with charisma almost invariably have a clear vision of who they are, where they're going, and what they're trying to achieve.

Great martial arts instructors and leaders have a vision of what they're trying to create and why they're doing what they're doing. They're focused on accomplishing some great purpose.

For instance, they may have a goal to enhance the lives of their students through the benefits of martial arts training. This higher goal is more motivating to them than a goal of simply turning a profit. This sense of purpose is critical to the development of charisma and all great martial arts leaders have it.

They're decisive about every aspect of their organization and their lives. They know exactly what they want and what they have to do to get it. They plan their work and work their plan. In more than 3,300 studies of leadership, and in every book and article I've read on the subject, the quality of purpose, or vision, was one of the qualities that was consistently used to describe leaders.

Leaders have vision. Followers do not. Leaders have the ability to stand back and see the big picture. Followers are caught up in day-to-day activities. Leaders have developed the ability to fix their eyes on the horizon and see greater possibilities. Followers fix their eyes on the ground in front of them and are so busy that they seldom look at their activities in a larger context. George Bernard Shaw summarized this quality of great leaders in the words of one of his characters: "Most men look at what is and ask, 'Why?' I instead look at what could be and ask, 'Why not?'"

You can enhance your charisma by setting clear goals for yourself, making plans to achieve them, and working on your plans with discipline and determination every day. The whole world seems to move aside for the person who knows exactly where he or she is going. In fact, the clearer you are about your purposes and goals, the more likely people will be to attribute other positive qualities to you. They will see you or perceive you as being an admirable human being. And when you have clear goals, you begin attracting to yourself the people and opportunities necessary to make those goals a reality.

The Power of Self-Confidence

Men and women with charisma have an intense belief in themselves and in what they can do. They are usually calm, cool and composed in their personal lives and in their work settings. Your level of self-confidence is often demonstrated in your courage, your willingness to do whatever is necessary to achieve

a purpose that you believe in.

People are naturally attracted to those who exude a sense of self-confidence, those who have an unshakable belief in their ability to rise above circumstances to attain their goals. One of the ways you exude self-confidence is by acting on the assumption that students naturally like you and respect you and want to learn from you.

The very act of behaving in a self-confident manner will generate personal charisma in the eyes of others.

The Power of Enthusiasm

The more excited you are about becoming a great instructor and helping your students grow through the martial arts, the more excited others will be about helping you to do it. The fact is that emotions are contagious. The more passion you have for your school, the more charisma you will have, and the more cooperation you will gain from others. Every great man or woman has been totally committed to a noble cause and, as a result, has had the encourage-

Instructors who develop great organizations and quality students develop charisma in the minds and hearts of their students and peers.

ment and attracted the support of others—in many cases, thousands or millions of others.

The best way for you to motivate others is to be motivated yourself. The fastest way to get others excited about learning is to get excited yourself. The way to get others committed to achieving a goal is to be totally committed yourself. The way to build loyalty to your organization, is to be an example of loyalty in everything you say and do.

The Power of Excellence

The more knowledgeable you are perceived to be as an instructor, the more charisma you will have among those who respect and admire that knowledge because of the impact it can have on their lives. This is why programs such as this certification are so important to your success and the development of your charisma. This is the power of being recognized by others as an outstanding martial arts instructor.

Men and women who teach extremely well and who are recognized for the quality of their students are those who naturally attract the help and support of others.

One requirement of leaders is the ability to commit to excellence. Just as a good general chooses the terrain on which to do battle, an excellent leader chooses the area in which he and others are going to do an outstanding job. The commitment to excellence is one of the most powerful of all motivators. All instructors who effect change in students and organizations are enthusiastic about achieving excellence in a particular area.

Many instructors and organizations still adhere to the idea that as long as they are no worse than anyone else, they can remain in business. That is just plain silly! It is prehistoric thinking. We are now in the Age of Excellence. Students assume that they will get excellent instruction, and if they don't, they will go to your competitors so fast that your head will spin.

As an instructor, your job is to be excellent at what you do, to be the *best*. Your job is to have high standards in serving students. You not only exemplify excellence in your own behavior, but you also translate it to others so that they, too, become committed to this vision.

This is the key to servant leadership. It is the commitment to doing work of the highest quality in the service of your students.

The Power of Preparation

The fifth power of personality that gives you charisma in the eyes of others is thorough, detailed preparation prior to undertaking any significant task. Whether you are preparing for a class, a belt exam or a public demonstration, or any other kind of presentation, when you are well-prepared, it is clear to everyone. Conversely, when you are not prepared, it is equally clear to everyone.

Whether it takes you hours or even days, every class is important. Take the time to get on top of the subject you plan to cover. Be so thoroughly prepared that nothing can faze you. Think through and consider every possibility and every ramification. Think about who will be in class and how you can present the material in the most effective manner for them.

Often, this effort to be fully prepared will do more to generate the respect of others than anything else you can do. Remember that the power is always on the side of the person who has done the most preparation and has the best notes. *Everything* counts. Leave nothing to chance. When you do something related to your school, take the time to do it right the first time.

The Power of Self-Reliance

The most successful men and women in America are highly self-reliant. They look to themselves for the answers to their questions and problems. They never complain, and they never explain. They take complete ownership of their situation and they accept accountability if things go wrong.

An amazing paradox of human nature is that when you behave in a totally self-reliant manner, others will often be eager to help you achieve your goals. But if you seem to need the help and support of others constantly, people will avoid you or do everything possible *not* to get involved with you.

One of the most admirable qualities of leaders, which gives a person charisma in the eyes of others, is the propensity to step forward and take charge. The leader accepts complete responsibility for getting the job done without making excuses and blaming anyone. When you become completely self-reliant, you experience a tremendous sense of control and power that enhances your feeling of well-being and generates the charisma that is so important to you in attracting and keeping students.

The Power of Image

There are two types of images that you need to consider:

1. Self-Image.
2. Image of Appearance.

Your self-image has an enormous impact on the way you perform and the way others see you and think about you. Your self-image plays an important part in your charisma.

Second is the image of appearance that you convey to others. The way you look on the outside will strongly influence the way people treat you and respond to you.

Successful instructors and martial arts leaders are very meticulous about how they appear to others. They take a good deal of time to think through every aspect of their external appearance to assure that it is helping them rather than hurting them. Remember that everything counts. If an element of your image is not building your charisma and your respect in the eyes of another person, it is lowering your charisma and your respect in the eyes of others.

Nothing is *neutral*. Everything is taken into the equation. Everything counts.

The primary factors in your personal appearance are:

1. Clothing.
2. Grooming.
3. Level of Fitness.

When you are choosing a uniform to teach in, ask yourself, "Do I look like one of the most successful martial artists in my field?" If you don't feel that you do look like one of the best people in your business, go back to the closet and change. It's natural to keep wearing the same uniform because you've broken it in and have fond memories of the bloodstains and holes as a result of your ring battles. However, to your students, it may look as though it's a dirty old uniform

with stains and tears in it. Wear a fresh, new-looking, pressed and properly hemmed uniform when you're in front of the people you want to influence.

Note the personal appearance of the most successful people in the martial arts—their grooming habits. How do they dress? How do they wear their hair? Pattern yourself after the winners in your field, the people who have personal magnetism or charisma. If you do what they do, over and over, you will eventually get the same results that they get.

Even more important than the look of your uniforms, is the condition of your body—your level of fitness. In the chapter on General Adaptation Syndrome (GAS), the tendency for the body to adapt to the activities it does over and over again is explained. Without reexplaining the contents of that chapter, let me say that it is critical to your image to maintain a fit, healthy look as a martial arts leader. Anything less

Personal conditioning is a primary factor in how a martial arts instructor is perceived.

than an image of an excellent healthy lifestyle by the school's leadership is, by default, an endorsement of an *unhealthy* lifestyle. This flies in the face of the martial arts image and is enormously destructive to your credibility and charisma.

The Power of Character

True martial arts leaders who possess the kind of charisma that arouses the enthusiastic support of others are invariably men and women with high values and principles. They have very high ideals, and they continually aspire to live up to them. They are extremely honest with themselves and with others. They speak well of people, and they guard their conversation, knowing that everything that they say is being remembered and recorded in the memory of the listener. They are aware that everything they do is contributing to the formation of their perception by others. Everything about their character is adding to or detracting from their level of charisma.

When you think of the most important men and women of any time, you think of men and women who aspired to greatness, who lived their lives by a high moral code, and who had high expectations of others. When you act consistently with the highest principles that you know, you begin to enhance your charisma. You begin to become the kind of person others admire and respect and want to emulate. You begin to attract into your life people who can give you help and support and encouragement, people you admire. You activate the Law of Attraction in the very best way.

Integrity is complete, unflinching honesty with regard to everything that you say and do. Integrity underlies all the other qualities.

Integrity means that when someone asks you at the end of the day, "Did you do your very best?" you can look him in the eye and say, "Yes!" Integrity means that when someone asks you if you could have done it better, you can honestly say, "No, I did everything I possibly could."

Integrity means that you, as a leader, admit your shortcomings. It means that you work to develop your strengths and compensate for your weaknesses. Integrity means that you tell the truth in all your relationships. Integrity means that you deal straightforwardly with people and situations and that you do not compromise what you believe.

Alexander the Great, the king of the Macedonians, was one of the most superb leaders of all time. He became king at the age of 20, after his father, Philip II, was assassinated. In the next 11 years, he conquered much of the known world, leading his armies against numerically-superior forces.

Yet, when he was at the height of his power, the master of the known world, the greatest ruler in history to that date, he would still draw his sword at the beginning of a battle and lead his men forward into the conflict. He insisted on leading by example. Alexander felt that he could not ask his men to risk their lives unless he was willing to demonstrate by his actions that he had complete confidence in the outcome. The sight of Alexander charging forward so excited and motivated his soldiers that no force on earth could stand before them.

The Power of Self-Discipline

Martial artists of charisma are highly self-controlled. They are well-organized, and they demonstrate will power and determination in everything they do. They have a tremendous sense of inner calm and outer resolve.

The very act of being well-organized, having clear objectives, and setting clear priorities on your activities before beginning gives you a sense of discipline and control. It causes people to respect and admire you. When you then exert your self-discipline by persisting in the face of difficulties, your charisma rating goes up.

Martial arts leaders, who display what others refer to as "charisma," are invariably those who possess indomitable will power and the ability to persist in a good cause until success is achieved. The more you persist when the going gets rough, the more self-discipline and resolve you have and the more charisma you tend to have.

The Power of Extraordinary Performance

The goal of extraordinary performance, of course, is to achieve extraordinary results. These results then serve as an inspiration to others to perform at equally-exceptional levels. People ascribe charisma to those men and women who they feel can most enable them to achieve their most important objectives.

We develop great perceptions of those men and women we can count on to help us achieve what is important to us. Instructors who develop great organizations and quality students develop charisma in the minds and hearts of their students and peers. They are spoken about in the most positive way. They develop what is called the "halo effect." They are perceived by others to be extraordinary men and women who are capable of great things. Their shortcomings are often overlooked, while their strong points are overemphasized. They become charismatic.

Summary

In the final analysis, becoming a charismatic and motivating leader comes from working on yourself. It comes from liking and accepting yourself unconditionally as you do the specific things that develop within you a powerful, charismatic personality.

When you become determined, purposeful and set clear goals, backed with unshakable self-confidence, you develop charisma. When you are enthusiastic and excited about what you are doing, when you are totally committed to achieving something worthwhile, you radiate charisma. When you take the time to study and become an expert at what you do and then prepare thoroughly for your classes and exhibitions, the admiration that others have for you soars. When you take complete responsibility for and accept "ownership" of problems or setbacks, without making excuses or blaming others, the example of control you set leads to the perception of charisma.

When you look like a winner in every respect, when you project the kind of image that others admire, you build your charisma. When you develop your character by setting high standards and then disciplining yourself to live in a manner consistent with them, you become the kind of person who is admired and re-spected everywhere. You become the kind of person who radiates charisma to others.

Finally, when you concentrate your energies on achieving the results that your students were seeking, the results that others expect of you, you develop the reputation for performance and achievement that inevitably leads to the perception of charisma.

You can develop charisma by going to work on yourself, consistently and persistently, and becoming the kind of black belt leader everyone can admire and look up to. That's what charisma is all about. ■

The Role of Discipline, Praise, and Punishment

By Gianine Rosenblum, Ph.D.

The Role Of Discipline, Praise And Punishment

The skills and strategies outlined in this chapter are primarily targeted at promoting discipline in children. However, the general principles are universally applicable and should be applied with students of all ages.

What is Discipline?

"Discipline" can be defined in two ways. It is:

1. An action we take to make another person's behavior conform to our standards, as in: "If you are out of line, I will discipline you to make you behave."
2. Something an individual possesses within themselves which keeps his behavior in line with certain established rules of conduct. As martial arts instructors, it is your goal to help students move from needing discipline from the outside to having internal, self-discipline.

What Is the Role of Discipline in the Martial Arts School?

Discipline is important on many levels. Martial arts instructors have a reputation for instilling discipline and teaching self-control to their students. Many parents bring their children to martial arts schools with the specific request that they learn to be more focused, concentrate better, and have more self-control at home and at school. Adults often come in looking for grown-up versions of the same thing. Through the martial arts, they hope to develop more self-discipline at work or in their commitment to physical exercise, or to develop a way to feel more self-confident and in control in all aspects of their lives.

An atmosphere of discipline is central to the successful functioning of the martial arts school. The school is an environment with a structure and clear rules of conduct. Much of the structure and rules of conduct are handed down from traditional martial arts training systems. Maintaining some of the traditional class structure is important, not for historical purposes, but because the traditional class structure, with its emphasis on external discipline, maximizes the likelihood that students will learn successfully and develop the desired self-discipline.

Certain elements are important for encouraging discipline. The important elements in a traditional class include: A clearly laid-out structure with well-defined rules and expectations for behavior; clear communication of these rules so that they are understood by everyone involved; role models who conform to the rules and standards; clear rewards for success in following the rules.

These elements are important for fostering a positive atmosphere which is conducive to learning. In contrast, when a student is unclear about the rules of their school, he often feels uncertain and anxious. In general, when someone is unclear about what is expected of him or her, they may feel confused. When an individual accomplishes a goal or does what is desired, but receives no reward or recognition, he or she is likely to feel frustrated and ignored.

KEY ELEMENTS FOR ENCOURAGING DISCIPLINE IN A MARTIAL ARTS CLASS

1. A clearly laid-out structure.
2. Well-defined rules and expectations.
3. Clear communication of the rules.
4. Role models who demonstrate the desired behavior.
5. Rewards for success and for following the rules.
6. Rewards for following the rules are consistently given.

An atmosphere of discipline, even fairly strict discipline, should not be confused with an atmosphere of harsh punishment, intimidation or fear. The most well-focused, respectful and motivated students can and should also be the happiest, most dedicated and least fearful. In a school that encourages discipline in a positive manner, students will learn most effectively and the negative side effects of punishment will be avoided.

Using Praise and Reward to Encourage Discipline

In general, an atmosphere that focuses on students' strengths, and that emphasizes praise and rewards for good behavior and minimizes the use of punishment, will be most conducive to long-term learning, high levels of confidence, and will maximize students' willingness to challenge themselves.

The fact is, the most effective and long-lasting way of changing someone's behavior is by rewarding the behaviors that are desired. In general, if a student is showing a variety of behaviors, some good and some bad, the most effective strategy is to actually *ignore* the bad behaviors while making considerable efforts to reward the good ones. Over time, the frequency of the good behaviors will increase because they are rewarded and the frequency of the problem behaviors will decrease because they are not rewarded. This is a "win-win" outcome. (There are, of course, times when problem behaviors cannot be ignored. This is discussed below).

Many people are familiar with the concept of reward or "positive reinforcement." When a person is doing something that is desirable, you reward them in order to encourage that behavior in the future. This might include giving a hard worker a promotion, a child earning a quarter every time she makes her bed, or just telling a student "good job" after a training session. The definition of reinforcement is anything that *increases* the likelihood of the behavior being repeated in the future. Praise and reward can be used successfully to help a student develop a particular martial arts skill, like a fast punch or a skillful form.

Reinforcement takes many forms, including verbal praise, prizes or trophies, doing something fun like a favorite drill, receiving compliments from one's fellow students, or a smile from the instructor. Anything that is valued by the student can be used as a reinforcer. That is why rewards can be very individual. While student A may love sparring and find it very rewarding to be allowed to spar, it may feel like punishment to student B, who still finds sparring a little scary.

As an instructor, be careful not to assume that all of your students will like what you like, or what you liked when you were their age or skill level. Try to observe what is enjoyed and valued by a particular student and use that as a reward. Sometimes you also have to look at the relative reinforcing value of two rewards.

For example, several parents told me that they had trouble getting their kids to come to class. "They have a great time once they're here, but it's a battle getting them out of the house," the parents said. Being a good psychologist, I did some further investigation. It turned out that all of these kids were doing one of their favorite activities, playing with friends, Nintendo, or watching a favorite TV show when the parents asked them to leave for karate. While the kids liked karate class, having to leave another favored activity made going to class seem like a punishment.

My suggestion was to simply change the schedule, making homework, a household chore, or some other less fun activity occur *right before* karate class. Since karate is much more reinforcing to the kids than cleaning their rooms, karate class turned into a reward! The result: No more battles, no more students late to class and no more unhappy parents.

Using rewards or praise sounds easy, and instructors are sometimes led to believe that a simple positive comment or pat on the back is sufficient. As with everything, there are better and worse ways to use praise and reinforcement.

When reinforcement is used improperly, there may be several unwanted results. If rewards are overused, students may become arrogant or overly dependent on the reinforcement to perform the behavior. A child may be unwilling to spar if there's no big shiny trophy waiting for her, for example. Too much praise may make a student think you're insincere, and dilute the impact of your praise.

Using rewards appropriately will maximize the likelihood that students will internalize the behaviors you want them to develop, begin to perform them on their own and learn to reward themselves.

Using Reinforcement Effectively

Don't wait to reward. Give your students positive feedback about a behavior immediately, as they're doing the behavior, if possible. Whether they are doing a powerful side kick, or being helpful by sweeping the mat, show your approval *right then*.

Use verbal clarification. Be clear about the relationship between the desired behavior and the reward. For example, don't just announce that Kenneth is the "Student of the Day" and will get a sticker to take home. In addition, explain what Kenneth did to earn this—"Today, Kenneth arrived on-time, stored his shoes and helped with line-up, he paid attention in class and tried hard. Because of his dedicated behavior, he is student of the day."

Reward a lot at first, then taper off. Praising a new white belt for each attempt at a technique would not be excessive and will help him learn. Rewarding a higher-level student in the same way would be excessive. Students need a lot of reinforcement when they are first learning. As a student begins to master something, you can slowly reduce the frequency of rewards or praise.

Reward "successive approximations." The entire belt-ranking system in martial arts schools is based on the principle of rewarding "successive approximations." This means breaking a skill down into small steps and rewarding students for behaviors that come closer and closer to the desired ones. This is an excellent way to help students develop new skills. It is common sense that you can't expect a white belt to have the same skills as a green belt. So, effective instructors reward students for everything they learn which brings their techniques and overall behavior closer to the goal.

Give rewards for *effort*, rather than final outcomes. One of the unique qualities of the martial arts is that it can be a lifetime pursuit. The ultimate goal of a committed instructor is to encourage continual effort and continual improvement. Training consistently and making a best effort should be the basis for rewards, not winning a tournament or besting others in class. If only a particular outcome—like winning a tournament—is rewarded the students may feel worthless if they are unable to achieve the specific goal. This will undermine their willingness to keep trying and their efforts to improve.

Never completely eliminate rewards. Don't assume that a student who has long mastered a technique, or who is the model of discipline won't benefit from occasional praise and recognition. The best way to keep a desirable behavior going strong is to reward it from time to time. Be sure to let your top students know that you recognize their efforts and provide them with a reward that they will value. This is particularly powerful when students are not expecting the praise. So don't wait until the next belt test to tell a student how well he or she is doing.

Don't dangle "carrots". Constantly reminding stu-

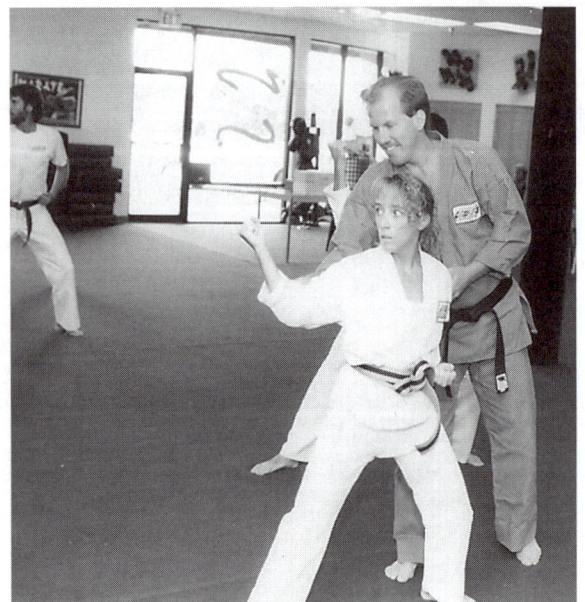

dents that a reward awaits them for a particular behavior may prompt the desired behavior at the moment, but it is not very effective for long-term learning. Students may learn to wait to find out what the reward will be *before* deciding how to behave.

Using Verbal Praise Effectively
Avoid "Good" and "Bad"

Often, when we give or receive praise, it is in the form of very general terms. We say: "Nice presentation yesterday, Lela," "What a beautiful picture you drew Christopher," "Nice roundhouse kick, Katie," or "Great sparring match, guys."

By expressing praise in terms of "good" (or negative feedback as "bad"), you are not helping the student understand his behavior, or what makes it worth praising. It also implies that the student is either all "good" or all "bad" when, in fact, he probably did several "good" and several "not-so-good" things that day.

Be Specific

When praising, provide the student with as much specific information as possible.

For example: "You showed excellent control on your punches in that match, Allison. You had good extension, but did not over-rotate your hip." While still a very brief statement, this comment not only praises the student, but gives him useful information about why what he did was worthy of your praise. This greatly increases the student's motivation and ability to do it again. It also helps students learn to evaluate their own performance and to praise themselves when they do well.

Explain what makes the behavior desirable. In addition to specific praise, tell the student *why* you value the behavior. This will further increase the student's motivation to perform the behavior and his ability to apply the principle to other situations. For example, telling the student: "Having good control in your techniques is important because it makes the matches safer, while allowing everyone to really test their skills," may help her realize that good self-control is important for safety in other activities as well.

Encouraging Disciplined Behavior

The principles described above can be very effective in helping students acquire new martial arts skills and adhere to specific school rules. However, helping students develop qualities like respect, dedication, focus, integrity, perseverance and honor is much more difficult. These concepts are much more complex and, while the same basic principles of reinforcement apply, these things are not as easy to teach through successive approximations.

Ideally, we want these behaviors and values to be internalized by the students and for the students to exhibit these values wherever they are. Obviously, we can't be with students at all times to reinforce these ideals. Students ultimately must put limits on their own behavior rather than being controlled by others' praise or outside rewards.

Helping Students Internalize Discipline
1. Be a Role Model

People of all ages learn naturally by observing. Allow students to observe you, your assistant instructors, and all students senior to them following the code that you wish them to adopt. Inspire, and give students abundant and varied reasons to want to be like you.

2. Use Persuasion

Use education, persuasion and motivation. Work to convince your students of the importance of the principles, instead of trying to command, control or use punishment to compel students to adopt certain school values. *Commanding* someone to be dedicated rarely works. Educating them about the benefits of dedication, nurturing and praising evidence of their dedication, and allowing them to observe dedicated role models is much more likely to be effective.

3. Be Accessible

Talk to students, formally and informally, about why you believe in the importance of the values, rules and principles of your school. Explain the ways in which they may have made a difference in your life. In this way, you make the principles come to life and take on personal meaning for your students.

4. Ask Questions

Encourage students (especially children) to come up with their own reasons why the rules and principles are in their best interest. For example, to encourage respect, ask a child how he or she would feel if they were treated disrespectfully by a classmate.

For example, compare the following students.
Student (A):
1. Observes the instructor treating others with respect.
2. Has been encouraged to think about the importance of mutual respect.
3. Has talked about the problems disrespect can cause.
4. Has come up with his own reasons why being respectful makes their life better.

Student (B): Is told by his instructor: "When in class, you must bow to me, and always address me by saying, 'Yes sir' or 'no sir.' You do this to show respect."

Student (A) will be much more likely to enact the value of mutual respect at most times, in most situations, because he will have come to understand the basic concept and importance of respect.

Student (B) has learned a specific behavior to be performed at a certain time and place. He has not necessarily learned about the *nature* of respect, its importance, or how to integrate it fully into his life.

What Is Punishment?

By definition, punishment is anything you do that causes a student to stop or reduce a certain behavior. Unfortunately, many instructors view punishment as the necessary path to discipline. They observe a student and determine which behaviors are unacceptable and must be punished. Take away all that negative behavior, the reasoning goes, and all that will be left is the good behavior that is desired.

How Effective Is Punishment?

However, punishment does not eliminate a problem, it only temporarily suppresses the unwanted behavior. The effects of punishment are often short-term, inconsistent, and limited to the situation in which the punishment was applied. Another problem with punishment is that it only teaches a person what *not* to do. Students are left knowing what they did wrong, but not knowing what to do instead.

Punishment can also have some unwanted "side effects." Using punishment can lead to increased aggressiveness and negative emotions like anger, hatred, and revenge, guilt, worthlessness and self-pity. A student may also learn when punishment is likely to occur and be sure only to act up when the person who will punish them is not around.

For example: Many instructors report that the class is well-behaved with the senior instructor present, but disruptive and lacking discipline with assistant instructors. This may be because the senior instructor administers punishment for bad behaviors. The students quickly learn not to act up when the senior instructor is around, but the problems reappear with the assistants because the students don't fear punishment. If the senior instructor had used other methods of instilling discipline instead of, or in addition to, punishment, the students would be more likely to behave well no matter who was teaching.

Students may also choose to lie to you or quit classes in order to escape being punished. In addition, punishment can cause the student to fear the instructor. This will undermine the atmosphere of respect and high levels of motivation you've worked hard to achieve.

When Is Punishment Useful?

Punishment is often useful and may be necessary when a problem behavior must be stopped immediately—to prevent harm to other students, for example. If a student is using excessive contact in paired exercises, has intentionally tried to insult, disrespect, humiliate or injure another student, immediate punishment would be appropriate. But before deciding what, if any, punishment is appropriate, consider the following factors:
1. Age and level of the student. Is the student too

young or inexperienced to be reasonably expected to change the behavior in question? For example, if a student is making contact, but is too young or new to have good control, punishment would not only be ineffective for changing the behavior, but is likely to damage the student's morale and self-esteem. A better strategy would be to change the exercise or increase supervision to minimize the likelihood of further contact.

2. Outside factors that may be influencing the student's behavior. Is a child's misbehavior perhaps related to problems at home, or bullying by another student, for example.

3. Degree of disruption or safety hazard that the behavior is causing. The smaller the problem, the lesser the need for punishment and the greater the need for reinforcement of proper behavior.

WHEN PUNISHMENT MAY BE NECESSARY

A student may require punishment when his:
1. Behavior is endangering self or others.
2. Behavior is disrupting the class to the extent that others can't learn or the instructor can't teach.
3. Behavior is harassing or abusing others.
   (Note: These examples apply to adult as well as child students.)

Acceptable Forms of Punishment
Verbal Reprimand

Instructors use verbal reprimands or "scolding" all the time. Telling students "No," or to stop what they are doing, can be very effective in halting them briefly in their tracks. Unfortunately, most instructors learn from experience that this is rarely enough to permanently cure a student of a bad behavior. Often, once your attention turns to something else, the problem starts right back up again. A verbal reprimand is most effective in changing behavior when backed up by other consequences.

For a verbal reprimand to have the greatest effect, you should include the following elements:

1. Express your disapproval strongly, *without anger*, and without demeaning the student.
2. State clearly what the student is doing wrong.

3. Tell the student what would be the correct thing to do, or what you expect the student to do next.
4. Give a warning. Clearly state what the consequences will be if the problem occurs again.

Example: I observe Kevin digging a hole in my mat with his fingernail. I say in a firm voice, without anger: "Kevin, I see that you are damaging the mat with your fingernail. Stop right now. You are damaging the school property by doing that, and damaging other's property shows great disrespect and will cost a lot of money to fix. This is very disrespectful and makes me very upset. When sitting, you are to keep your hands in your lap. If this happens again, you will have to clean the mat after class. Do you understand?"

Beware of criticizing or scolding students too often. Punishing in anger, or using personal attacks (for example, name-calling, using derogatory language) is particularly harmful. Disapproval is a very powerful motivator when it comes from someone whose approval the student badly wants. But if it is overused or misused, it leaves the student feeling worthless and disliked. This is the opposite of motivating, and can easily destroy an individual student's determination and damage the morale of the entire class.

Teach positive behaviors and allow the student to make amends. As mentioned before, one problem with punishment is that it only teaches people what not to do. When a student has broken a rule it is more helpful to do the following:

1. **Give the student an opportunity to make amends.** Example: A student intentionally damages another student's equipment. The student may make amends by apologizing and allowing her partner to use her equipment while the repairs are made.
2. **Have the student practice the correct behavior.** Example: A student repeatedly forgets to put away equipment after use. The student may be required to put away everyone's equipment for that week as a way of practicing proper behavior.
3. **Losing Privileges.** This is one of the most familiar kinds of punishments. A student breaks a

rule and as a result he or she loses something valued. This might be loss of a special job in the school, or the loss of an opportunity to spar, or do another favorite training activity.

This can be an effective form of punishment, but it must be consistently applied. Every time the rule is broken, the cost to the student should be the same. This is most effective when the problem behavior and its consequence are clearly spelled out and known ahead of time.

4. Time-out. Many parents are familiar with this one. "Time-out" actually means time out from reinforcement—or putting the student in a situation where he won't be rewarded for a while. The classic example is sending a child to their room, or to having them sit alone in a quiet place for a while.

In the martial arts school, having your student sit out for part of class, so that he does not enjoy the rewards of participation, would be an appropriate time-out. It is important that you keep the other students from interacting with the one in time-out. This is to prevent the student from getting any extra attention while in a time-out. It's not necessary to have the student miss the whole rest of class.

Brief time-outs work as well as long ones. Time-out is most effective when attention is also paid to rewarding positive behaviors.

Unacceptable Forms of Punishment

1. Corporal (physical) punishment.
2. Punishment by intimidation or threat.
3. Punishment by humiliation or verbal put-downs.

The above forms of punishment are considered unacceptable under *any* circumstances, for students of any age, for a number of reasons. Foremost, they are unquestionably damaging to the students, and are considered by many to be abusive practices. Practically speaking, they are no more effective than any of the strategies outlined above. All of them are highly likely to produce many negative side effects in students including, but not limited to, increased aggression, anger and hostility, decreased motivation, fear and anxiety, and feelings of worthlessness and self-doubt.

4. Punishment by physical exercise (for example, push-ups, sit-ups).

Punishment by physical exercise, as in, "Drop and give me 20"—boot camp-style—has long been used by instructors and coaches in many sports. However, it bears all the problems that the other forms of punishment share—temporary changes—teaching people only what *not* to do, etc. Using desirable exercises like push-ups and sit-ups as punishment destroys any hope of the student doing them with pleasure. Instead of choosing to challenge themselves by trying to do more push-ups and sit-ups each week, students are likely to avoid these exercises like the plague once they are thought of as punishment.

Using Punishment Effectively

There are times when using one of the acceptable forms of punishment is necessary to maintain discipline and order in the school. Keep in mind, however, that punishing a problem behavior will probably only result in a temporary change. To have students change their behavior and conform to the rules of proper behavior over the long term, and in all settings, punishment must be paired with other strategies discussed below.

1. Punish the Behavior, *Not* the Person. The goal in using punishment is to cause a negative, dangerous behavior to stop, and to pave the way to permanently introducing a desired behavior in its place. We must always be communicating the message that we believe in the student, respect him and have every confidence that he is capable of the desired change in that student's behavior. Therefore, one should never punish in anger, take a sarcastic or belittling tone, or in any way demean the student.

2. Use Verbal Clarification. Always tell your students what the rules are, and what the punishment will be if they violate the rules. This serves two purposes. By telling students about the rules ahead of time, you maximize the likelihood that they will follow the rules to avoid punishment. However, it is not enough simply to hang the "rules for sparring" or "school rules of order" on

the wall, or put them in a student handbook. You should remind your students of them often, particularly when they are broken. As part of administering punishment, spell out exactly what the infraction was, what rule has been broken and what the punishment is. Make very clear the relationship between the problem behavior and the punishment.

3. **Don't Wait to Punish.** If a behavior is bad enough to warrant punishment—that is, it's too dangerous to ignore or you can't take the time to try to get the student to exhibit a more positive behavior—then administer the punishment right away. The closer the punishment comes to the beginning of a behavior, the more effective it will be. If you wait until the problem's been going on a while, or if you don't punish until after class, long after the actual behavior ended, the punishment probably isn't worth doing.

4. **Be Consistent.** Once you decide that a certain behavior is punishable, especially a dangerous behavior, be sure to punish it *every time* it occurs.

This also means that your entire staff should also punish this behavior in the same way, each time. Otherwise, the students will learn that they can get away with the behavior from time to time and may test you and your staff to see whether they escape punishment. As well, it means that you must punish *all* your students for this offense. Punishing some students and not others for the same problem behavior will breed resentment and destroy the cohesiveness of your classes.

Be careful about playing favorites, and monitor your staff for their consistency. Students will actually appreciate this, especially when it comes to unsafe behaviors. Imagine how it feels to be a student knowing that occasional hard contact is overlooked by certain instructors or with certain students. This makes for a lot of anxiety on the part of students, because they fear having a particular instructor, or being paired off with a certain student.

5. **Don't Use a Weak Punishment.** Don't punish weakly first, thinking you will be more harsh if the behavior continues. Start with a moderate-intensity punishment right from the beginning. Otherwise, students will not take the punishment seriously and you will have to keep moving the punishment up a notch. You will end up needing to use a harsher punishment than if you had started with something more serious at first.

6. **Let the Punishment End.** Once the punishment has been given, allow the student to return to the class and resume his former status. Don't pretend that the punishment is over and then continue it by reminding the class of the student's infraction, taking a negative tone or attitude toward the student or removing them from their usual role in class.

Unless you have incorporated some type of "demotion" or loss of privileges into the punishment you described to the student, allow the student to return to his former status. Otherwise, you will be sending the message that punishment never really ends and that students cannot make up for bad behavior with good behavior. This undermines the students' desire to improve their behavior.

Remember, punishment only teaches a person what *not* to do. The most learning takes place when you combine punishment with training and reinforcement for the desired, appropriate behavior. If the desired behavior is *incompatible* with the undesired behavior, this combination is even more effective.

For example, a student cannot simultaneously cut-up in class while *kiaiing* loudly. Thus, reinforcing *kiai* may go a long way toward eliminating the problem of a student making inappropriate comments.

> I notice a child who is waiting for his turn at the kicking shield jostle with another child and shove him out of the way roughly, knocking that child to the floor. I stop the class immediately and say clearly and firmly, without anger: "Bobby, I saw you shove Charlie. That violates our rule of no hitting. Hitting is

dangerous and you could have hurt Charlie by doing that. The punishment for this is ten minutes out of class, starting right now. When the ten minutes is up, you may rejoin class if you apologize to Charlie and take the place in line behind him."

Notice the principles of immediacy, verbal clarification, use of a moderate-intensity, age-appropriate, punishment (for a more serious offense, full strength might have been having Charlie sit out the rest of class). The punishment itself consisted of a verbal reprimand, time-out of class, loss of a reward (participating in the kicking exercise), and a correction/restitution (having Bobby apologize to Charlie).

Once the ten minutes is over, Bobby would be told to rejoin the class, first apologizing, and then taking his place on line. The apology is *not* designed to embarrass Bobby; it is to restore mutual respect and allow Bobby to return to class with no ill will between him and the other student. Once the punishment is completed, Bobby's status should be restored and he should be treated as any other student.

At this point, my focus as instructor will be to reward any positive behaviors that are incompatible with Bobby's aggression. For example, praise Bobby for sharing, for cooperating, for appropriate levels of contact with other students.

"Bobby, you're making no contact with proper technique and control today, that shows real skill." Or, "Bobby, I noticed you helping a white belt get in a proper stance before. That shows excellent attitude, I'm impressed."

KEYS TO EFFECTIVE PUNISHMENT
Punishment should always be a method of last resort. Should you use it, remember these key points:
• Immediacy—Punish at the beginning of the behavior.
• Punish *without* anger, or personal attacks.
• Clarification—Explain clearly what the punishment is and what behavior it is connected to.
• Consistency—Punish every instance of the

behavior, in the same way with every student.
• Teach and reinforce desirable behaviors.
• Use a punishment of moderate intensity.
• Encourage restitution to maintain mutual respect.
• Allow the student to return to his former status after the punishment is completed.

Most people have a need for some structure in their environment, and a sense of predictability and consistency. Most people are comfortable with a moderate degree of routine and a smaller amount of variability in their environment.

When these needs are met, students will experience more rapid learning, lower anxiety levels, a feeling of psychological comfort and a sense of well-being. All of these elements can be found in a well-run martial arts school that encourages self-discipline and follows the general principles outlined above. A school that can foster responses like these is likely to develop a very dedicated group of students whose experience in the school is extremely rewarding. ■

References

Elias, M.J., Zins, J.E., Weissberg, R.P., Frey, K.S., Greenberg, M.T., Haynes, N.M., Kessler, R., Schwab-Stone, M.E. & Shriver, T. P. (1997). Promoting social and emotional learning: Guidelines for educators. Alexandria, Virginia: Association for Supervision and Curriculum Development.

Faber, A. & Mazlish, E. (1980). How to talk so kids will listen and listen so kids will talk. New York: Avon.

Gordon, T. (1975). P.E.T.: Parent Effectiveness Training. New York: Plume

Micheli, L.J. (1990). Sportswise: An essential guide for young athletes, parents, and coaches. Boston: Houghton Mifflin Company.

Pope, A.W.; McHale, S.M. & Craighead, W.E. (1988). Self-Esteem Enhancement with Children and Adolescents. New York: Pergamon.

Shapiro, L.E. (1981). Games to grow on. Englewood Cliffs, New Jersey: Prentice Hall.

Wyckoff, J.L. & Unell, B.C. (1991). How to discipline your six to twelve year old. . .without losing your mind. New York: Doubleday.

Teaching Character Skills Responsibly

BY SCOT A. CONWAY, ESQ.

Teaching Character Skills Responsibly

As a martial arts instructor, you may become the most influential person in the life of a child, right behind parents (but not *always* behind). Sunday School teachers only see a child once a week, if the child even attends Sunday School. School teachers only have influence over a child for one year, then the child moves on to the next grade, never to return. A martial arts instructor, on the other hand, may see a child two or three times a week, almost every week, for his entire martial arts career. Even if the child only stays until he becomes a black belt, that is nevertheless several years of influence.

Even parents often do not have the influence in their child's life that a martial arts instructor may have. If parents both work, then the child could feel as though the martial arts instructor is the primary leader and role model in his life. Ideally, this will not be the case. Ideally, both parents are cooperating together, investing themselves in their children and raising their children well. Nevertheless, there are some students who will respect their instructor more than anyone.

This should be a sobering thought for all instructors. Some of the young students you teach will follow you first, above parents, above teachers, above friends. They will learn much more from you than the martial art system you teach. They will learn a way of thinking. They will learn a way of looking at life, at people and at the world around them. You will teach this to your students either intentionally or otherwise, so it is best to give much thought to the course upon which you set your students.

Be a Role Model

If your students were going to become just like you, would that be a good thing? Would you want your children to grow up to do the things you do, to say the things you say, to believe the things you believe? If the answer to any part of these questions is "no," then you need to work on the first phase of teaching character traits, the first phase of leadership, you need to model what you want to see.

A guiding principle to remember is to imagine that your students will duplicate about *half* of what you do right, and *twice* what you do wrong. It might not actually be true in all cases, but if an instructor keeps in mind that a student will halve the positive lessons and double the negative ones, it should help keep an instructor in check.

The Big Difference Between Showing and Telling

Students pick up the mistakes of their instructors. A master-level instructor visited a school and noticed that nearly all the students made the same mistake. The instructor had been trying to correct the error for months, but with no success. Later that evening, the master instructor evaluated the teacher and found the head instructor was making the same mistake himself! The students were doing what they *saw*, not what they were told.

If you want to see a graphic example of this, try this experiment

that famed motivational speaker Zig Ziglar uses. Tell your students that you will count to three and then clap ("1-2-3"-*clap*). Then, in front of them all, count "One," "two," and clap when you say "three!" Most, if not all, of your students will clap when you clap—no matter what you told them to do! They will follow your lead, not your instructions.

An adult telling a child not to smoke while smoking does not work. Telling a child not to drink while holding a beer has little effect. If anything, it evokes the "Forbidden Fruit" syndrome and makes the child that much more curious. "You're not old enough" can be the worst thing to tell a child, because in the quest to feel "grown up," he will try all those things he's not supposed to be old enough to do.

Teaching character traits is not a matter of telling students what to do. Telling them will make little impact. You have to be the role model. You have to *show* them what to do. Be what you expect them to be. Show them the standard to which they ought to aspire.

If it sounds like a tough job, it is. None of us are perfect, and we all have our vices. For some, it might be as innocuous as not quite obeying all the posted speed limits. Others might have far more serious vices. Your vices should never enter the martial arts school. Do not let your students see you do anything you don't want them to do.

Even if there's nothing wrong with your conduct, if you don't want students to copy it, *don't do it.* If you smoke cigars, don't do it in front of students, lest a child want to smoke a cigar just like you. If you drink, don't do it in front of students. If all your students are adults, these might not be problems, but the children will want to emulate you. At the very least, when they do it, you will be their excuse. "Sensei smokes, so it can't be *that* bad!"

After you model the behavior you expect, then you want to tell them what is right and wrong, and give them some objective basis for listening. For example, "You shouldn't drink because it takes away your control, and a martial artist should always be in control. If you're young, it's illegal, and a martial artist should always obey the law." You might even add, "If you're an adult, it might be okay to have a drink once in a while, but you should never, ever get drunk."

The Mistake of Telling the Wrong Stories

Even excellent instructors who are masterful role models sometimes blunder into a mistake that many parents make: They tell stories about their past. Not just the type like, "I used to walk ten miles through six feet of snow to get to my martial arts school," but stories of "fun things" (read: stupid, irresponsible, wild) they did when they were younger. If instructors discuss these actions like they were fun, then students get the idea that any adverse behavior was acceptable. At the very least, it will give them a great story to perpetuate later.

> Even if the story does not relate to personal actions of the instructor, how the instructor handles stories when they arise will speak volumes to students.
>
> One instructor started telling a story about some people who had made obscene gestures at he and his wife while driving. He forced them off the road, got out of his car, and beat up all five guys in the car. "That taught them a lesson," he finished.
>
> Perhaps he didn't think about the inherent lesson he was teaching his students. He essentially told them it was okay to beat up people who do anything that antagonizes them. This is certainly not behavior that is sanctioned by martial arts instructors.

The stories of our irresponsible youth should not be told in fun—even if we really think they are fun or funny—but rather as object lessons. That same story cited above, if told at all, should have been an illustration of something the instructor regretted, an example of something a real martial artist should never, ever do. He should express his gratitude that he didn't really hurt anyone, that he didn't go to jail, and that no one in the car had a gun. Students should come away from the story knowing that their instructor made a huge mistake, and that they should learn from it.

If students are telling stories, instructors should put a responsible spin on the story.

An instructor overheard two students talking about some friends at another school who went to bars and picked fights to get some street-fighting practice. The instructor interjected about how dishonorable that conduct seemed to him. "A martial artist should never start a fight, and he should never go looking for one. Doing so missed the whole point of training."

It changed the attitude of the conversation, and it no longer seemed like such a good idea to the students.

Stories can be powerful illustrations. Whether used properly or not, they will have an impact. If they will influence so powerfully, they are best kept under careful control.

Teaching Specific Character Traits: An Example

Obedience. Teaching students obedience first requires, as already discussed, the instructor to lead the way. Show the students what you mean by obedience by letting them see how you obey your instructor. Show them how to treat their parents by letting them see how you treat, or talk about, your parents. Be the example.

The head instructor is in charge. Instructors should show obedience to the head instructor in the manner they expect to be obeyed. Then, by modeling obedience, the instructors have credibility to teach students the importance of obedience. Also, the head instructor must show that he has the best interests of his instructors at heart, and the instructors must do the same, which, combined with knowledge and skill at teaching, establish worthiness for the obedience expected.

Stories about achievement through obedience are powerful illustrations. It is most powerful if examples of people they know are used. Here's an example of one used at the Guardian Kempo Academy of Christian Martial Arts in San Diego.

Debora is a black belt who overcame countless medical disabilities to achieve a level of skill that led to her surviving two very violent physical attacks by criminals during her years in martial arts.

When Debora was a white belt, she never argued. In fact, she did everything she was told to do. Her doctor told her what she could and could not do, and she listened so she wouldn't hurt herself. Her instructor told her what to do and how to do it, and she followed the school rules about safety and let the teachers know when it was not safe. Then she practiced.

When her instructor said to do something 100 times, she did it 100 times the very best she could each and every time. When her instructor said to practice at home, she practiced at home every day. She did everything she was supposed to do.

When an attacker tried to strangle her 18 months into her training, she ended the fight in eight seconds and the police took him to the hospital. Less than a year after that, when drug-crazed criminals attacked her neighbors, she was able to protect them.

Even with all her medical limitations, Debora became one of the most skilled students because she obeyed her instructor, obeyed her doctor and followed the rules.

The Socratic method—teaching by asking questions and making students think through the answer, as opposed to just telling them—is a powerful teaching/discussion method for driving points home since it makes students give you the answer. Answers they give will have more impact on them than the answers you provide.

Example: Asking a class, "How many of you want to be master martial artists?" Hands go up. "Does a master obey his instructors?" Some answer, "Yes." "Does a master obey?" Most or all answer, "Yes!" "Should you obey if you want to be a master?" "Yes!"

Naturally, it plays a little differently with adults than with children, but the principles remain the same. For adults, examples of learning their trade by carefully listening to those that taught them, or obeying their employers to gain promotions in their career, often work better. For children, examples of doing what the teacher asks to get a good grade on an assignment.

Another important lesson in obedience is knowing when *not* to obey. It's easy to come up with examples here. An evil instructor telling students to go kill a man who the instructor doesn't like. Should the student obey? No, because the instructor is asking them to do something that is morally wrong. A boss asks an employee to prepare false reports to defraud a major client. Should the employee obey? The son of the instructor orders a young girl to perform a sexual act. Should the girl obey? Absolutely not.

Some instructions and orders should not be followed: Illegal orders (vandalism, murder); immoral orders (lying, rape); unsafe instructions (high dive rolls to cement, full-power punches on brick walls); orders beyond the scope of authority (personal life, religious beliefs); orders about things about which the person has no experience or knowledge (medical or legal instructions from laypeople with no expertise or outdated information). Students should know that there is a logical, moral and legal limit to the obedience owed to anyone.

Formulating Character-Trait Lessons

Respect; self-discipline; perseverance; goal-setting; working hard; working smart; honor; integrity; health; fitness; patience. . . Whatever the character traits, the principles of success and achievement, or the virtues the instructor hopes to instill in his students, there has to be more than lip service paid. One cannot claim to teach respect, mention it only occasionally in class, then do nothing else and have students learn respect.

Any lesson taught must begin, of course, with the example. Model it, develop stories about it, praise one another on the trait, teach it, and ask about it. Then don't be surprised when half the students have *no idea* what you're talking about. Remember, you aren't the only role model they are following, nor are you the only voice they hear. Your power is limited, but you

can, at least, enforce the behavior in your school and in your classes.

If you are not a good role model, then join the students in the work process.

> One instructor with a weight problem knew he had no credibility talking about health and fitness, nor about self-discipline (at least, not on that issue), but he was still able to get lessons across on how important it was to do it.
>
> First, he admitted to his students that he had a problem and explained that it was much easier to avoid having the problem in the first place than trying to overcome it later. He pledged to continue his personal battle with his weight and indicated that he was working on it. Then he used others as examples of success.

Of course, the above example only works long-term if the instructor follows through. If the students don't see his success, then it becomes their excuse for not even trying. After all, if even their instructor, their leader, their role model, cannot win the battle, why should they even bother to try?

The whole instructor team should be working together. If there is an outline or written form of the lesson to help guide the staff, then everyone can be teaching the same lesson. Parents can be a great help

recognize many of their own limitations. Often, adults can teach one another if you just let them discuss an issue during warm-ups. Bring up the issue of honor, for example, and ask them what they think of it. Keep the conversation going, prodding them along a certain direction if they stray off course, and let them teach each other about honor. Sometimes their insight will surprise you, and you will learn as much as they do in the conversation.

Is It Even My Job?

Is it the job of the martial arts instructor to teach character traits? For adults, maybe. For children, probably. Neither answer, you may note, is absolute.

You will teach character traits whether you intend to or not. Students, adults and children alike, will follow your lead if they respect you.

Children, of course, will pick up the character traits of anyone they admire, which, hopefully, includes their instructor. That means that children, moreso than adults, will learn from the instructor. Therefore, you want to especially watch what the children see in class. If an eight-year-old gets caught sneaking a beer, and his excuse is, "But my instructor drinks beer!" most parents won't be very happy. Many, however, will simply explain that the instructor is an adult, and it's okay for grown-ups to drink beer, but not kids. It really will depend upon your parents.

Whether you set out to teach character traits or not, keep in mind that you will still be a leader, a teacher, and a role model, whether you want to be or not. ■

as well if they know what you are doing. An explanation in a Student Handbook, in a newsletter, or even handouts can be of tremendous value to parents who would like to discuss the issues with their children.

Teaching Character Traits to Adults

Here's the simple advice for trying to teach adults character traits. *Don't even worry about it.* Often by adulthood, they have their own personalities and opinions, they have their own ways into which they have settled, and they don't much care for anyone telling them what to do. They come to learn karate, jujitsu, self-defense, fitness—whatever the sign says— and they don't want to be preached at.

Done with respect in open conversation, it can still be done effectively. While adults often do not like others telling them what's right and wrong, and they don't like being told what to do by someone they pay to teach them physical skills, adults are also the first to

THE CASE FOR RELIGION AND PHILOSOPHY

Many martial arts instructors claim that they do not teach a particular religion or philosophy. They claim that they teach honor, ethics and morality. Some do not even claim that much, only that they teach physical techniques. Some foundation, though, is necessary.

Martial arts instructors who teach combat systems may be doing worse than handing their students a loaded gun. They may be equipping students with the power to cripple or kill with no guidance on when the use of that skill is appropriate. Unlike a loaded gun, no one can take the martial arts knowledge away from the student if he abuses it.

No matter what the beliefs of the instructor might be, these beliefs are being passed along to the students in a thousand subtle ways. Even instructors who claim to teach no philosophy or religion are teaching their personal philosophy and world view. Students might be learning that there is no objective truth, that your beliefs are no one's business but your own, and that all morality is relative. They might be learning that religion and philosophy isn't important. They might be learning that it isn't worthy of thought.

Many instructors today do not see a place in martial arts for religious dogma or antiquated philosophies in their schools. The arts, to them, are purely physical skills, and so long as the student practices those skills, the rest is none of the instructor's concern.

Most of the ancient masters would strongly disagree. Most ancient traditional arts have a strong moral and ethical basis established firmly in a religion or religious philosophy. The early masters recognized that the more dangerous the art, the more necessary a code of conduct was in the use of that art. Thus, many arts have a Buddhist, Shinto or Taoist basis.

Some masters went so far as to require that only monks were permitted to learn a particular art. The Code of Bushido arose in the East as a religiously adhered-to philosophy for Japanese warriors. In the West, it was the Code of Chivalry. Whether East or West, those skilled at the arts of war recognized the need for an objective foundation of morality, lest the lands explode in never-ending war.

How to Teach Students With Attention Deficit Disorder

By Drenda Timmons-Schubert, Ph.D

How To Teach Students With Attention Deficit Disorder

Master Ron enters class and sees Johnny running around the training floor. He is kicking at his classmates, laughing, and distracted by the older students leaving the studio. Master Ron kindly but firmly speaks to Johnny, reminding him of the rules and tenets of courtesy and respect. Johnny continues his activity.

Finally, Master Ron stands in front of Johnny as he makes his final turn. Master Ron is in Johnny's line of site, and there is nowhere for Johnny to run! At last, Johnny stops and notices his instructor. As Master Ron kneels down to look Johnny in the eye, he again repeats his remarks to Johnny. Johnny responds as though he has heard these words for the first time today. Johnny complies with the instructions and class begins. Master Ron takes a deep breath, sprouts a gray hair, and makes a mental note to check in with Johnny's parents. Johnny's parents inform Master Ron that their son has been diagnosed with Attention Deficit/Hyperactivity Disorder, Combined Type. They report this busy, distracted behavior as typical. The parents and Master Ron brainstorm ideas to assist Johnny to have a successful martial arts experience.

Myth: Children outgrow Attention Deficit Disorder.
Myth: Attention Deficit Disorder only occurs in boys.
Myth: Children affected by Attention Deficit Disorder are always hyperactive.
Myth: Parents cause their children to be hyperactive.

Attention Deficit/Hyperactivity Disorder (ADHD) is a neurobiological disorder that affects approximately 5% of American children (Amen, 1995). "Neurobiology" is the study of the brain and all the nerves. ADHD is characterized by inattention, difficulty concentrating, and for some children, hyperactivity. Early detection and therapeutic and medical interventions prevent serious consequences of school failure, depression, poor peer relationships, behavior prob-

lems, and substance abuse.

This chapter will provide an overview of the definition of the diagnosis, as well as the causes, treatment interventions, and teaching strategies. Furthermore, the myths mentioned above will be dispelled. Understanding these aspects of ADHD will assist the martial arts instructor in becoming a more effective teacher to children affected by ADHD. Because of the emphasis on structure, self-control, and respect for others espoused within martial arts classes, the activity is often recommended for children diagnosed with Attention Deficit Disorder.

History

In 1902, the medical profession first identified ADHD. Since 1902, ADHD has been called by many different names including Minimal Brain Dysfunction, and The Hyperkinetic Reaction of Childhood. In 1980, ADHD was formally recognized in the Diagnostic Statistical Manual, Third Edition (DSM-III), which is the official diagnostic manual used by psychiatrists, psychologists and social workers.

It was popularly believed that children outgrew Attention Deficit Disorder. However, for 30-70% of those affected by the disorder, many symptoms continue into adulthood (Amen, 1995).

Definition

ADHD is a neurobiological disorder, which interferes with a person's ability to maintain attention, focus on a task, and delay impulsive behavior. Characteristics of ADHD occur during childhood. The Diagnostic Statistic Manual-IV (APA, 1994) defines ADHD in the following manner:

ADHD TYPES AND DEFINITIONS

The Diagnostic Statistic Manual-IV (APA, 1994) identifies three subtypes of ADHD. They include:
1. Attention Deficit Disorder with Hyperactivity (busy, moving).
2. Attention Deficit Disorder, Inattentive Type (distracted).
3. Attention Deficit Disorder, Combined (distracted and moving).

ADHD with Hyperactivity is characterized as inattentive and energetic. ADHD, Inattentive Type is characterized as difficulty paying attention, daydreaming, disorganized, complains of being bored, unmotivated, slow moving. ADHD, Combined Type is a mixture of inattentiveness and boundless energy.

ADHD with Hyperactivity is frequently noted in young boys. These children are very active compared to same-age peers. ADHD, Inattentive Type is often seen in girls and is easily missed because the girls display behavior consistent with acting like social butterflies, talking excessively with their friends (Amen, 1995).

In addition to the DSM-IV categories, Dr. Daniel Amen (1995) describes three more subtypes or styles of Attention Deficit Disorder. They include the following:
1. ADD, Over-focused (getting stuck on one thing).
2. ADD, Depressed (irritable).
3. ADD, Explosive (angry outbursts)

ADD, Over-Focused Type

Characterized as erratic attention span, easily distracted by stimuli, excessive worry, disorganized or very organized, argumentative, locked into negative thoughts, dislike change, hold grudges, trouble shifting from subject to subject, difficulty seeing options or opinions.

ADD, Depressive Type

Known for inattentiveness or erratic attention, moodiness, negative attitude, low energy, socially withdrawn, hopeless, helpless, sleep difficulties, forgetfulness, and low self-esteem.

ADD, Explosive Type

Depicted as having attention difficulties, impulse control problems, short fuse, periods of rage with little provocation, misunderstands comments as negative, periods of confusion, dark thoughts, frequent periods of deja vu, overly sensitive, history of head injury or family history of violence.

Some additional symptoms of ADD include:
1. Problems taking turns.
2. Shifting from one uncompleted activity to another.
3. Difficulty playing quietly. Children with ADD often use a loud voice.
4. Talking excessively.
5. Does not seem to listen.
6. Taking high risks.
7. Difficulty with handwriting.
8. Poor eye contact.
9. Decreased coordination.
10. Difficulty getting to sleep and waking up.
11. Less mature than same-age peers.

Children identified with ADD have an increased likelihood of grade retention, school drop out, academic underachievement, and social and emotional adjustment difficulties. Children with ADD are more vulnerable to failure in the two most important areas for developmental mastery, school and peer relationships. A significant percentage of children with ADD

are never properly diagnosed. Some sources estimate that up to 50% of children who are affected by ADD may be undiagnosed.

Children with ADD may not develop emotional problems. However, if the diagnosis is not obtained or treated, children can develop behavioral problems, low self-esteem, depression, and substance abuse.

THE IMPACT OF ADD ON LEARNING

Restless—Fidgets.

Easily Distracted—Limited attention.

Impulsive—Acts without thinking first.

Procrastinates—Puts off projects until the last minute.

Forgetful—"What was I supposed to do?"

"Stuck" on a Thought—hyper-focused on an idea.

Difficulty with Timed Situations—too much pressure.

Causes

Currently, the actual cause of ADHD is unknown (Barkley, 1997). Studies have examined the roles of neurological (the nervous system) factors, genetic factors, and environmental toxins to understand how ADHD is acquired. Neurological studies have indicated that lesions or injury to the frontal lobe (front

part of the brain) produce ADHD symptoms. Genetic research has indicated the primary transmission of ADHD is heredity. Investigations have revealed that between 10% and 35% of immediate family members of a child with ADHD are diagnosed with ADHD (Barkley, 1997). Research indicated that 57% of parents diagnosed with ADHD would have a child with ADHD (Biederman, et al., 1995).

A 1990 article reported the use of brain-imaging techniques to compare the brain metabolism between adults with ADD and adults without ADD. The results of the study revealed that those affected by ADD utilize glucose (the brain's main energy source) at a lesser rate than do those without ADD. This reduction of glucose was most evident in the areas of the brain important for attention, handwriting, motor control, and inhibition (stopping) responses. This was a landmark study and helped researchers, medical and mental health professionals and families know that a metabolic disorder, and not a chaotic home environment, caused ADD.

Other causes including exposure to environmental toxins, especially lead, alcohol, and tobacco, have been investigated (Barkley, 1997). However, these studies have been inconclusive for two reasons:

1. The investigations failed to use appropriate criteria to identify the children studied.

2. The researchers failed to determine the presence of ADHD in parents of children in the studies (Barkley, 1997).

Diagnosis and Treatment

A comprehensive evaluation is necessary for proper diagnosis to rule out other medical or emotional problems. An evaluation includes intelligence-testing and the assessment of academic, social and emotional functioning. Measures of attention and impulsivity and parent- and teacher-rating scales are also used. A medical examination is also an important element.

Treating children with ADD involves medical, psychological and educational interventions. Behavior management techniques are also useful. This type of multiple level intervention is referred to as a "multi-

modal" approach. A multi-modal approach includes:
1. Parent training.
2. Appropriate educational program.
3. Individual and family counseling as needed.
4. Medication, if appropriate.

The most commonly prescribed medications for ADD symptoms are referred to as "psychostimulants." Between 70-80% of children diagnosed with ADD respond positively to the use of medications (Amen, 1995). The medication can improve attention, decrease impulsive behavior and hyperactivity, as well as aggressive behavior.

Behavior management (which is an important part of parent training and educational planning) involves the use of consistent monitoring and rewarding of desired behavior to increase its frequency. The most important behavioral strategy for increasing compliant behavior is positive reinforcement. Positive reinforcement is defined as an immediate response (for example, verbal praise or tokens such as, stickers or patches) to a desired behavior.

So often, children with ADHD are acknowledged for their misbehavior and thus, rewarded for misbehavior. It is important that the martial arts instructor note when the child has performed or behaved in a desired manner. Charts that keep a visual record of the child's behavior can be developed to meet the specific needs of the child and instructor.

Prognosis

With proper early detection, diagnosis and intervention, children and adults can be successful and productive citizens. Intelligence, higher socioeconomic status, low degree of aggressiveness, positive peer relationships, emotional stability, and few family problems have also been identified as factors related to a positive prognosis (Amen, 1995).

Teaching Strategies

Attention Deficit Disorder can make learning a challenge. Children affected by ADHD (Attention Deficit/Hyperactive Disorder) are able to learn, but they may have difficulty with academics because of poor concentration, organization, and attention (Amen,

1995). Classes that are small and very interesting provide a successful learning environment for the child with Attention Deficit Disorder.

Martial arts classes can be an enjoyable, popular place for children to learn new skills, self-control and self-confidence. Children with ADHD will be restless, which can be irritating to other students and instructors. The restlessness can be disruptive to classmates who are distracted by the movement. Short attention span and being easily distracted impact a student's ability to follow the instructor's directions and perform consistently. The student may intermittently attend to the instructor's directions and, therefore, the student only hears pieces of the information presented.

Impulsiveness can cause the child to blurt out answers or begin a task before a teacher has fully explained the activity. Children with ADHD can be described as acting before they think. Procrastination can be a challenge for those affected by ADHD. Many people with ADHD wait until the last possible minute

to complete an activity. People impacted by ADHD can have problems shifting their attention from one activity to another (Amen, 1995). They are prone to becoming highly focused or "stuck" on an idea. As the instructor moves on to other topics, the child may be several thoughts, ideas, kicks, kata or poomse moves behind the instructor.

The child with ADHD is often described as forgetful. Children with ADHD have difficulty with timed situations because the pressure of the "timing" interferes with their ability to be successful. Therefore, instructors need to avoid using timed drills with the student with ADD.

> Brandon was having a positive day in class. Then the instructor announced a drill to see how fast the children could hop on one foot to the other side of the room. All of the children were excited and ran to the side of the room to prepare for the drill.
>
> Brandon lined up next to his friend, the instructor yelled, "GO!" The children began hopping. Brandon began to stumble and cry. He was loudly sobbing and writhing on the floor by the time the instructor ran to check on him. Brandon was having a "meltdown."
>
> The combination of timing and motor coordination required to be successful at the drill was beyond Brandon's abilities.

Due to these learning challenges presented to children with ADD, several modifications need to occur in their learning environment to help them be successful students.

Within the martial arts training environment, it is best to have the child placed near the front of the room. Such placement will increase the probability that the child is paying attention to the instructor and not distracted by other students. Since within the martial arts training situation, belt rank determines placement in the line up, it is recommended the child be placed near as few visual, auditory or physical distractions as possible.

Consider visual and auditory stimulation within the training environment (Amen, 1995). How many

posters and pictures are on the walls, how loud is the noise, how distracted are students by the audience of parents, and how loud are the phones, air conditioner, heater, and outside traffic? Reducing the amount of auditory and visual distractions will create a better learning environment for the students and save the voice of the instructor.

One piece of information the instructor needs to display is the rules of the dojang/dojo. Due to the forgetfulness and distractibility of the student with ADHD, a visual reminder of what is expected of the martial arts student in the training environment is recommended. Additionally, surrounding the children with ADHD with "good role models" can provide visual reminders of appropriate behavior. Finally, encouraging the child to attend the smaller classes can reduce the distractions and increase learning and concentration.

When training children with ADHD, the manner in which an instructor presents information is a key to a successful experience. Dr. Amen (1995) noted that people with ADHD absorb less than 30% of what is said. Children with ADHD need information presented in short, direct phrases. For example, "Line up!" gets the point across better than "Line up with your hands at your sides, looking straight ahead, toes pointed forward, facing the flags, stand there for five minutes." By the time you have ended such a sentence, the child with ADHD is thinking about how cold the floor feels on his feet, and how he is going to play with his video games after class. Furthermore, he probably only accomplished *one* of the requests you made. Commands to the children need to be short and straight to the point.

Also, consider what you say to the children. An instructor will be most successful eliminating the word, "Don't" from his vocabulary. Phrase directions, commands or instructions to describe what you *want* the child to do, rather than what you want the child to *stop doing*.

> Ashley was playing with the nunchaku instead of practicing her form. The instructor said, "Ashley don't play with the nunchaku." Ashley

kept on twirling. The instructor became frustrated and repeated his phrase. Ashley kept on twirling! Finally, the instructor said, "Ashley, practice your form." Ashley put the nunchaku on the wall and began to practice.

Children with ADD learn best when they are taught in a step-by-step manner. Break down the information in small, incremental steps. The information needs to be given in small chunks with one direction at a time.

Children with ADD tune in and out, so a teacher needs to keep it simple. For example, when teaching a form, inform and display the first move. Practice this several times, then move on to the second move. Once this step is learned, combine the two steps. Once this combination is learned, add the third move.

Follow this strategy throughout teaching the form. This strategy will extend the time it takes to teach a child with ADD. Therefore, the instructor needs to expand his expectations about the length of time it will take to teach the child a skill.

Children with ADD face many challenges and often experience a sense of failure and frequent frustration. These emotional experiences can have a negative impact on their self-esteem (Barkley, 1997; Amen, 1995; Fowler, 1993). Frequently, the children report feeling like they are "always messing up." They watch how easily their peers complete homework or a martial arts form, and it can make them feel inferior.

One of the benefits of martial arts is that the only competition is oneself. The child with ADD needs encouragement and positive reinforcement. Instructors can enhance self-esteem by providing praise and opportunities for the child to be in a leadership position. The simple act of smiling and welcoming the student to class can help the child feel like a part of your school and enhance self-esteem.

Furthermore, using visual cues (posters, worksheets) and movement (showing a child the step) enhance the child's ability to understand and learn concepts. Therefore, supplementing the instruction with worksheets, books, videotapes and posters can be invaluable.

In summary, there are four basic concepts to remember when teaching a child with ADD. An instructor needs to:

1. Reduce the number of distractions.
2. Expand the time frame for learning a new skill.
3. Compliment and create a positive environment.
4. Keep the instruction simple.

Summary

In summary, ADHD is a lifelong neurological disorder affecting boys and girls. The cause is unknown, but the most common form of transmission is hereditary. Treatment approaches include parent training, proper educational intervention, behavior management, and if appropriate, medication.

A martial arts instructor who has an understanding of ADHD, a willingness to be creative, and possesses a sense of humor can be a great asset in the life of a child with ADHD. When teaching a child with ADHD, there are four basic concepts to remember. An instructor needs to reduce the number of distractions, expand the time frame for learning a new skill, compliment and create a positive environment, and keep the instruction simple.

An easy way to remember these four basic steps is to think about the DECK. ∎

FOUR BASIC TEACHING STRATEGIES FOR ADHD CHILDREN

Decrease distractions.
Expand the time frame.
Compliment to create a positive experience.
Keep it simple.

Bibliography

Amen, D. (1995). Windows into the A.D.D. Mind. Farifield, CA: Mindworks Press.

American Psychiatric Association (1980). Diagnostic and statistical manual of mental disorders (Third Edition). Washington, D.C.: Author.

American Psychiatric Association (1994). Diagnostic and statistical manual of mental disorders (Fourth Edition). Washington, D.C.: Author.

Barkley, R.A. (1997). ADHD and the nature of self-control. New York: Guilford Press.

Biederman, J., Faraone, S.V., Mick, E., Spencer, T., Wilens, T., Kiely, K., Guite, J., Ablon, J. S., Reed, E. & Warburton, R. (1995). High risk for attention deficit hyperactivity disorder among children of parents with childhood onset of the disorder: A pilot study. American Journal of Psychiatry, 152, 431-435.

Fowler, M. (1993). Maybe you know my kid: A parent's guide to identifying, understanding, and helping your child with attention deficit hyperactivity disorder. New York: Carol Publishing Group.

Zametkin, A.J., Liebenauer, L.I., Gross, M., King, A.C., Semple, W.E., Rumsey, J., Hamburger, S. & Cohen, R.M. (1990). Cerebral glucose metabolism in adults with hyperactivity of childhood onset. New England Journal of Medicine, 323, 1361-1366.

How to Work With The Parents of Students

By Don Korzekwa, Ph.D.

Working With The Parents Of Students

It's 20 minutes after the last class for the day. You're still talking with the mother of one of your ten-year-old students. She wants him to participate in the next belt-promotion examination. You attempt to explain that he's not ready quite yet. You think to yourself, "Doesn't she understand? I'm the expert here. I'm the one in charge of belt promotions." She thinks to herself, "Doesn't he understand? I know my son. I'm the one in charge of whether he stays at this school."

As an instructor at a martial arts school, you recognize that working with the parents of your young students is a critical element in your success. Parents have an investment in their children's well-being at several levels, including physical and emotional aspects. Because of this investment, it is important to consider that your relationship with the child as instructor to student, also involves a working relationship with the parents.

Parents have expectations about your work with their child as a student at your school. They see their child as an individual with unique needs and characteristics, and expect that you will also. The manner in which you deal with the expectations of parents regarding their child's training at your school will have an impact on the motivation of the parents to keep their kids at your school.

Parents can also offer the advantage of years of knowing and understanding their child in a variety of situations. They have a first-hand perspective on what interests and motivates their child. They may also alert you to any changes, problems or sensitivities of the child which can have an impact on his training in the martial arts. The more proactive you are in gathering this information, the better equipped you will be to make the training experience a good one for everyone from the outset.

It is also worth consideration that you and the parents can be allies in working with the child. Training directed toward the goals of increased self-discipline, self-confidence, and others can either be supported or ignored by parents when the child is not in class. The extent to which you have a solid working relationship with parents can make a difference in the degree of success which is achieved in guiding the child toward these goals. If you and the parents are communicating about the child's progress, the consistency and continuity in your combined efforts are more likely to produce the desired results. If parents see you as a valuable ally in working with their child, they have added incentive in maintaining your relationship.

The bottom line is that it is important and advantageous for you to have a good working relationship with the parents of your young students. This can, however, be a difficult task. You may have many students, including children, in your school. The time which you have available to speak with parents is very limited. You may find that you have no difficulty in communicating with some parents, and a great deal of difficulty with others. Regardless of the challenges, it is up to you, as an instructor, to establish and maintain a good working relationship with the parents of your young students.

Establishing the Relationship

The first time the parents and child come to the school to talk with you, or to watch a class, is when the relationship begins to take shape. It is the first impression which they form of you as a potentially important person in the life of that child. If you do not connect with the parents and child in a meaningful way at that time, it is unlikely that the child will enroll to train at your school. They must feel confident in your abilities as a martial artist and instructor, and see you as a person who can understand and communicate with children and parents.

The following section deals with responding to parents' questions and concerns, gathering information, and parents' expectations related to their child's problem behaviors. Communication skills which are discussed here are also relevant to maintaining the relationship with parents, which is discussed in the next section. Also, several examples of questions which you might ask are given for illustration. Although the suggested questions often refer to the child as "your son/daughter," it is always best to use the child's name when talking with parents.

Responding to Questions and Concerns

At the stage of "getting to know each other," it is essential that you make every effort to listen carefully to the questions and comments of parents, and respond in a manner which addresses their unique concerns, interests and expectations. If you treat these issues as important when you first meet them, they will feel more confident that you will be sensitive to their needs as the child's training progresses.

Questions asked by the parents vary in content. Some questions require straightforward, factual information in response. Here are some typical questions:

- What is your method of teaching? What about discipline for misbehavior in class?
- Are the classes large?
- What age groups comprise the classes?
- Are beginners taught in the same classes as advanced students?
- Do you teach the classes, or do you have other instructors?

The answers to other questions may be dependent upon a number of factors, including the predisposition of the child upon entering the class, the diligence with which they train, and a number of other variables, some unpredictable.

- Will my child learn to defend himself?
- Will he learn how to avoid a fight?
- Will he become more self-confident and disciplined?
- Will my child get hurt?
- When will he test?
- When will he get his black belt?

In response to these questions, it is important to keep in mind that what you teach, and what the child learns may not have as direct of a relationship as you, or the parents, would like. You face the same concerns as any instructor. A child may sit in a Spanish class with an excellent instructor for nine months, and learn to say nothing more than, "*Adios*" ("Good-

bye"). If you begin to make lofty promises about what the child will learn, and this does not occur, "*Adios*" may be the parent's message to you.

You can more reliably talk about what you teach, and what you do to support each child in the learning process. If parents have specific goals for the child in martial arts training, you can suggest talking with them at appropriate intervals to discuss the child's progress. In this way, you and the parents are agreeing to a working relationship which assists the child in meeting these goals.

It is important to understand that each question the parents ask gives you information about their expectations and concerns. They may be concerned that you are overly strict or inflexible in teaching methods, or in disciplining misbehavior. Possibly they fear that their child will get "lost" in a large class, or be intimidated by older, or more experienced students. They may be anxious about their child's safety and want to know what they can expect from you in this regard. Listening carefully to the context in which the question is asked, the way in which it is phrased, and the parents' response to what you say can reveal a great deal about such concerns and expectations.

Answers which respond clearly and concisely to the content of the questions are good.

Answers which respond to the content, as well as the fears, anxieties and expectations of the parents are better. The reason that these responses are better is that this establishes a working relationship which shows an interest in understanding their personal concerns and expectations related to having their child train in the martial arts. If indeed you want the parent to know that this training will help the child on a personal level, the better job you do at communicating at this level, the more effective you will be seen by the parents as being capable of meeting their needs.

This simply means that you allow parents to talk more personally about concerns and expectations, if they wish to do so. If the question about "defending himself" comes up, once you've related what you teach in terms of self-defense, you may say, "It's important for kids to learn how to defend themselves in a variety of situations. Have there been some situations where you felt it would be good for your son to know more about defending himself?" If they choose to talk about the school bully picking on their child, you can begin to relate in a way that is more empathic and supportive of their needs.

Another example of responding at a more personal level may be if the parents ask about the size or make-up of the classes. Once you've talked about your class size and make-up, you may say, "We do our best to understand how each child responds to our group classes when they join, and give them the support that they need. What are your thoughts about having your son join in these group classes?" Again, you've opened the door for them to express any relevant personal concerns.

Parents of prospective students who ask, "When will my child test?" and particularly, "When will my child get his black belt?" may be communicating expectations which are best addressed at the outset of training. If you respond to such questions by talking about training and performance standards, you hope that the parents will be satisfied with this, and allow you to use your expert judgment as their child progresses at your school.

Parents who ask "when" something will occur, however, at times tend to be less concerned about "what" is required to make it occur. As these parents listen to your comments, they may make the assumption that their child will perform at the martial arts prodigy level, and most certainly receive their black belt within six months.

You can follow-up your response to this "when" question by saying to the parents, "I'd be interested in hearing some of what you might expect with regard to your child's progress." The goal of this comment is for you to become aware of their expectations, and to diplomatically clear, as needed, any misconceptions which could later become a point of conflict in the relationship.

Gathering Relevant Information

You can ask questions which show an interest in understanding the personal needs of the child and expectations of the parents related to martial arts training. Spend time getting to know the parent as well as the child. Your questions and conversation with the parent and child will, at minimum, help you assess the individual training needs of the child. They also allow you to talk with parents on a more personal level regarding these needs, and their expectations. You will gain an awareness of the mental, social and emotional development of the child, and begin to formulate in your own mind a "training plan" based upon the child's abilities. For example, issues related to how well the child can attend to instruction in a group setting, process this information, and respond accordingly, will certainly have an impact on the child's training.

In your assessment of the child's needs, and the related expectations of the parents, you will gain insight as to how this child interacts with peers, particularly if problem behaviors exist which can have an impact on the functioning of the class as a whole. Will the child be demanding of the instructor's time, possibly behaving in a manner which requires you to continually shift your attention to him?

Training in the martial arts places demands on the child to perform according to specified standards. It is important to assess the child's ability to cope with the frustration which may accompany these demands. At the same time, you must assess how the parent expects that you will deal with any of these potentially problematic issues, should they exist.

Your assessment of the child, and parents' expectations, can take the tone of a friendly conversation. Some questions for the parent may be:

- "How did your son/daughter get interested in the martial arts?"
- "Has your son/daughter trained before?"
- (If the answer is yes:) "What did you think about that training? What did you like? Was there anything you didn't like?"
- (If the answer is yes:) "Tell me about that."
- "Different people want to learn different things in the martial arts. What kinds of things might you want for your son/daughter to learn here?"
- "Are there some things which you would like to see emphasized in your son's/daughter's training?"

- (If the answer is yes:) "What are they?"
- "What does he like to do for fun?"
- "How is school going for him?"

The responses to these questions can engage the parents in a conversation which helps you understand the training needs of the child, and the expectations of the parent. If the parents tell you that they are interested in enrolling their child in the martial arts because, "The kid needs to learn some self-control," you had best gain insight into what they mean by this statement. Do certain problem behaviors exist which you should know about? If so, what are they? A simple "How so?" is a nice follow-up when parents make this type of comment.

Another scenario is that parents want their child to become more self-confident. Self-confidence can mean different things to different people. Are they bullied at school? Are they overly shy, or hesitant to speak up in class?

If you say to the parent, "Tell me more about that," not only do you show an interest, but you can more specifically define what it is they expect for their child to get from training at your school. The key is not to assume that you know what the child needs from general statements. If you really are interested in helping the child and parent, find out specifically what it is they need help with first.

As you gain insight into the needs and expectations of the parents and child, you can begin to relate how some of what you offer at your school can benefit them. This is an important element in establishing your relationship with parents. If you simply deliver a standard speech that you give to parents when they visit your school for the first time, they may feel that you are not interested in their individual needs and expectations, but only in "making a sale."

Regardless of what your school has to offer, unless you make a connection with what the parents want for their child, these nice features may be irrelevant in their mind, and so will the relationship which you are attempting to establish.

Responding to Expectations Related to Problem Behaviors

Some parents enroll their children in martial arts training because they want help. The child may have a problem managing his behavior when angry. Other concerns which parents express regarding their child are low grades in school, problems focusing his attention, or lack of appropriate respect for authority figures. Regardless of the problem, there may be a certain expectation that you, as his instructor in the martial arts, will play a major role in "the cure." These expectations may be supported by what parents see advertised by various martial arts schools.

Such expectations by parents must be appropriately managed. These parents need to know that martial arts training is *not* martial arts therapy. Also, your time with, and influence over the child is limited. Although training in the martial arts can be an excellent adjunct to other efforts which are being made to help the child, promising that martial arts training alone can solve personal and academic problems is risky.

When talking with parents, explain to them the role which training in the martial arts can play in helping the child with specific problem behaviors. Show an interest in how martial arts training will be used in coordination with other efforts to assist the child. Questions and conversation about the ways in which this problem behavior is being addressed at home, school and other areas allow you to understand their current efforts and needs. Do not allow the parents to expect that training at your school alone will be the miracle cure to all that ails the child. This is an expectation which can result in disappointment for all concerned, and a strained relationship between instructors and parents.

Maintaining the Relationship

If you have successfully established a good working relationship with the parents of your students, you must now turn your attention to maintaining that relationship. It is critical that you continue to apply the same communication skills discussed earlier in this chapter. If parents feel they can easily approach you with their questions and concerns regarding their child's training, and you will listen and respond with understanding and respect, you have made a major step in maintaining that relationship.

Parents have a variety of options when they are dissatisfied, or concerned about their child's training. Two obvious ones are that they can either bring these issues to your attention and allow you to respond, or they can pull the child out of your school. If the parents do not feel that they have a relationship with you which allows them to bring concerns to your attention, their most immediate response may be to terminate their relationship with the school. It is thus to everyone's advantage that you keep the lines of communication open with the parents of your students.

The Rarely Seen Parents

Maintaining a good working relationship with the parents of your students brings on its own challenges. Some parents can be quite busy. They may simply drop their kids off in the parking lot at the beginning of class, and return when class is over to pick them up, vanishing as quickly as they came. In essence, your contact with these parents may be limited to receiving a monthly tuition payment. Their child may be performing adequately in class, so you see no reason to have more communication with them than you do at present.

Although the above scenario presents an advantage in that these parents do not take up your limited time, there is a disadvantage in that you lack an understanding of how they view your school and their child's training. You might assume that as long as you get a tuition payment every month, things are okay. If, however, this is your *only* form of communication and contact with the parents, you may be missing out on some essential information.

There are some things you would benefit from knowing about these parents' perspectives.

- Are they satisfied with the school, and committed to keeping their child in training?
- Do they see their child as making adequate progress toward the goals which were discussed at the outset of training?
- Are they supporting your efforts with the child at home?
- Are there changes coming up in their family situation, schedule or other areas which may cause them to pull the child out of your school? These considerations, and others, can have an impact on the child's progress in training, as well as how long he remains at your school.

These parents also need information from, and contact with you. Some parents may not understand that training in the martial arts is not just "participating in another sport." If their kids disappear from your classes after six months, you may simply see this as a lack of commitment on their part to follow through with the training. It is important, however, that you assess your own commitment to maintaining a working relationship with parents which may preempt their departure. This includes helping them to understand that this training is more than a hobby or simple recreation.

There are some important considerations in this regard.

- Do you spend time talking with parents, reminding them of training goals and benefits, and reinforcing the commitment to keep their child in training and at your school?
- Do you talk with them about your efforts with their child, and check to see if there are problems with the school or training, of which you must be aware?
- Do they know how to support your efforts with the child at home?

The point is that if you, as the child's instructor, have this communication with the parents, you can do a great deal to maximize parents' commitment and support for their child's training. You also minimize the number of students needlessly terminating training at your school and thus enhance retention.

The Highly Involved Parents

Other parents may be quite demanding of you and their child. They continually express concerns to you about their child's lack of progress through the belt ranks. They may constantly "coach from the sidelines" while their child is in class, and admonish the child for what they consider to be inadequate performance.

In such instances, it is helpful to establish appropriate boundaries for the parents with regard to their child's training in the martial arts, and their interactions with you. These boundaries can be limits and guidelines which are set with regard to the behavior of the parent.

If you attempt to establish such boundaries, be aware that parents and their children tend to have their own special ways of relating to, and being in-

volved with, one another. This is part of the "family system." If you try to intervene in the way in which parents are involved in their child's training, you may be "bucking the system." There are some things that you can do, however, which may be beneficial to all concerned.

If you are setting boundaries for parents who seem to demand a lot from you and their child, the manner in which you frame this effort is critical. It is not that you want the parents to become less involved with the training, it's simply that you want to assist them in finding new ways of being involved. Recognize that these parents may feel they are being helpful, and showing an interest in their child's training. If you begin your conversations by voicing a sincere respect and appreciation for their desire to be helpful and supportive, you are building upon your working relationship.

One way in which you can begin to set limits on the frequent lengthy conversations in which you become involved is to establish regularly scheduled times when you can meet with them. You might explain that you regard these conversations as important, and setting aside specified times allows you to devote your attention more completely to the discussion.

Once you have established these appointments, keep them. It is also important that you specify the amount of time which you will spend in this discussion, and be consistent in beginning and ending on time. If these parents attempt to engage you in nonurgent matters outside of these discussions, remind them of your upcoming appointment, and assure them that they can bring this to your complete attention at that time.

Parents who continually coach from the sidelines, or admonish their child for what they see as inadequate performance, may believe that they are being helpful. Such behavior can, however, be disruptive to the child's training (as well as to the rest of the class), and prove discouraging to the child.

A private conversation with these parents can possibly modify this behavior. This is how to handle the situation:

- Acknowledge the fact that they want to help their child.
- Explain that progress in training typically occurs in small increments.
- Suggest a strategy which focuses and builds on the child's strengths, complimenting the child on the things that he does right.
- Ask that they hold their comments until the end of class, so that the child will be less distracted by other things that are going on, and more capable of hearing what they (the parents) have to say.

It is essential that these parents get the message, however, that you are the professional martial arts instructor, and in charge of training during class time.

Concerns about Belt-Rank Promotion

A common topic which parents bring to instructors is their child's progress through the belt ranks. Parents want to see their children succeed, and belt promotions can be an indicator of success to them. As with many conversations, this is one best held in the privacy of your office, away from other parents and children.

If this is a point of contention, it is best that you and the parent reach an agreement as adults, before discussing this with the child. In this regard, circumstances may or may not necessitate this discussion with the child. Typically, it is best that you talk with the child about his progress through the belt ranks in the same manner as you would with any other child of his age and skill level.

Meeting requirements to test and be promoted is not a foreign concept to parents. They understand that their child must meet certain requirements in academic settings to be passed from one grade to the next. Just as it would be a mistake to promote a child in school to the next grade if he has not met the academic standards, it would also be a mistake to do so in his martial arts training. This sends the wrong message to kids about their own responsibility, and sets them up for future difficulties. The better the working relationship which you have with parents, the easier it is to get this point across to them.

In these belt-rank discussions, it is important for you to understand that the parents are concerned about the best interest of their child. You can acknowledge this by telling them that you appreciate their interest and this opportunity to discuss their child's *training*. By doing so, you have opened the door for communication, and expanded this from a discussion about *when* their child will be promoted, to a conversation about their child's training in the martial arts.

This is how to handle the situation:
- Make the parents aware that *all* of you are working toward the same goal, making martial arts training a successful and rewarding experience for the child.

- Emphasize the child's current successes in training.
- Explain the elements which you look for, as a professional instructor in the martial arts, which would indicate that a child is ready to test.
- It is important to tell them specifically what you are doing with their child in training to assist him or her in meeting the requirements for their next promotion.
- If they press for a date, and you are not certain when the child will be ready to test, set a date for your next conversation with them to discuss the child's progress.
- Do not make promises which you are not sure you can keep.

Creating Opportunities for Communication

Communication doesn't occur unless there is an opportunity for it to occur. If you want to maintain a good working relationship with the parents of your students, it is beneficial to create opportunities for communication with them. There are various methods which can be used in doing so.

As discussed previously in this chapter, regularly scheduled meetings may be appropriate and desired by some parents. Other parents may not feel the need, nor have the time for these meetings. You can, however, initiate conversations with them when they drop their kids off, or pick them up from training. Be sensitive to their availability. If they have a few minutes, a pleasant greeting can open a conversation and allow them to express their thoughts, or to ask questions about their child's training.

Solicit feedback in the form of surveys. Although having these on hand at the school will get some results, mailings with self-addressed, stamped envelopes will allow the parents who only see your parking lot to participate.

Phone calls to parents whom you rarely see can open the door to increased communication. Unexpected phone calls, however, can be a little annoying or anxiety-provoking at times. If you talk with them about the fact that you like to receive feedback from parents, you can suggest occasional meetings or phone calls and gauge their response.

If you do have this type of contact, calendars, tickler files, or databases can be helpful in remembering when to make your next contact. Also, making a few notes when you do talk can provide consistency for subsequent contacts, as well as add to the value and importance of these conversations.

Newsletters can be used to acquaint parents with you, as well as other personnel at your school. Include articles that invite parents to contact you with comments or questions. Newsletters can also alert parents to any group activities, or an open house which you may be sponsoring. Such gatherings may become the forum for increased communication, and enhance the personal, friendly atmosphere of your school. Allow parents to volunteer to help at such functions if appropriate opportunities exist. This type of atmosphere does not detract from your professional reputation, and can be a point of added value for many students and parents.

It is also essential that your school is an inviting place for parents to stay during classes. Adequate seating which allows parents to watch the classes and have conversations with each other is essential. When they do come in, make them feel welcome. The message to them is that you appreciate them being there, and you want to make this a pleasant experience when they do come to your school.

Creating opportunities for communication might require some additional effort and creativity on your part. It does, however, send an important message to parents. It tells them that what they think about and expect in their child's training is important to you.

Summary

Establishing and maintaining a good working relationship with the parents of children in your martial arts classes is important to your success as an instructor. This relationship begins when you first meet them, and continues to develop throughout the child's training. It is your responsibility, as an instructor, to foster this relationship in a manner which allows open communication. This requires that you demonstrate an understanding of, and re-spect for, the needs and expectations which parents have with regard to their child's training. In doing so, you can maximize success in making the martial arts training experience a good one for everyone. ■

INTRODUCTION TO RISK MANAGEMENT

By Scot A. Conway, Esq.

"I've been teaching for thirty years and I've never had a problem."
—*A martial arts instructor who didn't think he needed waiver forms.*

True, some martial arts instructors have been teaching students for decades and never once encountered a legal problem. Many instructors have watched students get injured in class, and had no lawsuits filed against them. Even when instructors are negligent, students often do not make insurance claims, nor do they seek an attorney to pursue the matter in court.

Martial arts is combat. People get hurt. That's just the way it is. At least, that's what seems to be the collective attitude of martial arts instructors.

Then there are other cases where an instructor just opens a new studio. It's being run on a shoestring, with just bare essentials. The instructor didn't even get insurance because it wasn't in his budget yet. "Next month," he promised himself. He has no waiver forms, no insurance, no legal protection at all. All he has on his mind is how he is going to teach.

Then he makes a mistake with a student. Forgetting for a moment that little Timmy has a bad back, he has the students practice breakfalls on a mat. Timmy misses the mat completely and gets hurt. Not wanting to disappoint his new teacher, he gets up and does it again, somehow managing to miss the mat completely again.

That night, Timmy's parents take him to the emergency room, and the bills quickly add up. Timmy's parents take him out of the class and demand payment for the medical bills from the instructor. When the new school owner says he has no money to pay them, they file a lawsuit. The school closes, never to open again.

Whether you've managed to teach for 20 years without a single problem or you just survived the latest lawsuit as a consequence of a string of bad decisions, risk management is important. Training and conducting business without proper control of legal risk is gambling. Sooner or later, nearly everyone loses.

Think of it like this. Half of all driving fatalities involve alcohol. All other problems on the road *combined* kill only as many people as the one variable of drunk driving. The problem is that drunks often drive home safely. Some drive home safely night after night, year after year, without so much as a ticket.

That doesn't mean they aren't taking undue risks with their lives and the lives of everyone else on the road. They have changed the odds against themselves, and sooner or later those odds will catch up with them.

Risk management is a course in changing the odds. Nothing you do will completely protect you from all possibility of litigation. There will always be people who will sue you no matter how careful you are, and no matter how well you cross every "t" and dot every "i" someone will manage to wring a settlement out of you or win a case they had no business winning. By practicing sound risk management, you can greatly reduce the odds of being sued.

Most of risk management is protecting your students from undue risk. You get the danger level in your school under control. You fulfill your duties as a teacher and businessperson to protect your clients from harm. Parts of this book have already covered that. With safe training practices, you will greatly reduce the risk of harm to your students and, consequently, your risk of being put out of business by costly litigation or having your insurance cancelled after a costly claim against you.

The rest of risk management is purely legal. It deals with things beyond the scope of a safe punch or kick, beyond running a safe class and building a safe school. It deals with legal trends and paperwork, and it is too easily overlooked. Further, the purely legal aspects of risk management change from time to time.

Consider this: How many attorneys would have thought to warn a restaurant that it could lose over a million dollars if its hot coffee spilled in someone's lap? Since the widely publicized McDonald's Coffee Case, however, that possibility has become a real concern. Most people think that hot coffee is supposed to be hot, and if they burned themselves spilling it, they would consider it a normal risk of drinking hot coffee. All it takes is one person to sue, and one jury to grant an award, however, and the law changes.

In response to what they consider a ridiculous case, some legislative bodies have taken action to try to initiate tort reform. (Tort is defined as "a wrongful act which does not involve a breach of contract and for which the injured party can recover damages in a civil action.") Defining the law in this area is difficult, and most attempts fail to accomplish anything meaningful. Even when they succeed in crafting some sort of law, the challenges in the court system begin and it is years before the law becomes settled in any given area. Meanwhile, the battles continue, the insurance claims continue, and the lawsuits continue.

In the martial arts, we know that the best way to win a fight is to *not* have a fight. We learn how to beat people up with the completely opposite intention to avoid using that skill, if possible. Legal battles are an amplified version of this principle. We learn to defend ourselves against the start of the fight so we can avoid the fight altogether. The best solution to litigation is to avoid it.

Almost all of risk management is covered under two simple principles: 1) Keep your students safe; and 2) get all the paperwork done. Keep them in mind if you see a situation brewing that this book doesn't specifically deal with.

If you do risk management properly, then you can also be an instructor who will say, "I've been teaching for thirty years and I've never had a problem" — and it won't be by sheer luck.

Part IV covers eight vital subjects of particular legal importance to martial arts instructors and school owners. How important? Mismanagement or negligence in a number of these areas have resulted in past lawsuits against instructors. The generic examples cited throughout these chapters are based on actual cases.

There are many issues that are more important for the day-to-day operation of your school. Certainly, other issues are more important to keep your business running. Nothing, however, is more important than risk management for protecting the very existence of your school. Nothing is more important than risk management for protecting your own financial future. Even if you don't own the school, someone could sue you personally for something you did or didn't do in any class you taught. That could lead to wage garnishment, bankruptcy, or worse, it could result in criminal charges.

Protect yourself. You have a black belt in martial arts. You know how to defend yourself against a violent criminal assault. Be a black belt in risk management, and you will be equally prepared to deal with an attack that is as destructive to your financial future as a violent attack is to the body. Lawyers can be nasty adversaries, and the most powerful self-defense technique against them is risk management. ■

A Crash Course In Law

By Scot A. Conway, Esq.

A Crash Course In Law

Law school takes three years. The subjects covered in this chapter cover four one-year courses in law school, so don't expect to really understand it. Unless you are a legal professional, you should view a sense that you really grasp the subject with some suspicion. Even attorneys know that constant changes in law make it difficult to keep up with unless you work in the field constantly.

This chapter will deal with: Self-Defense; Defense of Others; Defense of Property; Criminal Liability (assault, murder, manslaughter, robbery, rape, sexual assault); related Tort Liability (assault, battery, false imprisonment, wrongful death); Citizen's Arrest; and a little on Criminal Procedure; Contract Law; Tort Law and Business Law.

This brief introduction to each area of law will not prepare you to do much more than recognize the issues of which you need to be aware. That should be sufficient to avoid any problems. You should consult an attorney for specific advice if you run into an actual problem. This introduction is part of the practice of preventative law, and is *not* intended to be used by instructors for dispute resolution.

Defense and the Law

1. **Self-Defense.** You have the right to defend yourself whenever necessary with as much force as required to ensure your safety. The critical elements to keep in mind here are:

   A) The defense must be necessary.

   B) The force used must be reasonable under the circumstances.

   In order for the defense to be necessary, you must be protecting yourself from *imminent* harm by unlawful bodily injury, sexual assault or unlawful detention. If the harm is not imminent, you do not have the right to use force. You must be in danger at the present time, not threatened with some future harm. Likewise, you cannot be retaliating for some past harm or attempted harm. For martial artists, an act may be considered retaliatory even if it followed the underlying assault *by seconds.* You must be responding to an ongoing, presently imminent threat.

   Reasonable force under the circumstances is a difficult matter to judge with any accuracy. If you use excessive force, you can be charged with a crime. If law enforcement has probable cause to believe you used excessive force, you will probably be placed under arrest even if you were defending yourself. This matter would be decided by a jury in a court of law, unless the prosecution decides the case is not worth pursuing.

   If you made a reasonable mistake of fact, you may still be able to plead self-defense even if you were in no danger. For example, if someone pointed an unloaded gun at you and threatened to kill you, and you killed him believing he could have and would have shot you, self-defense would still apply. The more innocent the person or unreasonable your belief, the less likely self-defense will still apply.

   Most states have laws against dueling or brawling, forbidding you from doing the classic "Let's step outside" routine for a challenge match. Unless there are rules and the match is akin to a sporting event, *both parties* may be guilty of a crime. This may also eliminate the possibility of someone legally coming to your aid, since neither side has the right to self-defense, and both are guilty of assault.

2. **Defense of Others.** You have a right to defend anyone who, in turn, has a right to defend himself, using as much force as that person would be permitted to use to defend himself. If the person didn't have the right to defend himself, then you don't have the right to defend him. If you made a reasonable mistake of fact, you might still be able to plead defense of others, but not always. You normally come to the aid of others at your own risk.

   Keep in mind that the same elements that apply to self-defense apply to defense of others. However, the standards are measured by and based upon the person being protected so far as the force permissible, but may be limited by your skill as a martial artist.

Defense of Property

Using force to protect property is generally frowned on by the law. The amount of force you use to protect property must be minimal, and generally speaking, progressive. You cannot start by breaking the arm of someone you see picking up your luggage at an airport. In fact, some places do not allow you to protect property at all, forcing you to stand by while, say, someone pounds a baseball bat on your car, causing thousands of dollars of damage.

You can avoid problems in almost all jurisdictions by first making a verbal contact, then moving to physically preventing the person from leaving with or harming your property without hurting them, and then moving on to holds, pain-compliance techniques, or other non-critical methods of protecting your property.

Defense of your "castle" is another matter entirely. If you are trying to keep a person out of your home or office, you normally have the right to resort to some degree of force to eject him. Physically pushing someone out will not normally result in any liability. If the person uses force to gain entry, or if there is a probable danger of the person harming any of the occupants, then the amount of force used may be higher. Once the person turns to flee, however, you *cannot* use any force against him unless he is leaving with your property or has been placed under arrest.

3. **Illegal Defense.** Never use illegal weapons to defend anyone or anything. If you use nunchaku in California outside a licensed martial arts school, you are committing a "felony," a serious crime punishable by one year or more in prison. Throwing stars are similar. An illegal handgun is a "misdemeanor"—a crime punishable by up to one year in jail—almost everywhere in the United States. Using illegal weapons to defend yourself will often get you in more trouble than the criminal against whom you used it.

Also, if the person has a right to do what he is doing, then your rights are curtailed. As previously discussed, this affects self-defense and defense of others, but it also affects defense of property. If the repo man is taking your friend's car, there's nothing you can legally do to stop him. If the landlord is coming into your apartment, he normally has a right to do so, and you cannot use force to stop him under most ordinary circumstances.

Violent Crimes

1. Assault

Any nonlethal violence that does not involve substantial risk of death will be an assault. The degrees of assault vary based upon instrumentality, numbers, or difference in ability to inflict harm.

"Simple Assault" is an unlawful touching, and simply grabbing a person by the arm during an argument may be sufficient to constitute a simple assault. Generally speaking, when we talk about assault, we are talking about someone getting hurt or potentially hurt.

"Excessive force," retaliatory strikes when there is no danger, will constitute assault. Anytime defense of self, others or property gets out of hand, it will be an assault (unless it rises to the degree of a "homicide" crime, the killing of one person by another). Of course, going after someone when there is no need for one of these defenses is assault. Anytime violence is used against another person, an assault is committed. This may also give rise to "civil liability" (found liable in a lawsuit and ordered to pay your victim for the harm done) for assault or battery.

2. Murder and Manslaughter

"Homicide" is when a person is killed. A killing in self-defense or defense of others, when justified, is still a homicide, but is excused by the law. The illegal homicides are murder and manslaughter.

An "Involuntary Manslaughter" is committed when a person is killed unintentionally, but with recklessness or gross negligence.

"Voluntary Manslaughter" is a mitigated murder. It may have been reduced due to provocation, heat of passion, drunkenness, or any other factor that indicates that there may have been no malice in the killing.

Murder, or murder in the second degree, is when a killing is committed with malice aforethought. "Malice" means that the person intended to kill or seriously harm, not that they *knew* they were doing a bad thing. It means they meant to kill the person, but it does not mean that they were *aware* that what they were doing was wrong. For example, someone pulling the plug on a crippled friend kept alive by machines—a so-called "mercy killing"—still has malice and intent to kill, even though he believes he is doing a great service for his friend or loved one.

Generally speaking, whenever a person is killed without mitigating circumstances, it is murder.

Murder in the first degree is premeditated murder or felony murder. Simply put, if the murder is planned, it is a first-degree murder. It doesn't have to be planned for very long. Simply taking a few minutes to think about how the person intends to kill his victim is enough.

3. Robbery

The unlawful taking of another person's property is a larceny, a theft. When force or the threat of force is used, then it is a robbery. Note that houses are burglarized, not robbed. People are robbed.

4. Rape

Any forced sexual intercourse is rape. Legally, anytime force or the threat of force is used to obtain sex, a criminal rape has taken place.

5. Sexual Assault

Whenever an assault is directed at sex organs, buttocks or breasts (on women), it is a sexual assault.

Rape or sexual assault against children is child molestation. Most states set the cutoff age at 13, so any sexual contact with a 13-year-old or younger will constitute molestation. Special care should be taken to see to it that molestation is

avoided in martial arts class. A periodic talk about the issue should suffice.

6. Statutory Rape

Actually called "Felonious Intercourse," statutory rape is sex while under the age of consent. The age of consent is often 18, occasionally 17, almost never younger than 16. Consent is irrelevant. Even if both people are below the age of consent, sex can still be illegal.

7. Citizen's Arrest

Any citizen may place a person under arrest if the citizen observed that person committing a criminal act. Citizens do so at their own risk. If he is wrong, or if he did not observe the criminal conduct, or even if he's right but the person can demonstrate that he is wrong in court, the citizen who made the Citizen's Arrest may be liable for false imprisonment. In most jurisdictions, a citizen will be listed as the arresting officer, and law enforcement is legally required to take an arrested suspect into custody even if they feel the arrest was unjustified.

A Citizen's Arrest should only be used as a last resort to prevent the departure of a criminal.

Criminal Procedure

Any person arrested for a crime has the right to be read his rights when he is arrested, which include the right to be silent and the right to an attorney. Suspects also have the right to a speedy trial, and in most cases have the right to bail.

If someone is arrested, he will normally be booked and then processed through a detention facility, either a city or county jail. He may have bail set at the jail, so if someone can post bail, that person can get out the same day. Bail is returned when the court appearance is made. If a bail bondsman posts the bond, they usually require a ten percent payment (nonrefundable) and collateral to cover the rest in case of default.

Then the suspect is "arraigned," which is your chance to enter your plea of guilty or not guilty. This normally occurs within three court days. An attorney will be appointed if you can't afford one or don't already have one. The prosecutor will normally have a "plea bargain" to offer at this time, or may drop the charges if they appear anywhere from inappropriate to insupportable. If you clearly acted properly but were arrested anyway, this is where it usually ends.

A guilty plea means that you admit you did it. A not-guilty plea means that you don't admit that you did it. There is a third plea, *Nolo Contendre*, or "no contest," that says you know the evidence is against you, but you still don't admit you did anything. Here, you can still be sentenced as though you pled guilty.

A guilty plea or criminal conviction automatically determines liability in a civil suit. *Nolo Contendre*, or a not guilty verdict, does not determine anything in either direction.

Trial may take weeks or months to get to, depending upon pre-trial motions, hearings, investigation and other procedural problems. It is not unusual for a case to drag on for a year before the actual trial. When the trial is over, a verdict will be reached. If it is not guilty, then it's over. If it's guilty, then you have other options.

If you are still convinced you are right and acted properly, you can appeal the case, and normally you can post bail pending a decision on the appeal.

If you feel your Constitutional rights have been violated, you can continue the appeals process to the high court of the State and through the Federal system.

Civil Law: Contract

Contracts are not as complicated as many people believe. All that is required is an offer, acceptance and consideration. If one person makes an offer to someone, the other person accepts that offer, and there is some promised exchange or actual exchange of value, then a contract has been formed. Contracts can be:

1. Written.
2. Oral.

Some contracts must be evidenced by a writing to be enforceable. These include contracts for the sale of real estate; incurring the obligation of another; goods over $500; or a contract that cannot be fulfilled in *under* one year. Note that it is a common fallacy, even among young attorneys or any attorney not up on his Contract Law, that the contract *must* be in writing. It does not have to *be* in writing, but must be *evidenced* by a writing. This can be a series of letters, notes or memos, signed by the person against whom it will be enforced.

There are a few rules when dealing with contracts. First, never make an offer unless you can and will fulfill your offer. This is especially true as an instructor, since it is possible you could inadvertently make yourself or your instructor responsible to fulfill an obligation on a contract you entered inadvertently. The need to watch your words is doubly true when you are dealing with writing. With spoken communication, you can always explain that you were heard or understood wrong. In writing, if you use the wrong words, you can inadvertently make an offer. Be careful.

Second, never *accept* an offer unless you want to enter a contract. Look for and read the fine print. Like dealing with making offers, acceptance can sometimes be inadvertent. This is often the most true when dealing with mailed solicitations. Some will send you a check, and cashing it enrolls you in a program. Be careful on the phone that you don't accidentally place orders when you are making an inquiry. Be careful about the price that may have a small print stating, say, "only 15 payments of" lost in the graphics, so the great $10 deal is actually a $150 rip-off.

Torts

Torts are defined rather simply as "any civil wrong other than a contract." Contracts are agreements between individuals, and legal issues arising from contract occur because of the agreement or purported agreement. Tort cases arise from any wrong action outside of an agreement.

Employers are often held responsible for the actions of the employees on a legal theory called "respondeat superior." The rule is that if an employee is acting within the scope of his employment, that the superior can be forced to respond *for* the employee. If an employee batters a customer while at work, for example, or if the employee makes a mistake at work that results in harm to someone, then the employer can be held accountable.

Basic tort rule: If you did it, settle. If you didn't do it, consider fighting.

Battery

Battery is the harmful or offensive touching of a plaintiff with intent to harmfully or offensively touch. It does not necessarily require harm, but as a general category includes all touching that is offensive, harmful, injurious or even potentially deadly, including rape, beatings, sexual touching, and harsh grabbing. There are some defenses to battery, such as the right to self-defense; reasonable touching; consent; implied consent; accident; mistake; and no intent.

If there is no harm and no criminal case, these are seldom pursued or won in civil law.

Assault

Assault is the "intentional creation of apprehension of an immediate battery." It's not a threat of some future harm, but a threatened *immediate* harm. You don't have to actually hit or even touch the person, only make him *think* you were going to.

Defenses are the same as for battery. As a practical matter, this tort is seldom pursued except in extreme cases of an attempted battery that missed, like a shot with a gun, a swing with a bat, or some other potentially serious attempted battery. Again, unless a criminal charge was made, and the accused was convicted, the civil case is likely to go nowhere.

Wrongful Death

If someone dies, the surviving family may file a wrongful death suit. This can be if an accidental death occurred, a murder, or anything in between. If there is some way to establish negligence or intent to kill, then the survivors can claim damages to them. Damages usually include lost earnings for the deceased if he was a financial supporter, and lost companionship in the case of a spouse.

There is not a connection with criminal charges, necessarily, since lethal accidents can happen without a crime committed. Defenses include: you didn't do it; self-defense; contributory negli-

gence; or mistake.

False Imprisonment

Holding or locking someone up without due cause is false imprisonment, often called "false arrest." Since damages can be hard to establish, this kind of case is seldom pursued by itself, but rather, it is done in concert with other cases, commonly intentional infliction of emotional distress. Defenses include a shopkeeper's privilege; lack of intent; accident; mistake; or ability for the person to leave, provided they had some way to know it. Keeping someone out of a place is not false imprisonment, only keeping someone within rather limited confines is.

Intentional Infliction of Emotional Distress

This one shows up in civil cases all the time, but is difficult to prove and damages can be hard to estimate. First, there must be intentional, outrageous conduct that is intended to result in serious emotional distress, and then actually does. This is the level of distress beyond what people are expected to bear, and sometimes there is a requirement for counseling.

If the tort is actually established, there is no telling what the damages will be. The most common defense is that the conduct was not outrageous, that there was no intent, or that there was no actual distress.

Most modern martial arts training techniques will not result in emotional distress, but a threat of a secret "delayed death touch" killing someone without healing techniques applied, if his contract for lessons isn't paid off, would probably be enough to cause emotional distress.

Defamation

Defamation comes in two basic forms:
1. Libel, which is defamation in writing or some other permanent means of recording.
2. Slander, which is spoken defamation.

Defamation is making false negative statements about someone that causes damages. For spoken defamation, the damages must be actual loss, and you have to prove harm due to a reputation change. For written or permanent defamation, damages may simply be harm to reputation.

Some public figures, such as political figures, are routinely exposed to negative evaluations, which do not amount to defamation, and the media has limited immunity from defamation cases, since "absence of malice" is a defense for the media.

A basic defense is *truth*. If what you are saying is true, that truth can serve as a defense to the defamatory statement, but you must be able to demonstrate the truth of your statement to the court.

Some statements do not fall under defamation. First, if the person was never named or his identity implied. For example, a negative statement against *all* Caucasians does not give rise to a defamation case by any Caucasian person if the statement was not on its face negative or intended to be negative. Something that is simply offensive to one person, but not considered so by the community at large, nor intended to be offensive, is not defamation.

There is no case if there was no actual financial or other harm for a spoken statement, or damage to a reputation for any statement (such as when the person already has a bad reputation). Finally, opinion statements do not amount to defamation.

Defamation cases are seldom pursued unless there is some ongoing defamatory statements or serious harm. If a person can't find a job because of negative evaluations by you, he may sue. Defamation cases are used primarily as a way to stop defamation.

Misrepresentation

In simplest terms, misrepresentation is fraud; that is, cheating or tricking someone. It involves making a false statement of fact, or failing to reveal information that the law requires you to reveal, in order to induce someone to do something. The individual must be damaged in some way, but damage does not have to be severe. Even if the person is induced to spend a single dollar he otherwise would not have spent, there are damages.

The biggest risk for misrepresentation cases is that fraud automatically gives rise to "punitive" (punishing) damages. If you prove the case, you prove the right to punitive damages.

To avoid committing this tort, all statements should be true or clearly stated as opinion. Some

things do not fall in the category of misrepresentation. Merchants are allowed to do something called "fluffing." Basically, they are allowed to exaggerate (such as "this is the *greatest* school in the world!") so long as they don't unfairly disparage others (including their competitors) falsely in the process. That's part of why you see so many comparisons that don't actually show you the brand name of the competitor product. Promises of future performance also do not fall under misrepresentation.

Trespass to Land

This is basically coming on to someone's land without right or permission. Emergencies allow people on land, and some people have a right to enter, such as police, postal, and such. If people come on land to approach a door, that is not trespass.

If someone enters a place of business, they have a right to be there if the place is generally open to the public or appears that it may be open to the public. Once an employee asks someone to leave, though, they are trespassing if they linger.

If someone is visiting your class and causing a problem, you can ask him to leave. If the person does not, inform them that they are now trespassing, and you would like them to leave before you have the police called. If the person does not leave, then you may call the police if you just want to get rid of him. Make a report even if he has left so the police will have some information on the troublemaker just in case he is doing the same thing elsewhere or he returns.

Harassment

(See Chapter 24, "How To Avoid Sexual Harassment Liability").

Harassing people because of their religious beliefs, or lack thereof, their race, their sexual orientation, their national origin, or other "protected classes" can be problematic. In some politically-correct areas, it can result in litigation. It should be altogether avoided.

Discrimination

The discrimination issues martial arts instructors need to be aware of are discrimination for:

1. Accepting Students.

2. Promoting Students.

We accept anyone we do not have due cause to reject, and when we reject someone, it is for objective reasons. You cannot discriminate against any member of a group because they are a member of that group, whether racial, nationality, sex, religion, etc. You must judge all people as individuals, ignoring any trait that does not deal with the matter at hand.

Just because a policy has disproportionate results for races or genders does not make it "discriminatory." If you, as an instructor, feel that relaxation and applied *ki* ("internal energy") are the important elements for rank, and you insist upon a certain level of relaxation and technique to let people get to higher ranks, it is not discriminatory just because men seem to have more trouble relying on relaxation. It is a disproportionate result for a rational policy, and that is permissible.

You are unlikely to see a lawsuit from students for improper promotion practices, since it would not reflect well on their character qualifications for rank. A more likely problem would come if you appear to discriminate in your policies for accepting students.

Negligence
(See Chapter 21, "Avoiding Negligence").
Negligence is the single most common basis for tort liability and the one instructors are most likely to encounter. Basically, negligence is a reasonably avoidable accident where someone made some sort of mistake that caused some damage to someone else. Car accidents are a common example. No one did anything intentionally wrong in many cases, but there was an accident that could have been avoided had someone taken appropriate precautions.
Negligence does not require personal injury, but personal injury is often included.

Business Law
The structure of the business and how it is run is beyond the scope of the ACMA goals for instructor certification, except insofar as it applies to potential liability. While certain elements, such as school layout (see Chapter 25, School Layout to Minimize Risk) and legal paperwork (see Chapter 27, The Proper Use of Release Forms) are covered in their own chapters, the forms of business and the pitfalls involved for owners, instructors and staff are discussed briefly below.

Types of Business
The first thing to note is that no business form will protect an individual from being sued or prosecuted for his own conduct. As a practical matter, people go after the "deep pocket," the person or entity with the money to pay. If there is no insurance, even being a student instructor could result in some danger of liability if you make a serious mistake or cause intentional harm to a student or visitor. The business will normally be named in a lawsuit, but the individual responsible for the harm will likely be a defendant as well. If there is no insurance, or if the business does not have enough money to pay, the individual could lose a lot of money, too.

1. **Proprietorship.** A Proprietorship is a business owned by one person, the most common form of business. That one person is responsible for *everything* at the school, and any instructors, staff or students under his authority that cause harm to others will make him the personal target of the lawsuit.

2. **Partnership.** Partnerships are businesses owned by more than one person, and all partners are liable for the conduct of all staff (except in limited partnerships). Be careful of becoming a "partner" in the operation and income of the school, since it could make you liable for everything in the school. Many stories exist of partners clearing bank accounts and disappearing, leaving their partner(s) with the bills.

All Partnerships should be in writing, and an attorney should be consulted. Doing it right may cost more, but, like a divorce, there are few things more expensive than doing it wrong.

3. **Corporation.** Corporations are separate legal entities under the law, and they are traditionally made to shield the owner(s) from liability. A corporation does so only if the proper procedures are followed, and failure to do so will allow someone to "pierce the

corporate veil." There are specific legal requirements for forming and maintaining a corporation, including the possibility of a minimum state tax, and even the "owner" as an employee. Consult with an attorney before attempting to form a corporation. ∎

Avoiding Negligence

By Scot A. Conway, Esq.

Avoiding Negligence

The most likely lawsuit brought against a martial arts school is for negligence. Negligence is simply having a duty to do something that will help maintain the safety of those present, and failing to fulfill that duty. Depending upon the State and the ideological bent of the Court in any given area, negligence may be easier or harder to prove.

Some areas of the U.S. are pro-business and understand that certain risks are so remote and fixing them so expensive, that the law does not require those measures be taken. Other areas are so pro-employee/consumer that a business owner may be found liable if someone is hurt in his business or during operations even if every conceivable precaution was taken.

Cases have gone to trial over spilled hot coffee in someone's lap (it was too hot, the jury decided). On someone slipping and falling on a tile floor after he walked in from the rain (no sign was posted advising people walking in from the rain that the tile would be slippery when wet). Even criminals have won lawsuits when they broke into a business and were injured. It doesn't matter who is hurt or what they were doing, if the danger existed, the owner was responsible.

At other times, in other places, what appears to be a strong case is lost at trial or overturned on appeal. A worker intentionally defrauded a customer, then injured the customer's agent when he tried to repossess the customer's car that the worker was using illegally. The Court refused to award any damages for the use of the car or the injury to the customer's agent. There are undoubtedly thousands of what might seem like cases with merit that still lose.

Many lawyers are known to openly admit that the outcome of trial is a "crap shoot," that it's a roll of the dice and you never know what's going to happen. To some extent, that's true. If a case goes to trial, it means that both sides are committed to the fight, that both sides think they can win. When two good lawyers (or teams of lawyers) think enough of their case to fight it out in Court, the outcome is difficult to predict. However, 95% of *all* cases settle before trial.

Avoiding Accidents

Taking the issue of accidents step-by-step, the first general issue to consider is avoiding accidents. No matter the present situation with documentation or insurance, if no accidents occur, then there will be no claims. There are three key areas to consider:

1. Safety of the Training Area.
2. Safety of the Training Equipment.
3. Safety of the Training Techniques.

Safety of the Training Area

(Also see Chapter 25, School Layout to Minimize Risk)

The first thing to do is evaluate the safety of your training area. Any potential dangers need to be addressed. If there is a tear in the mat that could catch someone's foot, then it should be taped down or the mat replaced. Look at your school from the standpoint of a nit-picking safety inspector. Do not dismiss things as "good enough," since, in a court of law, "good enough" often isn't. Carefully explore both the actual training area and the rest of your premises.

SOME COMMON TRAINING-AREA DANGERS
- Torn Mats.
- Uneven Floor.
- Protruding Objects (nails, splinters, etc.).
- Equipment Improperly Stored (stacked so it may fall over, weapons loosely mounted on a wall, equipment in training areas, etc.).
- Sticky or Slick Areas on Hard Floor.
- Chemicals (usually in restrooms, etc.).
- Poorly Lit Areas (especially Training Areas).

Safety of the Training Equipment

The second area to carefully evaluate is the safety of your training equipment. If weapons have splinters, then they should be sanded down or replaced. If the grips on sai are coming loose, then they need to be secured. If a cord on nunchaku is frayed or there is a crack in the weapon, it must be replaced. Sharp weapons should be stored well out of the way of curious visitors or students.

The standard here is the same. Look over every piece of equipment as though you were looking for an excuse to sue your own school.

Some common dangers:
- Splintering or Cracked Weapons.
- Old Kicking Shields.
- Stressed Chains on Heavy Bags.
- Fraying Cord on Speed Bags.
- Loose Grips on Weapons.
- Worn Mats.
- Sharp Weapons.
- Nunchaku, Three-Section Staves, Eight-Section Whips and other weapons with which the inexperienced can easily injure themselves.

If you find any potential dangers, address the problem as soon as time and money allow. Do not delay. Many problems can be partially addressed immediately, even if the problem cannot be completely resolved. If the nunchaku cord is frayed, get rid of them now. Even if you can't replace them for a while, it is better to go without the weapon temporarily than risk serious injury or damage to the school. If the cord breaks during high-performance use, imagine the harm it can do if it struck someone.

If an accident happens today because of a problem you meant to fix tomorrow, you will feel like a fool. If you've never had an accident, then *now* is the time to take care of the problems. You do not want to wait until a student is injured before you try to make your school safe.

Safety of the Training Techniques
The third thing to look for in avoiding accidents is your actual training. Martial arts, by its very nature, bears an element of danger. Students will get minor injuries through the course of their training. The injuries might be as slight as a hyperextended joint or a strained muscle, or as serious as a concussion or fractured bone.

Combat systems are especially prone to injuries, and training could not be made entirely safe without sacrificing the effectiveness of that training. The question to ask is this: Are there any unnecessary dangers in my training policies?

Some common dangers:
- Weapons Practice in or near traffic areas (a traffic area is not just a walkway, but anywhere that other students move through, even if they are training as well).
- Students wandering near or through other students' practice areas.
- Students holding kicking shields or heavy bags improperly (such as in front of the face, where they will hit themselves if their partner hits the shield hard.)
- Students holding kicking shields or heavy bags for others who hit too hard for them.
- Students training with sharp weapons without sufficient skill (even masters with decades of experience have nearly killed themselves practicing with combat-quality weapons).
- Sparring with excessive contact (often as a result of students sparring at a speed too fast for their level of control or a match getting out of hand).
- Sparring partners using techniques that cannot be safely performed in a sparring match (more than one full-speed shootfighting bout ended with a crippling injury because techniques were used that are difficult to control in a match).
- Rolling or falling on a hard floor while learning how to fall (recommendation: use a mat to learn, then the hard floor once some proficiency is developed).
- Wrist Locks, throws or self-defense skills practiced too hard (recommendation: practice very gently—even too gently—until you learn an individual training partner's pain and injury thresholds).

Mitigating Damages
The word "mitigate" means "to make less harsh or hostile." The principle of mitigating damages involves making sure that you take steps to reduce the level of harm. It is normally applied to "plaintiffs" (people who file the lawsuit).

An injured student has a responsibility to try to limit the severity of his own harm. In a martial arts context, that means that he should stop training when injured. He should not purposely expose himself to greater risk of harm. He should not execute kicks full speed with a bad knee, and he should not throw and be thrown with a bad back. Instructors must make certain that their school policies allow and encourage injured students to mitigate their injury, or the instructor and school could be held liable for pushing an injured student and causing even more harm.

Also, instructors should be able to treat minor injuries.

> Four students were injured at a tournament, as frequently happens. Two were injured while breaking. They struck the bricks improperly. The other two were injured during sparring, one with a bloodied nose. Despite the presence of many instructors from a variety of schools, there did not seem to be any ready care available for the injured students.
>
> One of the instructors recommended that the competitor with the bloody nose lean his head back, which is exactly opposite from modern First-Aid practices. It causes the blood to flow into the throat and can cause choking and illness (a person's stomach tends to throw up his own blood). Fortunately for the competitors, one instructor was on the floor with CPR and First-Aid certification and advanced martial arts healing techniques. She made herself available to treat the injuries of the competitors.
>
> Had there been no care available, or had the care been counterproductive (such as causing blood to drain into body cavities), then the injuries could have been much worse than they were.

There should be someone who can tend injuries available at all times. A First Aid kit should be handy. Red Cross certification in First Aid and CPR is recommended.

One big caution about martial arts-type healing techniques: *they had better work.* If an esoteric technique is used and makes matters worse, then instructors and schools could get in even more trouble.

The Best Defense Is a Good Defense

The best defense is having a good defense ready. If an attorney has to contact you to find out what happened in an accident eight months ago, and you are vague because you can't quite remember, that won't help your case much. If the attorney asks who else saw it, and you don't know, and if the attorney needs to know what was done at the scene, and you don't recall, then your case will be very difficult to prove.

The other side may have medical records, statements taken immediately following the accident, and pictures of the injury. You need to have your evidence as well. For most minor incidents—bumps and bruises—such detail will be unnecessary. When something serious happens, then you should put together a *complete* file on the incident.

Consider yourself your own private investigator. Be careful to collect only "objective" facts, though. That means treating facts without distortion by personal feelings or prejudices. You don't want to be accused of using your position as the instructor to badger your students into lying, embellishing or shading the facts.

Take note of what happened, who was around, what was done about it and by whom, and an account of the events and possible contributing causes. This will serve as a reminder to you, since memory can be inexact. It may be months before you have to give a "deposition" (testimony), and years may go by before a trial. If you rely on your ability to remember a two-year-old event, then you can expect to be expertly tripped up by a skilled attorney on cross examination.

If you have a good insurance policy, then your insurance company should take care of your legal defense. If you do not have insurance, then you should already have an attorney in mind to work on any case you might have. It might be a student, or a parent of a student, who understands martial arts and has some experience litigating.

Once you receive a lawsuit, your attorney typically has 30 days to file papers with the Court. If you spend 20 of those 30 days hunting for a decent attorney, then your attorney does not have adequate time to prepare your defense.

At times, attorneys have received case files the day before paperwork is due, and they have to rush on paperwork that can determine if you win or lose your case. Cases have practically been forced to settlement for more money than the case was worth, because the attorney wasn't given the Summons and Complaint in time to prepare the necessary paperwork.

What If It Really Is Your Fault?

You will want to take note of your conclusions on any serious accident, since you will have to decide if you are going to settle the case or defend. While we want to focus on avoiding accidents and defending our school if we are sued, we also need to consider our responsibility in some matters.

If you are responsible, tell your insurance company so. Let them know that you really believe that you owe these people, and you would like them paid. This might affect your standing with your insurer, and would probably affect your rates anywhere else you went, but that's what you pay them premiums to do. If a matter is small and easily within your budget, you might handle it on your own.

Sometimes we make mistakes, and those mistakes can lead to serious repercussions. At times, a matter might even be serious enough to warrant criminal charges.

> During a class, a fairly new student had serious problem with control. The instructor, in an effort to "Teach him a lesson," unleashed full speed on the student. While none of the strikes were full power, even with protective gear the student was knocked back, hit his head, and had bruised ribs.
>
> The student took no legal action, but the assault was potentially criminal and could have resulted in civil liability as well. If the family had made a claim, the instructor would have been well-advised to offer to pay for medical expenses.

Sometimes someone else does something criminal, and their ability to do so was a result of our negligence. Consider the case of the young girl sexually molested by the son of the school owner. The son is guilty of a crime, but the school owner could also be found negligent for allowing his son access to the young girls and making a place available to him for such conduct.

There would be additional factors to consider, such as previous conduct, known tendencies, and the reasonableness of precautions available. Still, the family could sue. The school owner in that situation might want to work out some sort of settlement with the family to cover therapy for the girl or some other form of compensation.

An attorney should help put together *any* settlement, since an improperly-worded offer may open the door to all sorts of problems in the future. In fact, a good-hearted, but improperly-done settlement offer could turn something that wasn't going to be a serious case into a major event.

A skilled attorney can avoid this situation, but make certain your attorney has some skill at diplomacy and negotiations, since many are overly combative and so focused on being a vigorous advocate for their client that they inadvertently pick fights and turn settlement discussions into Court battles. Some few do it on purpose to collect larger fees, but most simply haven't got the skill to deal with matters with courtesy and respect for everyone involved. If your insurance company is handling the matter, finding a good attorney is their responsibility.

Your insurance should cover the settlement on the case. If you don't have insurance, the fair settlement value of a serious matter might be more than you can afford. In that case, you may need to set up a payment plan. Called Structured Settlements, payment-plan settlements allow you to pay over time, and the total amount often does not change, since no interest is applied to the balance. There is also the possibility of obtaining an equity loan, selling a car and buying a less expensive model, or selling some personal property.

The lesson? Have insurance. Period. ∎

The Use and Maintenance of Safety Equipment

By Scot A. Conway, Esq.

The Use And Maintenance Of Safety Equipment

Martial arts are innately dangerous, and over the years many students have been hurt learning the arts. Punching makiwara boards or hard heavy bags with bare knuckles have bloodied many hands, and the damage done to the bones and nervous system has made some types of work difficult for old-school martial artists. Working with sharp weapons has cut many of us, and training without proper sparring gear has gotten noses broken, legs fractured and, in more cases than any of us would like, debilitating head injuries. Even simple but incorrect stretching methods have resulted in serious injuries in the past. Ballistic stretching, universally condemned today, has led to an industry-wide epidemic of torn knee ligaments among veteran black belts who started their training back in the 1960s and '70s.

Modern martial arts training is not like that. A litigious society, ready to sue even for the seemingly stupidest reasons, should motivate us to make things much safer than they once were. Not only are modern teaching methods better for business (with an apology to traditionalists who feel the art should never be about business), they are safer (same apology to those who feel "safe" and "martial arts" ought to be a contradiction in terms). Safer means "less risk to the student," and less risk to the student means less legal risk to the instructors and owners of schools.

With so many training aids and an incredible array of safety equipment, a Court of Law might find it unforgivable if you don't use them. Imagine the presentation to a jury of safety pad after safety pad, of safe heavy bags, gloves and kicking shields presented to them, and catalogs from two or three major martial arts suppliers handed out to each juror. Imagine the blistering accusation of recklessly endangering students by refusing to use any of them.

What defense could your attorney make? "It's martial arts. It's tradition." What do you think a jury of ordinary citizens will think about tradition when faced with a former student seriously injured or permanently disabled, because tradition was more important than safety?

Use of Training Aids and Safety Equipment

Most martial arts studios have some training aids and safety equipment. These must be used, and used properly, to minimize risk. The responsibility falls to the instructor to make certain that the students are properly trained in the use of equipment. The instructor should also make certain that students are appropriately matched when practicing sparring and even self-defense techniques.

Do the students know how to hold the body shields? A frequent problem is students holding the shields *away* from their bodies, then the impact drives their arm and shield into them. Another problem is holding it at improper angles for certain moves, such as roundhouse kicks, and getting kicked in the hand or arm.

Do the students know how to hold focus mitts? Shoulder injuries are common if focus mitts

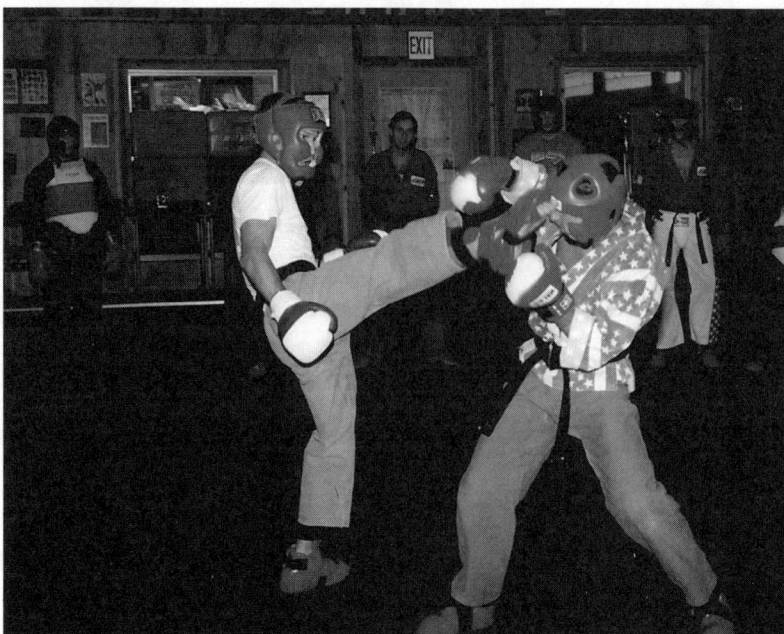

are held to the side, and if a student holds one in front of his face, he may get hit by his own hand.

Is the skill of the students equal to the drill? Practicing roundhouse kicks on a small shield may lead to kicks to the knees or other body parts not protected if the students don't have the necessary skill.

Is the piece of equipment the proper training aid for the drill? Using a small shield for a drill that should have a large shield may result in serious injuries.

Are the student pairs or groups suitable? If a child is hurt holding a shield being kicked by an adult, you may be liable because of the danger in which you placed the child. If mismatched pairs are unavoidable, the child should practice power techniques while the adult practices control.

Has anyone been hurt in the drill before? If someone gets hurt in a drill, the drill should not be used again until the instructor staff has carefully evaluated the drill to see if there are innate dangers in the drill, and those dangers should be eliminated before the drill is used again.

Safety Measures for Unsafe Lessons

When the class is practicing *any* kind of training drill, proper safety equipment should be used to minimize the risk of injury. Anything done that is potentially hazardous should be clearly related to the skill being taught or practiced, and students should have the right to excuse themselves. Whenever possible, however, some measures should be taken to make unsafe lessons as safe as possible.

Some martial arts practices do not lend themselves to excessive safety, such as breaking. However, even in that endeavor, rather than having students pound concrete on the first day they learn breaking, have them practice on easy rebreakable boards, or let them put substantial padding on the bricks (a folded up towel, for instance) so they cannot hurt themselves while they learn how to break. Then steadily reduce their padding until they are breaking the way you would like them to break.

Also, never permit students to attempt breaking feats beyond their level of skill. A white belt, for an exaggerated example, should not be trying to break

boards with an advanced kicking technique. Likewise, the degree of difficulty created by the number and composition of the material to be broken should always be closely monitored. Do not allow unqualified students—no matter how big and strong they are—to attempt to break too many boards or dense objects like bricks, cinder blocks and ice. And permitting any student to break objects with his head could be a shortcut to disaster, legally and otherwise.

Once, at a tournament, a competitor nearly knocked himself unconscious by smashing his head into a pile of bricks that didn't break. If such advanced breaks will be attempted, then instructors had best know what they are doing and be prepared for the consequences.

On other lessons, start safely and build from there. If students are learning rolls, for example, start simply, on the ground, and then work steadily to kneeling, standing then jumping rolls. If students are learning breakfalls, start them practicing from a roll, then a trip, then a dive roll, then a hip throw, and finally a shoulder throw.

Many of the skills and teaching techniques discussed in other chapters throughout this book are also excellent for risk management. They help introduce students to skills slowly, guiding them to greater skill, helping them grow as martial artists. As so many of them help students learn safely, they also help to reduce the risk of liability as well.

Maintenance of Safety Equipment

Most of us have seen an old kicking shield, battered by years of use, wrapped with duct tape that is separating. Some of us may even have them in our schools. If you kick them wrong, you could catch a toe and break it. Even if you hit it right, you could hit the soft spot and really hurt your partner.

If it's old, if it is no longer serviceable, get rid of it. Keep it as a souvenir if you like, but when it becomes easy for you to imagine a first-day student hurting himself on it because of its condition, it's time to retire it.

Likewise, torn mats can be dangerous. Replacing them can get expensive, and taping them may add a few years to its life, but at some point, the benefit is not worth the danger and the mat must be addressed.

> At one school, the original mat covering the floor was brand new—a decade ago. The tarp covering the mat had torn in some areas and separated in others. From time to time, a student would catch his feet and stumble or fall. The instructor, as wise as he hoped his student would become, saw that the mat was now more of a danger than a training aid, and he got rid of it. Soon, double-padded athletic carpet replaced the mat.

Keep up on your equipment. When you see a problem, fix it. When a student or a parent brings a problem to your attention, fix it. If you address problems when they are small, the repair can be simple. Other problems might be more difficult to fix, and you should try to maintain a fund for those, or parents and fundraisers can often be a tremendous help when something big needs to be done.

Sparring

A young man was sparring in a martial art in which the groin is a primary target. He had forgotten to wear his cup, but neglected to mention that to anyone. Then, wham! He got hit in the groin and landed on the ground. As far as anyone knows, he recovered completely.

A cup cannot protect you if you're not wearing it. Neither can chest pads, head gear, gloves, shin pads or anything else. Equipment must be *used* to be effective. Students should have sparring equipment with which to spar, whether provided by the school or purchased by the students. If the school owns the gear, the school is responsible for keeping the equipment in good condition and disposing of it when it is no longer effective.

Instructors should maintain a policy of requiring students to inform their partners when they are missing important pieces of equipment that are not obvious, such as groin cups. The time for discovery is not when the kick lands.

Likewise, students should be required to inform

others of any physical limitations or injuries they may have, such as a headache, shin splints, sore shoulder, etc., that might affect the techniques used. Students should also be required to tend to their own limitations, by wearing knee braces, wrist wraps, bandages, etc., as their condition warrants.

An instructor that maintains a "No excuses!" policy might generate tough students, but he is just as likely to generate seriously-injured, sometimes permanently-disabled students. It is better to forbid a student to spar without proper equipment than it is to allow a student to go ahead and fight without an important piece of protective gear and get hurt.

Adult students can be granted more flexibility in what safety gear they use, especially in extra-curricular sparring (before and after class), if they have the experience and skill to take care of themselves. Anyone, though, who injures another, must be severely limited in what he is allowed to do. Allowing someone with a known track record of hurting others to fight without gear, may be construed as negligence on the part of the instructor. If the sparring partner did not know about the tendency in his partner to hurt people, and the instructor did, then the instructor could be held responsible.

Safety equipment is an important aspect of modern martial arts instruction. From a risk-management perspective, it is critical to have safety equipment for any exercise that may be dangerous without it. Tradition will not be an excuse in Court if a student is seriously injured. It is likewise important to remember that equipment must be in serviceable condition, and, finally, that safety equipment must be used to protect the students from harm, and to protect the instructors and school from lawsuits. ■

The Proper Use of Student Instructors

By Scot A. Conway, Esq.

The Proper Use Of Student Instructors

The $25,000 Volunteers

Probably since Abraham put his servant Eliezer in charge of his 318 trained men in ancient times, senior instructors have put senior students in charge of training junior students. It has been a tradition in martial arts that has endured through the centuries, from master to disciple, and now from head instructor to senior student. The State of California has other ideas, though.

> A California instructor, using a long-standing tradition, had his black belts teaching classes at his studio. In exchange for their commitment, he no longer charged them a fee for classes. Most of the black belts had regular teaching duties as part of their black belt-level training. This continued until one fateful day when the Chief Instructor and a black belt student had a disagreement. The student, vindictive, contacted the California Labor Board and reported his instructor.
>
> The State of California came down to the school to investigate. The Chief Instructor complied with all the requests. The investigators concluded that the Chief Instructor, over the years, had a total of 25 black belts teach classes. They defined them as "uncompensated employees," which is illegal under the laws of California, and fined the instructor $1,000 *per incident*.
>
> The final bill: $25,000 for the volunteers.

Defending Against the State

When someone sues you, they have to hire a lawyer, file a complaint with a Court, have you served copies, and they have to prove their case in front of a jury or judge. In turn, you have to hire a lawyer and bring your witnesses and your evidence to the court and show it to the jury or judge. They will decide who wins.

If you have a good insurance policy, and the case has to do with negligence, then your insurance company will hire the lawyer for you. Of course, if you know you did something wrong, you or your insur-

ance company negotiates a settlement.

That's the easy version.

When the State comes after you in this context, (meaning *any* government entity), it has the power to send someone out who takes a look at your operation and decide if you're guilty. Then the investigator issues his finding and you are found innocent or guilty. It's not an adversarial proceeding. It's not a fight. It's the State deciding whether you win or lose. The best you can hope for is to convince the investigator that you're innocent. Sometimes you can convince him to give you a break because you didn't know you had done something illegal, and assure him that you won't repeat that mistake ever again. Sometimes, however, you can't.

Here's where things may seem odd.

If you disagree with the finding of State bureaucracy, then the way you appeal the decision is to go to the State bureaucracy and they will look at your case again. The same organization that found you guilty before it gets to decide if you're *still* guilty. In many cases, the bureaucracy that finds you guilty sets the fine, and you pay that fine to it or to the State. That fine is credited to them—either to their operating budget, or to them politically—for being a revenue-generating body.

The State has full-time investigators who are being paid whether they're looking into you or not, so it doesn't cost the government anything more than it already spends to investigate you. Even when expenses are incurred, its resources are enormous. Only *after* you've exhausted your administrative remedies are you permitted to take the State to court. Unlike dealing with another person or business, you have to pay the government first, and then fight them to get it back. Not only are you out of the money for the fine, but now you have to pay for the legal battle, too.

Even if you run a very successful school, an attorney's standard fee of $150 to $200 an hour can add up very, very quickly. Further, it's hard to find a good defense when the government is after you. Many people find it's just easier to pay the fine, no matter how high, than it is to try to fight it. Imagine the instructor who lost $25,000 to the State of California. He might get 125 hours of an attorney's time for the same money. How many billable hours will the fight take? Who knows? You might win and still lose all the money.

Use of Black Belts

As with many other things such as lawsuits and nuclear war, the best defense is to avoid the fight. By keeping documents and records straight, and maintaining policies that conform to whatever the various levels of government might be demanding at the time, you can normally avoid these problems. Maintaining good relations with people can minimize the risk of someone reporting you and putting you through the hassle of an investigation. Even if you're innocent, investigations can be time-consuming and stressful.

To solve the problem of Black-Belt-Instructors-as-Uncompensated-Employees, like the California case above, you should have on file a document that essentially reads as follows (feel free to copy this):

"I understand that advanced training at this school requires exercising responsibility for others, which may and often includes being put in charge of classes, learning how to teach what I know, and practicing leadership through teaching. This is part of my normal training, and whether supervised or not, is part of my rank requirement for advancing to upper ranks. I understand that I am not an employee and that I am learning valuable skills by teaching. If I am not available to teach, or if there are no classes available to teach, then I may exercise my teaching and leadership responsibilities in some other way by mutual agreement with my instructor."

This will make it clear to both the advanced students and the State, should they investigate, that the high-ranked students engage in teaching to earn higher rank. By

also allowing black belts to engage in their teaching and leadership responsibilities outside the school, you are also demonstrating that you are not making them "uncompensated employees" (the violation for which the California instructor was fined), but honestly giving them leadership experience. If you do not allow them to fulfill their responsibilities elsewhere, you are demonstrating that they must work for you, which could get you in trouble with the State.

If you structure the leadership responsibility correctly, you could make it so easy for them to carry out their leadership and teaching functions at the school that few will take the other option. You should have these policies in writing. Some who lead clubs on high school and college campuses, or lead church groups, or are working on their Eagle Scout (Boy Scouts) or Cadet Gold Award (Girl Scouts), might fulfill the requirement. They might also be required to assist in classes they attend to demonstrate they know their material well enough to convey it to others, but they won't have to be responsible for teaching classes.

High-ranked students should still be charged a monthly fee, even if a token fee, and the fee should be the same whether they are teaching at the school or performing their black belt leadership elsewhere. If the fee is different for instructors who teach at your school and black belts who do leadership elsewhere, then you are effectively "paying" them the

difference in fees. That means that the various taxes and fees that apply to employees must be paid to the State, "paid" students must be listed as employees when applying for a Business License (where applicable), and that "pay," the difference in fees, may be considered taxable income to the black belt who is teaching classes.

Owner Liability for Instructor Conduct

An instructor got an emergency phone call from his wife and had to leave the studio. He informed his senior student, a fairly new black belt, and left the class to his supervision. The black belt took it upon himself to try some of his "improved" exercises, and a student was seriously injured in the process. The owner of the school was legally responsible for what happened, even though he wasn't present at the school and had no idea what the black belt was going to do.

Whether you are teaching personally, a paid employee is teaching, or any person you authorize to teach is in charge, the owner of the school is legally responsible for *anything* that happens in class. In law, this is called an "Agency Relationship." Essentially, if someone is acting as your business "agent," it means that they are acting on your behalf.

All employees are considered agents, period. Anything that they do within "the scope of their employment" is attributable to the business in general, and in a proprietorship (individual owner) that means the owner is responsible. "The scope of their employment" means anything that is work-related in any reasonable way (and sometimes *not* reasonable ways, depending upon how good the other lawyer is).

If a paid instructor makes a mistake in class, then the owner is liable. If an employee is helping a student get his car started and accidentally runs the car into the car parked in front of it, then the owner may still be liable. If an employee gets in an accident on his way home from dinner after a workout, that is beyond the scope of his employment and the owner will not be liable (which doesn't necessarily stop some lawyers from trying to blame the owner.)

Volunteers are typically considered agents if they derive their authority in any way from the owner. A notable exception might be if some students (not employees) decide that they are going to paint the school window with the school logo as a surprise for the owner. If they have an accident while they are doing that, then the owner is probably not liable, since the students were not directed to paint the window by the owner. Had the owner *requested* them to paint the window, then they would have derived their authority from him and would therefore be agents for the owner.

If an employee with the authority to make the decision so directed the students, then the owner would also be liable. If any employee was involved, then agency would be in question. That means a legal fight could ensue, which, as stated before, can be expensive, even if you win.

Because school owners are legally responsible for the conduct of the people in charge of their business, the owner should make certain the people in charge are capable, trustworthy and responsible. The people left in charge should understand how to conduct a safe class (watch out for "old school" black belts who might push your students to injury) and should permit students to withdraw from any exercise or drill they—the students themselves—feel is unsafe. Even if school policy allows students to back out of anything they feel is unsafe, if the instructor in charge belittles or badgers those students who drop out, or orders them to do it, then the assumption of risk may be nullified. That would leave the owner open to any claim arising from an injury during that workout.

Also, if standing protocols determine who's in charge (for example, the highest-ranked student is in charge if an instructor must be absent for any reason, or the senior person on the Leadership Team is in charge if the instructor must leave the room, etc.), the instructor must make certain that those protocols put *only* capable people in charge. Limiting leadership to National Black Belt Club members, Leadership Team members, or adults will help minimize the risk of harm.

Leaving Minors in Charge

There are several innate dangers in leaving a minor in charge of a class or in charge of your studio, not the least of which is negligence, per se. Minors are often presumed to lack the necessary skills to assume high levels of responsibility, and the younger the student, the more likely the presumption of negligence. That presumption can be overcome by showing the level of maturity and responsibility of the student through their experience, overall performance in the school, their grade-point average, and their general behavior.

Imagine this claim made before a jury:

> "Ladies and gentlemen of the jury, the owner of this school left a class full of children, teens and adults under the leadership of a fifteen-year-old girl. A fifteen-year-old girl! She got to decide what everyone was going to do in that martial arts class, and while she was leading the class, my client got hurt. The girl was fifteen! What did the owner expect?"

Imagine how much more serious the above problem might be if the teen was found to drink underage by testimony of some partying friends (of course, the instructor wouldn't know about this), or worse, use drugs. What if the girl had poor grades or had been in trouble before? What if she had only been training in the martial arts for two or three years?

Of course, you can envision how the jury would react if the girl had a 3.85 GPA (grade point average), was a black belt Certified Instructor with ACMA Certification, had been a supervised junior instructor for two years and a martial arts student for five years—and she didn't smoke, drink or use drugs. The jury, then, would react much differently, but her competence would still have to be shown.

Another problem arises not so much due to age, but lack of a driver's license and vehicle (which is a concern for older instructors who can't drive, too). If there is a serious problem and a student needs to be taken to the emergency room, the instructor can't do anything about it. While calling an ambulance is always an option, it is an expensive option for what might be a relatively simple matter.

> In one actual incident, a senior student managed to break his arm while making a serious mistake during practice. He needed to get to the hospital emergency room for an x-ray and cast. He and the instructor were the only two present who could drive, and with his arm broken, his instructor had to take him to the hospital. Calling for an ambulance or waiting for a ride to show up would have delayed care by up to an hour, or cost up to $800 dollars for the ambulance ride.

If there are several drivers in the class, though, this is not normally a serious problem. School owners should make certain that their instructors, without regard to age, are competent at the responsibility entrusted to them. The younger the student, the higher the standard, since even things that do not seem to directly affect the school *can* affect issues of liability.

Protecting the Students

The ultimate purpose for all school owners who practice risk management is to *protect the students*. Since martial arts is such a physically-demanding activity, and it necessarily involves combat skills, people *will* get hurt. There is little we can do to totally eliminate the risk of injury. All owners and head instructors must, however, take all reasonable measures to keep their students safe. Knowing the capabilities of the person left in charge is paramount.

If an instructor is known to have problems, whether emotional-control issues, physical-control issues when training with students, or an instructor has gotten students injured before, the school owner must either remove that instructor or place him under careful supervision for a period of time that fits the degree of harm done. Sometimes the order of rank places that person in charge of a class. But with the very existence of the school at stake, sometimes rank protocol must give way to the safety needs of the students.

Also, instructors should *never* choose an inadequately-prepared instructor to teach class as a matter of convenience. You certainly would not entrust the cash box in a major retail outlet to someone you didn't trust. Likewise, don't delegate authority for your classes to someone whom you cannot entrust with the safety of every student in the class.

A Note to Student Instructors

Without any regard whatsoever to your age, your rank, your experience or your preparation, when you are placed in charge of a class, you are entrusted with a sober responsibility. It is easy for young student instructors to play around with their friends a little more than they otherwise might, or to let people horse around or try difficult techniques, but you must know your own limits and your own abilities. You are in charge. You are responsible. You represent the head instructor and owner of the school both legally and as a teacher.

If you mess up, if you blow it, if your negligence gets someone hurt, not only can your instructor be sued, but you can, too. Accidents will happen, but you have to know what, and how much, you can observe. Maybe you can't spar and watch the class at the same time, like the master instructor can. If not, then just watch. Make sure no one gets hurt.

If someone is practicing a technique that you don't know enough about to really keep everyone safe, then tell that person not to practice that technique. You are responsible not only for what you *tell* people to do, but also for what you *allow* people to do while under your authority.

And if anyone argues, remember, your authority derives from your instructor. You are in command. When put in command, take charge.

And if you have any questions about how much authority you have, ask.

Proper Use of Student Instructors

Student instructors can be the greatest asset an instructor has, especially at a small one-instructor school. Used properly and carefully, they can be a tremendous benefit, allowing the head instructor a level of freedom unknown since before the school was opened. Used improperly, they can cost students, get the school closed down, and knock the owner into bank-

ruptcy. Used improperly, they can get the government after the owner, and then even bankruptcy won't protect the owner from the fines levied for violation of the law, no matter how innocently done.

Even if a school isn't closed down, student instructors, no matter the rank, who take improper advantage of their position will reflect upon the owner. Imagine the case of the 20-year-old instructor arrested for child molestation. What if he went to court and offered a plea bargain to testify against his instructor, and explain how his instructor taught him how to use his position to get the girls, even the young ones. The instructor might have nothing to do with the situation, and had he known, he would have gotten rid of the person immediately. What would happen if the headlines read, "'My Teacher Taught Me How,' Karate Instructor Claims." Suddenly you're on the defensive with no idea how it all happened.

Remember the $25,000 problem cited at the beginning of this chapter? It started with a problem between the head instructor and a student instructor. The student instructor reported his teacher, and it cost the instructor $25,000.

You must be careful to whom you give that responsibility. When you grant someone authority over your class, you are placing the fate of your school, your financial future, and maybe even your freedom in the hands of that person. Make sure they can live up to that responsibility. ∎

How to Avoid Sexual Harassment Liability

By Scot A. Conway, Esq.

How To Avoid Sexual Harassment Liability

Authors' Note: Certain material within this ground-breaking chapter may disturb you, but in order to serve your best interests, it was, in all good conscience, entirely unavoidable. The following contents are, ultimately, solution-oriented. But understandably, sound solutions cannot be proposed unless the problem is presented first. And the problem is the disturbing trend in the martial arts industry involving sex and, to a far lesser extent, sex crimes.

Sex is a serious subject whose written communication demands acute sensitivity and adroit literary skill. Sex and the law is a serious subject whose written communication demands acute knowledge and brutal frankness. Legal expert Scot Conway, we believe, achieves all of them.

Even when lawsuits do not arise, even when arrests are not made, sex is an issue in the martial arts school. Some critics go so far as to make the statement, "Martial arts instructors have the highest incidence of sex crimes of any profession." What is alarming is that some people who make statements like this are martial arts professionals who would have cause to know. While this is not verifiable in any way, it is also a very powerful statement of how bad things look in our industry.

The incidence of improper sexual conduct, child molestation, statutory rape and abuse of power are prevalent enough to inspire such a statement. This is one element of the reputation of the martial arts that desperately needs to be turned around.

Whenever you mix men and women in any activity involving physical activity, there is a possibility of sexual interaction entering into the equation. An instructor might be caught up in the adoration of a pretty young student, or students might create relationships and liaisons on their own. Certain immoral types of people might learn that your school offers coed classes and your style allows groin contact and grappling, and consequently sign up for reasons other than honest martial arts training.

Short Advice: Keep it professional. This applies to owners, instructors and all support staff.

Problems

A young, female junior instructor wanted to learn grappling skills. Her older, male instructor agreed to teach her. Since both were occupied with students during regularly-scheduled classes, the training would have to take place after those classes were finished. A man and young woman together, practicing all manner of grappling techniques alone after class, is a formula for disaster. It didn't even matter if nothing happened, rumors and allegations would be enough. The solution: witnesses.

The students and other instructors were routinely gone shortly after classes, so the instructor invited the young woman's family to come watch as often as they might like. They were given an open invitation to arrive unannounced, and to observe the training. The girl's grandmother attended the first several sessions.

She watched her granddaughter being pinned to the ground. She watched the arm bars, the head locks, the rolling around jostling for position. The grandmother watched this man throw the girl to the ground and she watched her granddaughter wrap her legs around him and push his face back. She watched attacks, escapes and counters.

"That reminds me of some dates I had in my day!" she exclaimed.

Even though the system made extensive use of groin grabs and other techniques that might appear questionable by some non-martial artists, the family was satisfied that the young lady was learning real self-defense. After a time, they stopped visiting, and they just trusted that all was well.

Not all is always well everywhere, however.

In Texas, a female martial arts instructor

was arrested under suspicion of child molestation. In California, a male instructor in his twenties was arrested in connection with felonious intercourse (statutory rape) of two students, 13 and 15. Across the country, martial arts instructors are arrested, tried and convicted of statutory rape, sodomizing young students, molesting girls, and more.

Two "martial arts masters" were caught by a female instructor sharing techniques for using their rank to get sexual favors, including "private, personal lessons," "showing loyalty and obedience," and flat-out trades of rank for sex.

Even baseless accusations can have a severe impact.

A disgruntled parent of a former student once called Social Services to report abuse by the instructor. She didn't claim that her daughter had been abused, but that the instructor was abusing another girl. Social Services launched an investigation, but the interviews indicated that the case was groundless. The instructor even offered to give any investigator six months of unlimited classes to see first-hand, but Social Services indicated that it was not necessary.

The case was closed. Nevertheless, the family of the child was terrified they might have their child taken away from them and placed in State custody. It took a lawyer to calm their fears.

Had the false accusations been about his own daughter, and had the daughter lied about it and made up specific allegations, the instructor could have been in very serious trouble, even though he committed no improper actions.

Crash Course in Sexual Harassment

Sexual harassment is normally considered a workplace power problem. There is unlikely to be a lawsuit filed by a client (student) over sexual harassment by a business person (including a martial arts instructor) unless it is a severe case. Most states would not even allow such a suit, since there are no real damages suffered and the student is free to withdraw her patronage. There may be damages if there was a registration fee, since the student may not have received full value for that fee. Also, if a contract is enforced against a student, then that might constitute damages.

Between staff members, however, it could become a legal problem. If any person on paid staff harasses another, charges of sexual harassment might arise. Generally, a person in a senior position has to be responsible for sexual harassment, but the law varies considerably.

Damages in such a case might also be limited, unless the employee is very well-paid and feels she can no longer work in such a hostile work environment. If a man fires a woman for cause, that cause should be thoroughly documented.

Just because lawsuits are unlikely under the circumstances does not mean that sexual harassment is not a problem in martial arts schools. For instructors, image and reputation can make or break a school, and allegations, true or not, can have a major impact on enrollment. In the current climate of lingering radical political correctness, sexual harassment issues will likely arise, and the instructor needs to know something about the subject.

Unfortunately, even legal scholars are still working on understanding modern sexual harassment. At one time, it was a request or demand for sex in exchange for a job, raise or promotion. The classic statement, "Be *extra nice* to this man, he's an important client," as a veiled instruction with an implied threat that her job was on the line, is an example of the "old" sexual harassment.

Today, sexual harassment is *anything* that makes a woman feel harassed. There is no objective standard. If a woman is offended by the look, comment or gesture of a man, then she has been harassed by him. It does not matter that the 90-year-old gentleman has been calling every woman he knows "sweetheart" since *Casablanca* first hit the big screen in the 1940s, it is harassment if one woman does not like it. Of course, if another finds it endearing, then the same action is *not* harassment to her.

In most areas of law, something called "the reasonable person test" helps normal people understand even ambiguous areas of law. If sexual harassment was in this category, then we could judge by what the reasonable person would find offensive under the objective circumstances. Sexual harassment, however, has its own rules. What matters is how a person—male or female—*feels* about what happened. The objective facts are irrelevant.

Many schools have a friendly, open, even affectionate culture. Men and women work side-by-side with kind, sometimes flirtatious comments made to one another. Instructors hug, chat, comment on one another's appearance, talk about personal matters, and build teamwork in dozens of different ways. If someone entered this culture and found it offensive, the whole school's culture could be declared a "hostile working environment," and the "victim" could file a suit for sexual harassment.

Obviously, some rational thinking must be brought to the subject. However, while the majority of both men and women find the current sexual-harassment climate somewhat ridiculous, it is, nonetheless, the climate in which we live.

Many women who have been married for over ten years report that they met their husbands at work, and that the conduct in which their husbands engaged might be considered sexual harassment today. Even a request for a date and an offer of lunch could be considered sexual harassment if the woman didn't like it. The men reported that they would not have asked their current wives out under the present standards for sexual harassment.

Sexual Harassment and the Law

Make no mistake about it, sexual harassment of students by instructors—and by other students—is an issue in martial arts studios. While lawsuits against instructors may be less likely in a commercial, private school, it can have an impact on enrollment. It can also set the stage for criminal conduct, notably sexual battery and child molestation, which will be discussed later.

Maintaining a professional but friendly atmosphere is important in any business. Students should be comfortable in classes. Depending upon the makeup of the student body, higher or lower degrees of distance must be maintained. The standard is "Friendly Professionalism."

1. Instructor-Student Dating. Instructors should not use classes or seminars as dating services and, to be bluntly truthful, many have used self-defense and/or rape-prevention seminars for precisely that. If there are any relationships within the studio (boyfriends or girlfriends join the class, wives or husbands start training, etc.), those relationships should be left outside.

> In one exceptional case, the boyfriend of an instructor joined the class. No one was told they were dating. Months later, when the instructor announced her engagement, no one knew who she was marrying! The man she meant to marry had been in the school for five months, but they did such a good job of keeping a professional distance in the class, that no one, not even her head instructor, suspected that they were anything more than friends.

This professional level of conduct between all students, involved or not, maintains a professional atmosphere. It keeps intimate private relationships out of the school. Often, newer students, not realizing the degree of relationships involved, make assumptions about appropriate conduct. When they feel that they can be affectionate to other students, or they feel that they are expected to be affectionate to senior students or instructors to get ahead, it creates an atmosphere in which sexual harassment is practically unavoidable.

Instructors and senior students should not ask new students on dates. When dating relationships go bad, the junior student, unable to face the "ex" in class, will usually quit. Women are especially prone to this behavior, and even if she was the senior student, she will often quit.

Anytime a person in a power position makes an

unwanted sexual advance, even as simple a thing as asking a junior person on a date can be considered sexual harassment under the current law in most states. For practical purposes, it would be hard to litigate a single incident, but a pattern of behavior permitted by the instructors may lead to a claim. Remember, it all comes down to the feelings of the harassed, *without any regard* to the intent of the person asking the question.

Hopefully, in the current legal climate on this issue there will be some sanity returning to it, but until that happens, it is by far better to be safe than sorry.

How dating policies are handled in a school is up to the instructor, but in all cases, the instructor should take measures to ensure that the school is not becoming a dating service. This includes giving out phone numbers to students who call and ask for another's phone number for non-martial arts purposes.

2. **Minor-Female Crushes.** One element that is certain is dealing with underaged students. Always, when minor females are involved, adult male instructors absolutely must maintain a professional distance. These emerging young ladies are already prone toward crushes, and their martial arts instructors will be likely candidates. If there is any conduct to support or reinforce their romantic fantasies, they will cling to it. The resulting relationships have caused unending problems for many instructors and must be avoided. Too many instructors are already in jail because such relationships went too far.

3. **Sexist/Sexual Remarks.** Sexist and sexual remarks should be completely eliminated from the school. Remember that not all statements one gender would find objectionable is sexist. It may offend some men that we train to beat up men when women can be violent too, but 90% of all violence *outside* relationships is committed by men. (Note: Violence *inside* a relationship appears to be 50% male- and 50% female-initiated, according to several studies. Law en-

forcement is just finding this out.)

It may offend some women when an instructor brings up the fact that they tend to be smaller and weaker than the average criminal, but it is statistically true.

Nothing sexual should be brought up in a class unless it is somehow related to training (such as a rape-prevention class).

Sexual Battery

Sexual battery is "unwanted touching in a sexual area or in a sexual way." The "touching" can range from a grope, grab or caress to an attack. It is sometimes included under the generic banner of sexual harassment. In society, this is easily defined and avoided. Just *don't* touch someone where you *shouldn't* touch them, period.

In martial arts, this is much more difficult.

At my school, the groin is a primary target. Students who study the art are routinely struck in the groin during sparring and self-defense technique practice. At middle levels, we add grappling skills and students grapple as well as strike. Groin-grabs during matches are common.

But what happens when men and women train together? What about adults and minors? There will be intentional contact with the groin (normally protected by cups on men, but not women), and incidental contact with the chest and buttocks.

1. **Groin Contact.** Students should not be caught by surprise by groin contact. They should be advised at the beginning about certain elements of the system and then given time to grow accustomed to the idea before they need to hit or be hit. Most students and families recognize the innate sensibility in learning to protect such a sensitive area, and most people already know it is a good place to attack in self-defense.

Some students recognize it as training, and they will have no problem fully participating. Others might need some time, but no one should take longer than six months if he is serious about training in martial arts. If any student is still squeamish about it, then he might wish to study an art that does not use that area as a target.

2. Technique Abuses. Students must also be given the ability to complain about improper use of training.

> One woman felt that a man in class was abusing the lapel grab in a technique. The man may not have been doing anything wrong intentionally, but the woman was uncomfortable. She even admitted that he may not have meant anything by it, but she still felt uneasy.
>
> She was permitted to train with another student. Even though her new training partner was another male, she didn't get the same feeling and she could focus on her technique.
>
> Another young boy was generally known for not being able to keep track of too many things at once. When he was doing kicks, he was oblivious to where his hands were. When he was punching, he had no idea what was happening with his stances.
>
> When he practiced techniques with women, he was so focused on the grab and his moves that he seemed completely unaware that he was grabbing the women's chest as he reached for the lapel grab in training. While the female instructors knew he didn't even realize he did it, it had to be addressed before any female students were offended.

Instructors must do what they can to keep sexual issues out of training. So long as students feel that an activity is pure training, they will have little problem with groin-grabs, grappling, incidental breast contact, or anything else that might come up in class. When men and women can train together, even with contact to normally private parts, and no one thinks of anything other than the techniques being applied, then the issue has been dealt with successfully.

Child Molestation

Similar issues apply with children, except the consequences are much higher if there is abuse. The solution for dealing with problems on the training floor is similar to dealing with sexual battery, except that parents must also be informed. Children may need more time than adults to grow accustomed to groin contact, especially in light of the molestation training they often undergo in school. Eventually, though, even kids come around.

1. Changing-Room Abuses. The biggest problem with child molestation is likely to arise in the changing area. If men and boys are using the same locker room, there is the opportunity to abuse.

A child molester is not likely to report himself as such if he signs up for classes, and instructors cannot routinely conduct background investigations on every new student. If such a person is alone in a locker room with a young boy, problems might arise. One such incident could cost a school *every* young student.

Protecting against such behavior is difficult without treating everyone like a suspect. One simple technique is frequent walk-throughs by instructors. If people know that others will wander in and out randomly and often, they are less likely to try anything.

Also, students need to know they can talk to instructors about any uncomfortable circumstances or incidents.

Single-person changing rooms, similar to those found at clothing stores, will effectively address most of this problem. Obviously, for existing studios with locker rooms, this may not be practical, but for any new or remodeled school, this is an excellent idea. This issue is dealt with in more detail in Chapter 25: School Layout To Minimize Risk.

Unlawful Intercourse

Laws vary from State to State, but it is generally illegal for adults to engage in sexual behavior with minors. In some states, the age of consent is 16, while in most states it is 18. Sometimes there will be legal loopholes for those close in age, such as a nearly 18-year-old girl with her just 18 boyfriend, so that what was acceptable before his birthday does not become a felony on his 18th birthday. In other states, California being one of them, no one has the right to have sex before they turn 18. The difference in age and the age of the minors involved will simply affect the severity of the crime.

The simple solution is to avoid *all* sexual contact and intimate social contact that may lead to sex or may create the appearance of sexual activity with minors. If one member of the party is young enough, it may constitute child molestation. Imagine the shock of the 14-year-old boy who just "scored" with his 13-year-old girlfriend, suddenly arrested for being a child molester!

Adults should have relationships with adults. All problems associated with sex issues are best avoided by reserving the act for marriage, or at the least, monogamous relationships.

Note on Disasters Waiting to Happen

Instructors who use their position to gain sex and sexual favors from students are being very, very unprofessional. They are asking for trouble, and sooner or later trouble will come. Martial arts schools are a "people business," so anything that has a powerful impact on personal relationships will also have a powerful effect on business. It undermines the school and the martial art system, it destroys morale, and it can destroy a school even without criminal activity or a lawsuit.

One school was torn apart when one of the senior instructors was found to be having an affair with another instructor's wife. Another system was undermined when many of the senior instructors were found to be sleeping with students, and those students seemed to be gaining rank faster than those who trained harder. A school lost many students when an instructor's boyfriend was promoted to black belt in about half the time it would normally take a student to earn a black belt, and he didn't have to take a belt test like everyone else did.

In each of these cases, the disaster happened. The impact is far reaching. Even in schools where nothing wrong happens, exposure to the problem in the martial arts community can affect the perception the public has of the rest of us.

One woman was burned by her previous system. She discovered that many of the instructors were sleeping with students, trading rank for sex, and making passes at any attractive woman around, even underaged girls. Her eyes were suddenly opened when she accidentally stumbled across two "masters" discussing how to do it, and the head of her system, a married man, asked her to join him on a "school planting trip" for several weeks without his wife. She declined and left that system.

She declared openly that any instructor at any school who wanted her respect would have to prove himself to her. She would show no respect to any man who had not earned it. She was distant, callous and even nasty at times, which was not behavior acceptable in a martial arts school. When asked to leave, she chalked it up to "another man problem," even though it was due to her disrespectful attitude.

So, not only can harassment and inappropriate sexual conduct bring litigation, each can lose students even when lawsuits are not filed. They can also cause harm to schools, instructors and students not affiliated with the problem school or system.

Also, senior instructors who become aware of wrong conduct in their junior instructors and leaders should take it very, very seriously. Imagine the impact if people are talking about the activities going on at your school. What kind of clientele would that attract? What kind of problems could that create?

And if criminal activity is found to be happening at or through your classes, and you assisted in any way when you knew, or should have known, what was going on, you could be sued or arrested for aiding and abetting criminal activity.

Sex and Martial Arts

We are dealing with physical activities that involve men and women, and sometimes target body parts that are normally private. We are dealing with high levels of energy, respect shown between ranks, and people generally in good physical condition. Taken as a whole, it is a problem waiting to happen.

We have to remember that we are professionals, and we must conduct ourselves accordingly. We have to remember that students are human, and in today's culture, sex is rampant and will likely become an issue in *any* large school.

I have addressed the problems and some potential solutions in this chapter. It is a volatile subject, however, and it must be handled with sensitivity. Remember that a serious mistake in this arena can totally devastate a student. While we are discussing it in terms of risk management, we must always remember that risk management is best accomplished by putting the client—the student—and all the people for whom we are responsible, first. ∎

GENERAL GUIDELINES TO AVOID PROBLEMS

Rule #1
Head Instructors must lead the way by example. Do nothing that can be perceived as improper or illegal. Maintain the integrity of the school and set the example for the expected behavior of everyone in the school.

Rule #2
Have written policies for all instructors and staff. All instructors should know exactly what the school policies are regarding their conduct with students. A complaint process should be instituted if someone thinks a staff member is engaging in harassment, sexual battery or any form of abuse.

Rule #3
Students must be informed and consent to the bodily contact that will take place in class. If the student is a minor, then the parents must consent.

Rule #4
Students need to have the freedom and power to complain if they think someone is doing something wrong. Students and their families must have the freedom to leave (let out of a contract, if they have one) if they perceive a problem.

Prime Directive
Always keep it professional!

School Layout to Minimize Risk

By Scot A. Conway, Esq.

School Layout To Minimize Risk

Many instructors and owners have no control over school layout. If your school is already operational, or if your budget for remodeling is limited in a new school, there may be nothing you can do to change the fundamental layout of your school. That's okay. This isn't a command to spend enormous sums of money to change everything, but, rather, suggestions to consider when you do have control over the layout of your school.

Offices for View of Door and Floor

When you're busy at work in your office and the front door swings quietly open, can you see who it is? When students are training before or after classes and you've gone to do paperwork in the office, can you see the floor? When you're on the floor and someone steps into your office, can you see them?

> A school owner stepped out briefly to patronize a nearby business. He was only going to be gone for a few minutes, but there was a small problem with the customer in front of him and he was gone for nearly ten minutes. When he returned, he found two boys, both preteens, in his school playing with the weapons. They were startled, dropped the weapons and ran. Had they injured themselves, the owner would have been liable.

This spectator viewing area is partitioned from the classroom with break-proof plastic.

In the above case, the lack of supervision was due to a momentary absence, but had he been in his office and the same thing happened, he would also have been liable. (Note: Always lock up if you are leaving, even for a few minutes.) Also, if you are working in your office, what's to stop someone from doing a snatch-and-run coming inside, grabbing an expensive weapon or piece of equipment, and running off with it?

Even for pure business considerations, you want to be able to see your front door from your office. If a prospect wanders by and they can't see anyone, most won't come inside. If you can't see them at your front door, you can't wave hello and go talk to them. That's one more student you may never sign up just because you couldn't see them.

Imagine making an appointment to meet an excited potential student, but he shows up, peers through the door glass, and sees no one. Assuming you're not there, your potential student leaves. What happens then? Because you could not be seen from the window, you lose a student.

Also, when students are on the floor, you want to be able to see them. For risk management, it is more important to see student activity than it is to see people coming and going. If students are performing skills or drills improperly and you don't see it, they may get hurt. If students are violating school rules and they hurt someone, the owner may be held liable. If a visitor who has not signed any paperwork is working out (or just playing) and get hurts, the owner may be held responsible.

You want your office in view from the floor. Keep in mind that the office may be used improperly if you can't see in your office from the floor.

You need to be able to see your front door, and you absolutely *must* be able to see your workout floor. If you cannot see the floor from the office, then some responsible instructor or staff person should be in view of the door and the floor at all times when the school is open and the floor is available.

You should be able to see in your office from the floor, and others should be able to see you if you are in a meeting. While some privacy might be preferred, total privacy can lead to any number of problems, such as those above. Some judgment is required here, since to err on the side of privacy can lead to sufficient privacy to commit crimes or sexual misconduct (or the appearance of one or the other, even if never done). And erring on the side of openness can lead to others overhearing what you are doing and seeing what you have in your office.

> A school owner's son raped a young girl in the school office, and no one saw it. The office interior was not in view from the floor, and an innocent young student suffered for it. While you might have a policy that forbids students from going into your office, this case involved the son, someone the owner presumably trusted.
>
> In another matter, senior students were often used to supervise the class when the instructor staff was occupied. One of the instructor staff was graduating from high school, so the senior staff attended the commencement exercise. A trusted high-ranking student ran the class that evening and, that night, calls to phone sex services occurred, using the credit card numbers of students gained from the financial records of the school. The senior student had used the office, unseen by the others in the school.

Dressing Rooms

Locker rooms are often the preferred changing areas in many schools, but there are some potential problems that may arise. Who supervises the activity in the locker rooms? If young boys and older men are changing together, what security is there that the child will be safe? Imagine the temptation for a molester to find a martial arts school where young boys routinely undress in a locker room, especially a locker room with some privacy. If he signed up for classes, he could gain access to the boys.

Naturally, students will need some place to put their clothes, and near-floor cubbies or lockers are ideal. An inexpensive alternative is simply designating a place on the floor for students to put their equipment bags. Be certain to keep it away from the workout area so students do not trip or stumble over them during the workouts.

Some students will be too shy to change in these changing rooms, just as some will be too shy to change in locker rooms with others around. These students should be invited to arrive and leave in their training clothes, or they should use the restroom or restroom stalls for changing rooms.

High shelves must be securely mounted, and objects perched on them should also be secured. Mounting tape or adhesive should help. Bookcases must be secured against a wall, possibly bolted to the wall, or kept where young students and guests do not have access to them, such as in the office.

Display cases must likewise be secure, and any sharp edges from cracked glass must be repaired or covered in some manner to prevent cuts. Pictures must be firmly secured on the wall so that they will not fall down even with a sharp impact to the wall, or, if you live in California, an earthquake.

Care of School

Another layout consideration is your ability to care for your school. The layout must make simple tasks such as cleaning, vacuuming and other mundane activities possible. Some have managed an artistic layout, but they cannot get a vacuum cleaner into their crowded lounge, and they cannot get to parts of their floor. Keep in mind what you need to do for maintenance when designing or remodeling a school.

Color coded rings, boundaries and pathways assist in providing safe traffic and class flow.

Control

We don't always have control over the layout of our school. Often, the existing layout is all we have, like it or not. Money will often be the determining factor in most layout decisions. However, sometimes we have a choice. When we move a school, when we open a school, and when we remodel, we have a chance to do something different. When we can control school layout, isn't it prudent to consider all the issues?

If you have locker rooms, people should come and go through them with such frequency that no one can expect to have even a few minutes of certain privacy to do anything to anyone. If students are not constantly moving in and out, instructors or staff ought to.

For legal and security considerations, the type of one-person dressing rooms found at most clothing stores is ideal. The door should be low enough so a small child can change with sufficient privacy, and high enough to afford similar privacy to very tall adults. This is the NAPMA (National Association of Professional Martial Artists) recommendation, and it solves many potential problems, including molestation concerns, theft of student belongings, staff knowing who is in the school at all times, and slip-and-fall accidents in tiled locker rooms.

Shelves, Bookcases, Display Cases and Pictures

Some schools have shelves mounted on the wall well above head level to display trophies (at least, those short enough to fit). Bookcases with pictures, and display cases with more trophies and awards, often adorn schools. Certificates and photographs often hang on walls.

All these things must be carefully secured if they will be anywhere near visitors, students or staff. Imagine a visitor leaning back against a wall and bringing down half-a-dozen certificates and photos, with glass shattering on the floor. Imagine a student losing his balance during a workout and falling against a wall, and two or three trophies with marble bases topple down on top of him. Imagine a kid climbing on a shelf to get at some interesting object higher up, and the whole bookcase tumbles down on top of him.

Training Area Apart from Traffic Area

Keeping your training area apart from the traffic area is critical. If someone walks into your school, and they are immediately in the line of fire for punches, kicks, weapon attacks, even grappling partners toppling into them, then you are asking for a lawsuit. Sooner or later a visitor is going to get hurt.

If the path to the bathroom takes visitors through a workout area and subjects them to danger, you are asking for a problem. If students have to walk through others practicing to get to the dressing rooms, or to the water fountain, or to anything else they need, you

Weapons for sale are kept out of children's reach with this counter top pro shop design.

are as much as asking for someone to get hurt—and when they do, you will be found negligent.

Important Point: Even if students sign forms assuming the risk of harm, you could be found liable. If the layout of your school gives them no choice but to be in harm's way during ordinary, necessary activities, then the form may be invalidated because you rendered it impossible for students to see to their own safety.

Support poles should be padded to avoid injury.

Either the visitors lounge, bathrooms, water and dressing rooms have to be accessible without entering the floor, or the training floor must have a clear, safe walkway through it. On a tight budget, this can be accomplished by a task as simple as putting cloth tape on the floor about two-and-one-half feet from the wall and designating that area as walkway. Students should then be forbidden to have their training exercises pass over the tape, with punches and kicks stopping short of the tape at all times.

Since a solution is so simple, the Courts may actually find you negligent if you fail to take even these elementary precautions and someone is injured.

Weapons Out of Reach of Visitors

Visitors, especially children, are often enthralled by weapons. They often want to see the weapons up close, to handle the sword, to check the weight of the staff, or to play with the nunchaku. If the weapon's rack is within easy reach of the visitor's area, they are likely to do so. In one school in a single week, this became plain.

While the visitor's lounge was apart from the weapon's rack, the bathroom was not. Three

separate visitors that week stopped by the rack, picked up a weapon, and started playing with it. The instructor saw this in seconds and asked them to put the weapons back, but even in those brief moments, an injury could have resulted in a lawsuit.

They were guests, not students, and there was no signed paperwork protecting the school. They were only supposed to use the restroom and get some water. Instead, they played skillessly with some of the most dangerous objects in the school.

Not only should the weapon's rack be out of reach of visitors, it should be in view of the instructors at all times, whether on the floor or in the office.

Even an exceptional martial arts instructor, an expert of many weapons, managed in a freak accident to seriously injure himself practicing with weapons. So severe was his injury that he required hospitalization.

With one so skilled finding himself in the hospital, imagine what damage someone with *no control* over the weapon might do. Think not only of harm to himself, but the harm to other visitors and guests when the hotshot teen grabs the nunchaku and swings them right into the face of another visitor!

Avoid this problem. Keep weapons out of reach. Only students should even have access, and only students trained in the weapons should have permission to use them. In the case of very dangerous weapons, all sharp-edged or pointed weapons that can easily cut or pierce—and perhaps even nunchaku, three-section staves and other difficult-to-control weapons—should be locked up or stored in "instructor-only" areas such as the office.

Allowing students with no training in a weapon to play with them may eliminate the effectiveness of the assumption of risk forms (see Chapter 27: The Proper use of Release Forms), since a student cannot adequately provide for his safety or the safety of others if he has no idea what he is doing.

Mirrors

Many schools have mirrors. It should go without saying that mirrors should be professionally secured to the wall. In one studio, the large mirrors were essentially *leaning* up against the wall, with small screws holding them in place. In another, a large, heavy mirror was affixed to the wall with mounting tape. Fortunately, it didn't land on anyone when it fell.

Sparring, and certainly weapons practice, must be carefully monitored when there are mirrors adjacent to or near the training area. One slip with the nunchaku or sai, a moment's thoughtlessness with a bo, or an aggressive match that sends a student toppling toward the mirror can spell disaster. When mirrors break, they have a tendency to rain glass shards on anyone in close proximity.

If the mirrors are glued to the wall (professionals will often glue the mirrors with industrial adhesive in addition to any mounting brackets that are used), then a shattered mirror will probably still be held to the wall and only a little glass will fall. You should request this type of mounting from your mirror vendor.

Naturally, in the event of a broken mirror, the class should be stopped, all students should be instructed to put on shoes or train well away from the broken mirror, and the instructor or staff should see to an immediate and very thorough clean-up. Remember that small splinters of glass can cause extreme discomfort. If you conduct workouts on the ground, as in jujitsu, the danger is multiplied.

Imagine a young student who unknowingly gets a few glass splinters on his hand, and later uses that hand to rub his eyes. Blindness could result. Imagine the foolishness of blinding a student, losing the school, losing your home, car and all other assets just because a clean-up job after an accident was incomplete.

Don't take chances with broken glass! ■

The Importance of Water For Student Safety

By Scot A. Conway, Esq.

The Importance Of Water For Student Safety

Dehydration

Martial arts is a physical activity, and the body needs water to perform high intensity workouts. The more intense the workout, the more water the body needs. The hotter it is, the more water the body needs. The dryer the climate, the more water the body needs. If you run an intense workout in a hot, dry part of the country, you had better have a lot of water on hand and you had better make certain that students drink often.

Students should be encouraged to drink water often and only drink a little each time. Large amounts of water during a hard workout can result in side aches and an upset stomach. Moderate amounts of water will keep students hydrated and minimize the problems associated with high water intake during heavy exercise.

An ordinary person in a comfortable climate needs half a gallon of water even if he is completely inactive. This amount can easily double or triple with exertion or an arid climate. If you were to run a class outside in the middle of Death Valley, California, your students would need more than four gallons of water to get through the day. (Of course, there would be heat and sun problems to go with it, so please don't do it).

The first sign of dehydration is thirst. If students are thirsty, they should be allowed to drink. It seems obvious that the feeling of thirst is an indication that the body need fluids, but this fact is often ignored, even by martial arts professionals, in the name of "being tough." Thirst may mean that the body is down by as much as a quart of water, which is not difficult to lose in a good cardio workout. Also, many people gain a sensation of thirst early in a hard workout when their muscles start to demand water to operate at such high performance levels, but there isn't enough water in the body to fulfill the demand.

Some students may have grown so accustomed to a slowly worsening dehydrated state that they do not feel thirst, or they have been conditioned to believe that the drinking of *any* liquid fulfills the body's need for water. Many fluids—alcohol, milk, and sodas among them—do not meet the body's need for water. The actual useful water in those substances is so low that a person can continue to dehydrate even though liquid is consumed frequently.

As dehydration grows more severe, the blood thickens and the muscles fatigue quickly. This level of dehydration is also normally accompanied by headaches. Students may grow light-headed and muscles will reach failure quickly. In a sparring match, a student may also lose some of his control. Also, the dehydration-induced fatigue may contribute to errors such as hyperextending limbs or twisting joints through improper body control on spinning motions. By this time, students may require as much as a gallon of water to fully rehydrate, which is not an amount of water someone can drink at one time. A student this dehydrated should be told to get some water and should be excused from class.

It is highly unlikely that a martial arts instructor will ever deal with cases of more severe dehydration. With the loss of even more water, a student would be dizzy and would stumble, breathing would be difficult with minimal activity, and speaking clearly would be problematic.

Obviously, a person in such a condition could not train in a class, and if a student tried, it should be obvious to anyone that he should not be permitted to participate. By this time, medical attention may be required, and it would be unlikely that this person could get to a school on his own. Should a student have walked a long way to class in severe heat, though, it may be possible to encounter such a student in certain climates. Call the emergency number you should have on file and get that person some help.

As unlikely as it is to come across someone as dehydrated as described above, no martial arts instructor should ever expect, no matter the part of the country in which he teaches, to ever have a student more dehydrated. Still, a complete description of the onset of dehydration requires further elaboration.

A person who may require up to two gallons to fully rehydrate will likely have a swollen tongue and be delirious. Balance will be difficult and muscles will start to spasm. As it gets worse, a person collapses, the swollen tongue shrivels, and the skin begins to dry out, crack and bleed thick blood. The eyes will have sunk in, the vision will grow dim and fuzzy, with all colors bleaching, and hearing will be nearly gone.

Death is imminent. As this stage is approached, the body will be several gallons short of fluid and drinking water will not stave off death. Hospitalization is required.

Reaching such a severe state of dehydration would require a full day in a hot desert working out with no water at all. Obviously, no instructor will encounter such severe conditions in class, but it does serve to demonstrate how serious a condition dehydration can become.

Simple technique: have your students drink water.

Diagnosis and Treatment

Mild dehydration is not a serious medical condition. Letting thirsty people drink isn't exactly a medical diagnosis or treatment. This is a fitness condition within the responsibility of a martial arts instructor to address. If dehydration gets more serious, then it leaves the arena of fitness condition and becomes a medical condition.

More severe dehydration may require special drinks or intravenous rehydration. If dehydration has resulted in physical symptoms, such as headaches, muscle fatigue and dizziness, and it does not go away within half an hour of drinking a pint of water, you should recommend the student see a physician.

Unless you are a medical professional, you should not try to diagnose and treat moderate or severe dehydration. These are medical conditions and the student should be referred to a doctor. Practicing medicine without a license is illegal and can lead to liability.

General Notes on Water

These issues have nothing to do with liability directly, but they are nonetheless important.

1. **Room Temperature Water.** Room temperature water is better for students than cold water. The body needs to warm up water to body temperature to absorb it. Drinking ice cold water might help burn calories as the body warms it up (8 glasses of ice water could burn 100 calories in a day), but that time delay won't help students in a workout.

2. **Filtered or Bottled Water.** Most tap water contains enough contaminants that it is not healthy, and most tap water does not taste good enough to inspire students to drink adequate amounts of it. With the exception of those few areas that might have good, quality tap water, students should be provided with filtered or bottled water.

An inexpensive option is a water dispenser, some bottles, and regular trips to a water-dispensing machine or relatively pure water source (the filtered water at home, etc.) to get more water. Owners of large schools may also invest in a water fountain. Bottled water is expensive, and it would probably not be worth the expense unless you have a very, very small school with only a few people drinking water.

Something else to keep in mind is the controversy over fluoridated water. Many communities are adding fluoride to water, and many bottled water companies are adding fluoride to bottled water. Fluoride is known mostly for a beneficial effect upon the strength of teeth when applied topically (fluoride toothpaste, fluoride painting by dentists, etc.).

When you eat or drink it, however, the studies are less certain. Ingesting even moderate amounts of fluoride on a regular basis has been linked to several problems, such as brown spots on the teeth. While many dentists consider this a minor problem, it may also indicate a systemic problem in the body. Other alleged results have included depressed intellect and behavioral disorders. Until this is cleared up one way or another, it might be safer to avoid fluoridated water.

3. **When to Drink.** Ideally, students should be fully hydrated before they come to class. This might involve drinking a quart of water about half an hour before class, using the restroom about 15 minutes later, and then working out. Several endurance studies have shown that fully hydrating before a hard workout, and frequently drinking small amounts of room-temperature water

during the workout, doubles, and sometimes triples endurance for aerobic exercise over drinking only when exercising or not drinking water at all.

4. **Passing Along Illnesses.** Most common illnesses are not passed through coughing and sneezing because the germs are so dispersed in the air. A sick person who shares cups or waterbottles can pass a contagious illness to another student. A sick person who had coughed into his hands and touches something, such as the handle on a water fountain or water dispenser, will pass the germs to the hands of the next person who touches it. If that person rubs his eyes, then the germs can get into the body through the eyes. Unlike the lungs and mouth, the eyes have no defense against germs.

That means that if any students are sick, they should not share cups or bottles. Ideally, someone else should fill the water bottles or cups for them, and someone else should hold the handle on a drinking fountain. This isn't always practical, in which case instructors will have to clean the dispenser handles frequently when students are ill. A disinfectant cleaner is ideal for this. During hard workouts, the water supply will be used by all students. Instructors need to keep it clean to minimize the risk of ordinary illnesses being passed through all your students.

5. **What Is Water?** Soda is not water. The carbonation severely limits the body's ability to draw useful water from it. Alcohol is not water. Alcohol will dehydrate you. Beer and sparkling wines are both carbonated and contain alcohol; you get hit twice on each one. Milk is not water. It is a food in liquid form. It has some water in it, but it isn't very effective for satisfying the body's need for water.

So, what is water? Water is water. Nothing beats actual water for providing your body with water. Juice is water. It is high in water content, but too much juice can provide too many sugars for the body. Vegetable juice is often high in

salts. Tea is water. It's basically leaf juice in water. Be careful of the herbal effects of the leaves used to make the tea, however. Punch, lemonade, and flavored water drinks are water. They may be heavy in sugar, but at least they have real water. Coffee may technically qualify, but you shouldn't be drinking half a gallon of coffee a day.

Short-form advice: Have water available.

Liability for Dehydration

Martial arts instructors have a duty to the students to run a safe workout. If martial arts instructors routinely drive students in hard workouts, and students get thirsty, then light-headed, and someone passes out, the instructor and school owner may be held liable. Pushing students to the point of collapse will probably not be considered a safe workout.

Normally, simply passing out won't give rise to liability. Financial liability requires *damages*. While the Court may consider it negligent to push students in a workout until they pass out, if the student recovers quickly, there will be no damages. However, there are a number of complications that can arise, such as head injuries in a fall, that might lead to expensive injuries.

Also, keep in mind that untreated dehydration, and pushing a dehydrated person in a hard workout can create complications in an otherwise mildly dehydrated person. It could also result in seizures, brain damage, or it might make an existing condition worse.

Students should be permitted to drink often, and if there are no breaks for the whole class, any individual student who feels thirsty should be allowed to bow out of class *at will* to get some water. If students are permitted to drink often, then the instructor is probably fulfilling his duty to the students regarding this issue.

This kind of lawsuit would be a rare and unusual thing, but we don't take care of our students only to avoid legal liability. We owe it to them as teachers. As teachers, we are not helping students learn as people if what we do and the way we do it results in more harm than good. There are no practical reasons students need to be trained to even mild dehydration.

Again, keep plenty of water on hand, and have students drink often.

Collateral Water Issue on Liability

This doesn't directly pertain to how important water is for your students. It is technically part of Negligence, but it is worth mentioning.

Keep an eye on your water supply. If there is a spill on a tile floor, it could become a slipping hazard. "Slip-and-fall" lawsuits are relatively common. While you take care of the water needs of your students, don't accidentally expose yourself to a slip-and-fall claim. If there is a spill, get it cleaned up right away. ∎

The Proper Use of Release Forms

By Scot Conway, Esq.

The Proper Use of Release Forms

Release Forms are known by several names, including Waivers, Liability Waivers, Assumption of Risk, and others. Whatever the name, it is essentially intended to be a form in which the students and parents agree not to sue the school if something goes wrong.

"Release Forms," as they are popularly called, are essential in martial arts classes. There are no exceptions. There are many martial arts instructors who have taught for years, sometimes decades, without having a single problem. There are others, however, who have serious accidents in their first week of teaching. The importance of having a signed, properly-executed release form cannot be stressed too loudly or too often.

When to Get a Form Signed

"But he's my best friend!"
A black belt was on vacation and visited his best friend's studio to say hello and train a little. During his visit, the two of them sparred. They had a medium-contact match and he got hurt. The pain continued for the whole vacation, and when he got home, he learned it was more serious than he thought. It required medical care, and that care would cost a few thousand dollars.

He understood that they were just two black belts sparring, so he didn't plan to sue. But his wife insisted. "He has insurance," she said, "and you didn't sign anything. We can't afford to pay all these bills ourselves." Consequently, the school owner lost thousands to his friend and, further, he was surcharged by his insurance company.

There may be many practical reasons to wait before someone signs a release form. You may not want to scare off a prospect who is afraid of getting hurt. The person may be a good friend, or even a family member, and you know they would never sue you. You might run out of copies. You might just forget.

No matter the fear of the student, no matter the relationship, you *always*, repeat, you *always* get a release form signed before the student, guest, or prospect does anything even remotely dangerous in your school. If someone is borrowing your bathroom for a moment, okay, you'll probably be fine without paperwork. But if they are going through a class, sparring, or just working out on the bags, get a signature. If someone gets hurt, that form is your first line of defense against a legal attack or insurance claim.

Three Exceptions: None, none and none.

Who Signs?
In the case of adults, the student signs the form.

For children, the parent signs the form. If both parents are available, then both sign the form. Do not make this a hard policy, however, or you will create serious problems with students from divorced families. If the child is in the custody of someone else (a legal guardian or grandparent, for example) then the responsible adult will sign the form, with a parent signature gained when and if practical. Foster parents and adoptive parents normally sign as parents.

If a student was a minor, and then turns 18 (legal adulthood), then the student needs to sign a new form on his first class after his birthday. This is essential, since an adult is now personally responsible and able to sign contracts, and the parents are no longer responsible in the same manner as before.

If the form recommended in this chapter is used, then both the student (if he is old enough to understand the form) and the parent sign the form. There are clauses in the recommended form that show warning and agreement, even though the children themselves cannot be legally held to a contract. Their sense of honor and morality will often be more powerful than the law.

Who Gets Copies?
The school must maintain a copy of the paperwork. The owner must be able to prove that the parties to be bound (the student or parents) signed the form. If the family would like a copy, then let them have one. It is an easy matter to provide them with a blank copy, which is usually enough to satisfy most people. Sign-

ing duplicate originals (two different copies both bearing signatures) will satisfy others. Never allow someone to take the *only* signed copy away to bring back later unless it is a trusted staff member.

Once Is Enough, But. . .

Except when minors become adults, getting a signature on a good release form is valid indefinitely. However, for several practical purposes, you should update your paperwork on a periodic basis. Updating paperwork annually or at certain key rank or belt-levels reminds students and families of their agreement, and it minimizes the risk and impact of losing paperwork. Usually you don't discover a piece of paper is missing from a file until you need it.

When you get new forms signed, always keep the old forms. If a student has an accident, but the injury isn't discovered until later, they might make a claim. If the only release form you have on file is one dated after the accident, you have a problem.

What About Loss?

"Where did it go?"
A letter from an attorney led off the attack. They hired an attorney to counter. Problem: the defenders didn't have a signed copy of the contract that was supposed to settle the dispute. The defending attorney had to try to enforce a contract that the other side claimed was never signed and wasn't the actual agreement. What could have been solved easily with a signed document then mushroomed into a seven-month odyssey through a dozen court appearances.

Sometimes paperwork disappears. Often, there is no explanation. Maybe someone wanted to see the file and it dropped out. Maybe it got misfiled somehow and it's in another file, never to be seen again. Maybe it got thrown out for some unknown reason. It is an unfortunate fact that sometime, somewhere, there will be an instructor who knows he got the form signed by the student, but somehow he doesn't have it now.

A missing form does not always mean you have no hope. It complicates things somewhat, but if you know the form was signed, you can provide your insurer or attorney with a copy of the blank form and indicate that the original signed copy is missing. If the claimant (the student) does not deny signing the form, then that is as good as the signed form. If the claimant says that he never signed the form, then it becomes a question of fact to be determined at trial. Your attorney will take over from there.

Normally the process includes showing that you routinely collect forms from everyone who trains at your school. (You do, right?) Then whomever witnessed the signing can testify that they personally recall the student signing the form (if they honestly remember). The other side will probably claim that they never signed it, or that they saw it and declined to sign it, or that they lined out certain clauses, or whatever else their story might include. The judge or jury will then decide if they think the form was signed or not. Of course, if you are sloppy about whether or not you get forms from students, or if you regularly accept changed copies of the form, then you will have some trouble at trial.

Keep the forms on file, however, and you will avoid this mess completely.

Content of the Sample Form

The Release Form contains 11 items. They are:
Item #1: Signatures and Initials
Item #2: Authority to Treat
Item #3: Advisory of Rights and Responsibilities
Item #4: Assumption of Responsibilities and Risk
Item #5: Notice and Consent to Instructors
Item #6: Notice of Physical Contact
Item #7: Consent to Physical Contact
Item #8: Indemnification by Parents
Item #9: Arbitration Clause
Item #10: Severability
Item #11: Durability

Item #1: Signatures and Initials

There are multiple signatures required on the form, and initials required at each heading. The purpose for the multiple signatures is to distinguish the "Authority to Treat" portion from the rest of the document. This will be covered under Authority to Treat.

Initialing shows that the particular section was actually read and understood by the person against whom it will be enforced. The signature at the end covers the entire document except Authority to Treat, but the initials will give additional support to the validity of the particular clause. Also, it will make people more aware of the clauses and less likely to sue. Otherwise, you have to wait until you get to court to debate the validity of each clause. Also, in some areas, certain types of clauses must be set apart, and the required initials will help fulfill that requirement.

The witness signatures are for whatever staff member handled the intake. That signature should only be affixed by someone who actually witnessed the physical signing of the document. Even a minor may sign as witness. If a minor wants to take the form home to be signed by a parent, that minor may act as witness to the parent's signature, and the parent may act as witness to the minor's signature.

You can see the potential for forgery here. It is best to have the form signed in front of a staff member. If the document does turn out to be forged, however, that may constitute fraud and give rise to a countersuit if they sue.

Item #2: Authority to Treat

A child sat in an emergency room for four hours crying. His arm was broken. No one gave him any pain killers. No one put a cast on his arm. It was obviously broken, but the hospital would not even X-ray and set the arm. It turned out that there were no parents available. The school teacher had brought the child in, and the parents could not be found. Without parental consent, the doctors could do nothing.

There are laws that limit a medical professional's ability to treat someone without consent. If someone's life is threatened, medical professionals can take action to save the person's life. If they are unconscious, many jurisdictions take that to be implied consent. Children, however, cannot give consent to their own treatment. In many parts of the country, a child with a broken arm must wait until someone arrives who has the legal authority to authorize treatment.

Having authority to treat is especially important when you have children in the class. Authority to Treat gives instructors, staff and responsible adults the power to consent to a child's treatment, or even an adult who might be confused after an injury, provided medical professionals don't deny treatment, which they always have the right to do).

Item #3: Advisory of Rights and Responsibilities

This section details the rights and responsibilities of the students and parents. A careful reading of this section details the recommendations of the school, even though for practical purposes we all know that almost no one will actually check with their physician before beginning a martial arts program. Those with known medical conditions, however, might need to.

Also note that students are given the right to be excused from any class activity they feel is too dangerous, and given the responsibility for their own safety and knowing their own limitations. If students do not have the right to excuse themselves for safety reasons, it is difficult for them to assume the risk for any given activity.

This right helps make them responsible, and it makes their assumption of the risk meaningful on an activity by activity basis. If they can't get out of something, it may be more difficult to maintain your claim that they assumed the risk of harm. It also advises students to carefully limit their training when they are injured or even mildly impaired in any way, or to desist training altogether if it is medically advisable to do so.

This clause puts the burden of responsibility on the student and on parents. The instructors still have a duty to run a reasonably safe class. They still have the duty to avoid negligence. This clause simply shifts some of that responsibility to the students. It makes them co-responsible for what happens to them during class.

Item #4: Assumption of Responsibilities and Risk

This clause is where the student and/or parent acknowledges the rights and accepts the responsibilities explained in the previous clause. Here, they agree not to file claim or suit even if they get injured, and they agree specifically to bear any costs of medical attention required and maintain their own health insurance.

Item #5: Notice and Consent to Instructors

This clause is to inform students and parents of the instructor's management structure. It advises them that the head instructor may not always teach every class, and that assistant instructors, and perhaps even student instructors may teach a class. It explains that all agreements with the head instructor and school in this document apply with equal force when any other person is teaching classes. With this clause, students consent to any instructor teaching the class.

Item #6: Notice of Physical Contact

This clause explains the nature of contact in martial arts. The clause, as drafted, covers total body-contact systems that include both strikes and grappling techniques. If your system does not target every area of the body, you may still use the form as written. It will simply cover more techniques than your system employs.

This clause puts all students and parents on notice that physical contact in martial arts is an ordinary part of training, and it may involve intentional or incidental contact with portions of the body ordinarily considered private or sexual. It also explains that if any student feels uncomfortable with the physical contact, particularly if the student feels someone is abusing the ordinary training in martial arts for improper purposes, that instructors shall attempt to make allowances and accommodate the student.

It is very important that instructors actually try to accommodate students. Some students who have experienced sexual abuse in the past may not give instructors that information, but they may be very, very sensitive to contact with certain parts of their bodies. Other students may have been raised physically very conservative, and they will need time to adjust. Not only could failure to accommodate students result in the loss of the student, it is also possible that a psychological episode could result, triggered by a particular type of physical contact. That would disrupt an entire class and may disrupt training at the school for some time.

Item #7: Consent to Physical Contact

This clause is where the students and parents consent to the physical contact they were just notified about in the previous clause.

Item #8: Indemnification by Parents
INDEMNIFICATION BY PARENTS

It is important to remember that minors cannot be held to any contract or agreement they sign. It doesn't automatically make the contract null and void, but rather, it makes the contract voidable at the option of the child. That means that they can hold you to it and abide by the contract as long as they like, but then they can cancel the contract at any time. Thus, a minor who signs an assumption-of-the-risk form can cancel the form at any time.

If a minor were to sue, the waiver form could be voided at his/her discretion. Minors should sign the forms because it remains enforceable *until* it is voided, and a sense of honor and duty may keep a child from voiding the contract.

Often, parents are asked to sign waiver forms on behalf of their children. Schools, clubs, and many other organizations do this. A waiver form signed by a parent has tremendous psychological force to prevent the filing of a lawsuit by a family, but it has no legal force to deny a child the right to sue. No one can waive another person's rights, *not even a parent.*

Think of it this way: Could your friend sign a document taking away your right to sue someone? In the same manner, a parent cannot take away a child's right to sue. That right belongs to the child, not the parent, so the parent cannot take it away. A person can only waive his own rights.

The indemnification clause is our way around that problem. It is intended to make litigation a high risk venture for a family. Parents will normally be the initiators of lawsuits on behalf of their children, but indemnification means that they would have to pay the school for any financial loss to their child. In short, if they win, they lose. This clause may not always be enforceable, but they would be gambling if they helped their child file a lawsuit anyway. Unlike wondering if they can win by defeating a document, they have to wonder if they can avoid losing. When people have something to lose, they are far less willing to gamble than if they simply may not win.

Parents will often ask about this clause. When they do, you can simply explain to them that it is intended to make the assumption of the risk legally meaningful for their child. Let them know that they are always welcome to show it to an attorney if it would make them feel more comfortable.

Item #9: Arbitration Clause

In the event a lawsuit is brought against you, you want to avoid litigation in court in front of a jury. This gets expensive. Trial attorneys typically earn $150 to $250 per hour. Imagine a five-day trial, plus preparation time. A five-day trial could cost 80 billable hours. Imagine paying $12,000 to $20,000 to prove you were right.

Arbitration is much faster. An attorney or professional arbitrator hears the case instead of a judge or jury. The rules of evidence are more relaxed. The same matter might be resolved in half the time. Both sides still get to present their case, but with easier rules of evidence and the arbitrator actively participating in the effort to uncover the truth, it goes much more smoothly. Certainly, arbitration is a better alternative to a full-scale, all-out court battle.

In this clause, the student agrees to binding arbitration in the event of a legal dispute.

Item #10: Severability

This clause simply states that each clause and each sentence within each clause are severable, and the unenforceability or invalidity of any single phrase, sentence or clause is severable from the rest. In regular English, that means if a court decides that any one part of the document isn't going to be allowed, any part that *is* allowed will stay enforceable. Without a clause like this, it is possible the whole agreement could be thrown out if *any* part was found to be illegal, unenforceable or against public policy.

Item #11: Durability

This simply states the time for which the document applies. Basically, this clause indicates that it is infinitely retroactive and continues indefinitely. This by no means allows you to dispose of previous forms. The retroactive clause may or may not be enforceable. It is there to help offer some protection to the school in the event a previous document is lost.

HOW TO HANDLE THE TERROR OF THE FORMS

"Well," started the man in the chair, "I was going to sign myself up, and my wife, and all three of my kids, and I was going to bring my niece and two nephews and my best friend. . ." Then here it comes. "But these forms! What am I signing?"

Many instructors are concerned that prospects will take one look at the legal forms and balk.

"How dangerous is this?" the mom thinks. "What do you mean my daughter might be grabbed in her private area?" dad asks.

If you try to explain your program, that all these risks and issues are part of normal martial arts training, and that nothing really unsafe and nothing improper will happen in your school, the next question is, "Then why do you need all these forms?"

That's easy.

It's the lawyers fault.

Lawyers who take stupid cases, lawyers who make big trouble out of little problems, and lawyers who create problems out of nothing. If it wasn't for lawyers, none of the paperwork would be necessary. If it wasn't for lawyers, clients could just pay their tuition and you could just teach your classes.

But there are lawyers, a *lot* of lawyers, and a lot of the many, many lawyers would be more than happy to squeeze the school for a few thousand here, a few thousand there, and they would keep looking for the big score, the one that would finally put you out of business.

Maybe it's not that bad. But it could still be a problem. Because of all the lawsuits out there, you have to have this paperwork to complete your files, just in case a lawyer shows up with a piece of paper demanding thousands of dollars. Even if it's another student, even if it's an old student, you have to show that you *always* get the paperwork. You'd rather not need it, but you have to have it. Scot Conway, your ACMA lawyer, said so. So you're just doing what the lawyer told you to do.

Most people don't mind blaming the lawyer. Even lawyers understand how annoying many lawyers can be. While most are professional and only take the most worthy cases, there are too many crooks, too many liars (li-ar/law-yer; maybe we should call the good ones "attorneys"). Even attorneys know that they have to protect themselves against lawyers.

Here's the blame-the-lawyer letter we use at my school, the Guardian Kempo Academy in San Diego. I use it as a cover sheet for the Risk Agreement. ∎

Dear Students and Parents,

There was a time before lawyers got involved in martial arts training that martial arts instructors only had to worry about teaching students. From time to time someone got hurt, but everyone accepted the slight risk of injury in return for effective martial arts training.

Then the lawyers came. Lawsuits were filed. Instructors went bankrupt. Schools closed.

To protect themselves from the lawyers, many martial arts schools and entire martial art systems started to water down their training. While there were fewer accidents and few lawsuits, many students were not properly trained. Then students started paying the price on the street, when they were unable to defend themselves. Criminals won. Students lost.

At the Guardian Kempo Academy of Christian Martial Arts, we want to ensure effective training of all our students. As of 1998, we are seventeen for seventeen in effective street defense for our students. We have a perfect track record against violent criminals. We want to make certain that the criminals keep losing when they initiate assaults on our students.

We choose to take slightly greater risks in class to keep our students safe from robbers, muggers, rapists and other criminals. We feel it's better than coddling students in class only to have them unprepared to confront a real-life violent situation. This means that we still have an element of risk in our training, and we need to be protected from litigation.

We do our best to be safe without compromising the quality of our program. While most people understand this, there are a rare few that are inclined to blame anyone they can, and sue. It just takes one of those to shut down the whole program, so we must protect ourselves.

That's why we have to have all this paperwork.

With over 140,000 lawyers in the State of California alone, self-defense against them with paperwork is almost as important as self-defense against the criminal on the street.

We thank you for your understanding.

If you have any questions, you can call Scot Conway at (619)582-8770.

The following release form is intended to be a comprehensive document. This is what we use at my studio, but some studios might not have a need for every clause in the form. Depending upon your State, your martial art, and your individual teaching style, you can pick and choose which clauses you need. So, please take what is useful and discard the rest.

One caution, however. While the form may seem long, if in doubt about any clause, leave it in. Many people think that students will balk at signing a four-page form, but when you blame the lawyers and explain each clause, most people see that it really is for the protection and understanding of the student as well as protection for the school.

RISK AGREEMENT

Student Name: _____

Parent Name(s) (if student is a minor): _____

Address: _____

City: _____ State _____ Zip Code: _____

Phone (H): _____ E-Mail: _____

Phone:_____ (W): _____

Workplace: _____

Emergency Contact: _____ Phone: _____

AUTHORITY TO TREAT

I, the undersigned, give the instructors, staff and responsible adults the power to authorize medical or other treatment of the person named above under "Student Name," subject to the limitations listed below, if any. If I am not the person so named, I am the parent, guardian or adult responsible for the person named, and I have the legal right to grant this power. Treatment may be made without regard to whether I or any other parent, guardian or adult responsible has been contacted or has consented to the specific treatment, provided it does not conflict with the limitations outlined below. This authority begins on the date signed and continues indefinitely.

Limitations to Treatment:_____

_____

Information of Medical Significance: _____

_____

_____

By giving my authorization, I assume responsibilities for all decisions made, provided they are reasonable decisions under the circumstances based upon the knowledge and understanding of the person making the decisions, and I trust their judgment and offer the benefit of the doubt to them in any claim or legal proceeding. This presumption may only be overcome by clear and convincing evidence that they acted with malice or willful gross negligence, and, if so, they may still be liable.

_____   _____
Signature   Date

_____   _____
Print Name   Relationship (if other than self)

I understand that the instructors, senior students, or others may have some skills in first aid, CPR, and, at their discretion, I authorize them to use those skills and techniques to assist in any circumstance in which they judge their skills would be necessary or helpful.

_____   _____
Initials   Initials

ADVISORY OF RIGHTS AND RESPONSIBILITIES

Safety is not the sole responsibility of instructors and staff. Everyone in class is responsible for their own safety and the safety of those around them.

All students have the right and responsibility to excuse themselves from any exercise they believe will be harmful to them. All students must evaluate each situation in the context of their skill and current physical condition, and conduct each drill in a manner that is safe. If an instructor gives an instruction that is unsafe for the student, it is the student's responsibility to inform the instructor that the skill may be unsafe. The instructor will routinely excuse the student from unsafe exercises and drills. The instructor may ask for an explanation, and the student is expected to provide one.

All students have a responsibility to train and conduct themselves in a manner that helps all students and instructors remain safe. Students must give those who are training enough room to avoid interfering and avoid being accidentally struck by someone else practicing, which is especially important when others are practicing with weapons.

In the event of an injury, students have the right and responsibility to evaluate the extent of harm, stopping what they are doing even if it includes a partner, and determining if it is safe to continue. Unless a student is certain that further practice will not create or worsen a problem, all students are encouraged to stop what they are doing and inform an instructor. In the event of a serious injury or appearance of a serious injury, all students, instructors, staff and visitors, notably parents, have the right to call a stop to a particular training exercise.

If a student notes an unsafe training situation, which may include a student performing a skill incorrectly, a student not being careful about others, a defect in a piece of training equipment, a potentially dangerous obstacle or condition on the floor, or anything else that may cause or lead to harm of students, instructors, staff, visitors or guests, then the student is expected to correct the situation if within his ability or notify an instructor or staff member immediately. If something is simple to correct, such as picking up a weapon left on the floor, the student should correct the situation. If the situation may require the authority of the instructor or staff, or if it is not a simple matter, then an instructor or staff member should be notified immediately.

_____   _____
Initials   Initials

ASSUMPTION OF RESPONSIBILITIES AND RISK

Martial arts is a potentially dangerous activity. Bumps, bruises, scrapes, scratches and soreness are commonplace, and most students will encounter this sort of minor injury from time to time in their training. More serious injuries are possible, including sprains, strains, twists, cramps, and injuries of similar magnitude, and students can expect to encounter these injuries infrequently. The possibility of more serious injury exists, including fractured bones, broken bones, torn ligaments, though not all students encounter such serious injuries. There remains, despite safety precautions, the remote possibility of crippling or death, though this is certainly not expected in this martial arts class.

I understand the above statement of risk, and I understand the rights and responsibilities of students. I assume responsibility for my own safety (or the safety of my child), understanding and accepting the risks involved with martial arts training. Even if the instructor has informed me that no serious injuries have ever happened in this school or with any of the instructors, I understand that this does not mean that there is no possibility of harm. By assuming this risk, I completely absolve all instructors, staff, guests, students, landlords, management companies and any and all other parties of liability for my harm, unless intentionally caused in criminal conduct.

_____   _____
Initials   Initials

NOTICE AND CONSENT TO INSTRUCTORS

This school seeks to make use of highly-trained, professional instructors, with both expertise and experience both in the art we teach and in teaching. Classes may be taught by the head instructor or any other qualified instructor. Should an instructor be unavailable for a given class, a junior instructor, senior student or guest instructor may teach. The choice of the instructor is left to the discretion of the school.

I understand that I may not always have the instructor I desire, but I shall seek to learn from whomever is teaching, to show the respect due the position of teacher to whomever is teaching, and to conduct myself in accordance with the etiquette established at this school. I understand that I have the responsibility for my own safety without regard to who is teaching the class. I specifically consent to any instructor the school, instructors or staff feel are sufficiently qualified by any standards they set to teach the class. I specifically understand and agree that the full force of this document applies no matter who is teaching.

_____   _____
Initials   Initials

NOTICE OF PHYSICAL CONTACT

Complete martial arts training involves a wide variety of skills. While practicing these skills, students may have contact with any portion of the body. The groin may be the target of kicks, strikes and grabs. The chest, buttocks, groin, or any part of the body may be contacted by any part of the training partner's body during training by martial arts techniques, or incidentally contacted while performing a martial arts technique targeting another portion of the body.

When male and female students train together, or when adult and minor students train together, and in any other training combination, the purpose and intent of the school, instructors and staff is to provide an environment for all students to learn and practice martial arts and self-defense. Students are expected to conduct themselves appropriately at all times to ensure the best training results for everyone.

Should any student feel a training partner is engaging in contact beyond the scope of training, or a training partner is taking undue and unacceptable advantage of training contact, or if a student is made uncomfortable by any training exercise or partner, then that student has the right to withdraw from the exercise or drill. If the conduct of the training partner appears inappropriate, the student should inform an instructor privately. If the conduct of the training partner or any training partner appears criminal, then an instructor should be informed and the authorities may be notified either by the student or the instructor, or both.

_____   _____
Initials   Initials

CONSENT TO PHYSICAL CONTACT

I understand the nature of physical contact in martial arts training, and I understand that I have the right to immediately withdraw from any exercise or drill in which the conduct of any party seems beyond the scope of training or makes me uncomfortable. I agree to abide by school etiquette in all matters pertaining to training, and I shall not in any way conduct myself inappropriately or take inappropriate advantage of the contact martial arts training allows.

_____   _____
Initials   Initials

INDEMNIFICATION BY PARENTS
Applicable only to Parents Enrolling Minor Child

I agree not to bring any claim or suit against the school, instructors, staff, guests, students, landlord, or any other parties on behalf of my child for any injury or harm sustained by any event short of a criminal act, and then only the criminal shall be the subject of such a claim. I further agree that I will not cause to be brought, nor encourage a claim or suit. I also agree not to cooperate in the bringing of such a suit or claim except insofar as I may be legally required to do so. Finally, I shall indemnify the school, instructors, staff, guests, students, and any and all additional defendants covered by this agreement for all judgments, costs, attorney fees and other expenses incurred as a result of a breach of this agreement.

_____   _____

Initials   Initials

ARBITRATION CLAUSE
Should any dispute arise between me, my child, or anyone acting on behalf of my child, regarding this school, then I specifically agree that the dispute shall be resolved in binding arbitration. Should a suit be filed in Court, I specifically authorize the Court to order the case to binding arbitration.

SEVERABILITY
If any clause, sentence, phrase or statement is found unenforceable or invalid by any Court of law, the remainder of the document shall remain valid enforceable and the invalid clause, sentence, phrase or statement shall be considered struck from the document.

DURABILITY
This document is effective from the date signed with no expiration. Furthermore, the terms of this document are retroactive to the beginning of training and visiting the school if this document was signed after that date.

I have read this document, and I understand the content of it. I agree to abide by the terms of it.

_____   _____

Student Signature   Date

****

For Minor Students

_____   _____

Parent Signature   Date

_____   _____

Parent Signature   Date

****

_____   _____

Witness Signature   Date

GLOSSARY

ARREST, CITIZEN'S — The act of a citizen placing a person under arrest when the citizen observed that person committing a criminal act. Citizens do so at their own risk. A Citizen's Arrest should only be used as a last resort to prevent the departure of a criminal.

ASSAULT — The intentional creation of apprehension of an immediate battery. It's not a threat of some future harm, but a threatened immediate harm. You don't have to actually hit the person, or even touch him, only make him think you were going to. The degrees of assault vary based upon instrumentality, numbers, or difference in ability to inflict harm.

ASSAULT, SEXUAL — Whenever an assault is directed at sex organs, buttocks or breasts (on women).

ASSAULT, SIMPLE — An unlawful touching. Simply grabbing a person by the arm during an argument, for example, may be sufficient to constitute a simple assault.

ATTENTION DEFICIT DISORDER (ADHD) — A neurobiological disorder which interferes with a person's ability to maintain attention and focus on a task. ("Neurobiology" is the study of the brain and all the nerves.) ADHD affects approximately 5% of American children.

BATTERY — The harmful or offensive touching of a plaintiff with intent to harmfully or offensively touch. It does not necessarily require harm, but as a general category includes all touching that is offensive, harmful, injurious or even potentially deadly, including rape, beatings, sexual touching, and harsh grabbing.

CALISTHENICS — A series of rhythmic exercises which use the body's own weight as resistance in order to develop muscular strength, muscular endurance and flexibility.

CHARISMA — A personal quality of leadership arousing special popular loyalty or enthusiasm for a public figure. Charisma is also a quality of magnetism that many people have and use.

CHILD MOLESTATION — Rape or sexual assault against children. Most states set the cutoff age at 13, so any sexual contact with a 13-year-old or younger will constitute molestation.

CONTRACT — An oral or written agreement between individuals composed of an offer, an acceptance and a consideration. If one person makes an offer to someone, the other person accepts that offer, and there is some promised or actual exchange of value, then a contract has been formed.

COOL-DOWN — Light exercises performed after the main workout that help to prevent or minimize muscle tightening.

CORPORATIONS — Separate legal entities, "persons" under the law. Corporations are traditionally made to shield the owner(s) from liability.

CUE WORDS — Words that focus the students' attention on just the key components of a given skill.

DEFAMATION — Making false negative statements about someone that causes damages. Defamation comes in two basic forms: (1) Libel, which is defamation in writing or some other permanent means of recording; and (2) slander, which is spoken defamation.

DEFENDANT — Someone against whom a lawsuit is filed.

DEFENSE OF OTHERS — The right to defend anyone who, in turn, has a right to defend himself, using as much force as that person would be permitted to use to defend himself.

DEHYDRATION — Excessive loss of water from the body or from an organ or a body part, as from illness or fluid deprivation.

DETRAINING EFFECTS — What one gets when he stops training. When one stops training, the gains in performance will be lost.

DISCIPLINE — An action we take to make another person's behavior conform to our standards. See also: SELF-DISCIPLINE.

DRILLS, LIMITED SPARRING — A classroom sparring match with a strategy other than winning as the goal. For example, one student might be limited to executing only a jab to the forehead, while the student's partner could be limited to using only footwork and head movement as a defense.

DUNGEON DOJO (Slang) — A school that is typically small, smelly and soiled. The instructor doesn't teach as much as command and the atmosphere in the school is intimidating. The demands on the new student far outweigh his confidence or skill. All of which result in a massive dropout rate.

ENDURANCE, AEROBIC — Type of endurance for which a large contribution of oxygen is needed, such as in distance running. In the martial arts, this is typically seen in forms practice, sparring or in martial arts training in general.

ENDURANCE, ANAEROBIC — Type of endurance for which there is no major contribution of oxygen needed. As a result, anaerobic endurance is characterized by brief periods of activity, as opposed to aerobic endurance, which may last for hours.

FEEDBACK, AUGMENTED — Information that the student would not normally receive as a result of just the skill performance. Two examples are verbal feedback that is provided by the instructor on some aspect of the skill performance, and visual feedback by use of a videotape or mirror.

FEEDBACK, INTRINSIC — Information that the student receives as a normal consequence of a movement. For example, the student can "feel" if his foot made solid contact with a shield or can "see" if the foot landed with accuracy on the target.

FITNESS, THREE COMPONENTS OF — Muscular strength, muscular endurance and flexibility. Muscular strength and muscular endurance are important to withstand the resistance offered by opponents. Participants must also develop flexibility so that they can bend and twist with ease when executing martial arts movements.

FLEXIBILITY — The range of motion of a joint or a series of joints. Three factors influence flexibility: (1) The amount of connective tissue around the joint; (2) structure of the joint; and (3) muscle, tendon and ligament elasticity.

FORCE, EXCESSIVE — The use of retaliatory strikes when there is no danger.

GENERAL ADAPTATION SYNDROME (GAS) — Term explaining the reactions that people display as a result of physical and mental training stress. The General Adaption Syndrome has three distinct stages, which define a martial arts student's response to training: (1) Alarm Phase; (2) Resistance Phase; and (3) Exhaustion Phase.

HIERARCHY — (1) Categorization of a group of people according to ability or status. (2) The group so categorized.

HOMICIDE — When a person is killed. A killing in self-defense or defense of others, when justified, is still a homicide, but is excused by the law. The illegal homicides are murder and manslaughter.

KISS PRINCIPLE (Acronym) — Keep It Short and Simple. Proper teaching method in which the instructor spends no more than one minute on the explanation and demonstration of *simple* skills.

LEARNING STYLES — How a person receives information and the mode in which the information is perceived and organized internally. The different styles of intaking information include: (1) Hearing (auditory); (2) seeing (visual); and (3) doing (kinesthetic).

LEARNING, THREE STAGES OF — Beginning stage - cognitive; intermediate stage - associative; and advanced stage - autonomous.

LIABILITY — Something for which one is liable; an obligation, a responsibility, or a debt.

LOADING — The application of force to a body part. Loading of joints, for example, occurs every time you throw a technique or even when you take a walk.

MANSLAUGHTER, INVOLUNTARY — When a person is killed unintentionally, but with recklessness or gross negligence.

MANSLAUGHTER, VOLUNTARY — A mitigated murder. It may have been reduced due to provocation, heat of passion, drunkenness, or any other factor that indicates that there may have been no malice in the killing.

MISREPRESENTATION — Fraud; cheating or tricking someone. It involves making a false statement of fact, or failing to reveal information that the law requires you to reveal, in order to induce someone to do something.

MOTION, RANGE OF (ROM) — The comfortable range through which the muscles may move a joint. When the ROM is exceeded, the associated muscles may be strained. At worst, a tear in the muscle or its tendon may result.

NEGLIGENCE — A reasonably avoidable accident where someone made some sort of mistake that caused some damage to someone else. Negligence is simply having a duty to do something that will help maintain the safety of those present, and failing to fulfill that duty. It is the single most common basis for tort liability and the one martial arts instructors are most likely to encounter.

OVERLOAD — An increase in training load to meet the new training status of the student. Overload is accomplished by four factors: (1) Frequency; (2) duration; (3) intensity; and (4) mode of training.

PARTNERSHIP — Businesses owned by more than one person, and all partners are liable for the conduct of all instructors and staff (except in Limited Partnerships, which must be properly created under the law).

PEDAGOGY (*ped'a-go-gee*) — The science of teaching.

PHYSIOLOGY — The biological study of the functions of living organisms and their parts.

PLAINTIFF — Someone who files a lawsuit.

PRACTICE, PART — Practice method allowing the instructor to break the skill or skill sequence down (for example, jab, reverse punch) into logical parts. In the part method, practice of each part of the skill is performed before the parts are recombined into the whole skill.

PRACTICE, PROGRESSIVE PART — Practice method allowing students to "add on" movements to existing movements by putting skill sequences together. Forms are the best candidates for this practice method.

PRACTICE, WHOLE — Practice method referring to teaching a single skill (for example, a round kick), or to a series of skills (for example, a form or a series of movements in a sparring sequence — spinning front kick, jab, reverse punch).

PROGRESSION, PLANNED — Method of teaching by breaking the specific skill down into the smallest possible, practical component of the complete technique or movement.

PROGRESSIVE OVERLOAD — Method of strengthening the muscles by increasing the workload beyond that usually demanded of those same muscles. With repetition of the greater workload, the muscles will adapt to the stress and become stronger.

PSYCHOLOGY — (1) The science that deals with mental processes and behavior. (2) The emotional and behavioral characteristics of an individual, a group, or an activity, such as the psychology of war.

PUNISHMENT — Anything you do that causes a student to stop or reduce a certain behavior. However, punishment does not eliminate a problem, it only temporarily suppresses the unwanted behavior. The effects of punishment are often short-term, inconsistent, and limited to the situation in which the punishment was applied.

RAPE — Any forced sexual intercourse. Legally, anytime force or the threat of force is used to obtain sex, a criminal rape has taken place.

RAPE, STATUTORY — Actually called "Felonious Intercourse," statutory rape is sex while under the age of consent. The age of consent is often 18, occasionally 17, almost never younger than 16.

REINFORCEMENT — Anything that increases the likelihood of a behavior being repeated in the future. Praise and reward, to cite two positive examples, can be used successfully to help a student develop a particular martial arts skill.

RELEASE FORMS — A form in which the students and parents agree not to take action against the school if something goes wrong. Release Forms are also known as Waivers, Liability Waivers, Assumption of Risk, and others.

RETENTION — The keeping of students, as opposed to their dropping out.

RISK, ASSUMPTION OF — See RELEASE FORMS.

RISK MANAGEMENT — Conducting business with proper control of legal risk and protecting your students from undue risk. Risk Management deals with enacting safe teaching and classroom procedures and building a safe school, as well as observing legal trends and paperwork.

ROBBERY — The unlawful taking of another person's property is a larceny, a theft. When force or the threat of force is used, then it is a robbery. Note that houses are burglarized, not robbed. People are robbed.

SELF-DEFENSE — The right to defend yourself whenever necessary with as much force as required to ensure your safety. The critical elements to keep in mind here are: (1) The defense must be necessary; and (2) the force used must be reasonable under the circumstances.

SELF-DISCIPLINE — Something an individual possesses within him which keeps his behavior in line with internal and/or external rules of conduct.

SEXUAL BATTERY — Any unwanted touching in a sexual area or in a sexual way. The "touching" can range from a grope, grab or caress to an attack. It is sometimes included under the generic banner of sexual harassment.

SEXUAL HARASSMENT — Anything that makes a woman or a man feel harassed. There is no objective standard. If a woman is offended by the look, comment or gesture of a man, then she has been harassed by him. What matters is how a person — male or female — feels about what happened.

SOLE PROPRIETORSHIP — A business owned by one person, the most common form of business. Unique in that the business and the owner are considered one entity. The liabilities and assets of the business become those of the owner.

SPARRING, LIGHT-CONTACT CONTINUOUS — Conventional point fighting without stopping to decide who scored a point.

SPECIFICITY — Overloading the training components that are most important to the martial arts involved. For example; practicing sidekick in order to improve the sidekick is training with specificity.

STRESS — The response of the body to any demand placed upon it. In martial arts training, this demand is of both a physiological as well as psychological nature.

STRETCHING, BALLISTIC — Improper bobbing-and-bouncing movements used when stretching, which causes a reflex muscle contraction that makes stretching difficult and risks injury because the elastic limits of the muscle may be exceeded.

STRETCHING, CONTRACT-RELAX — Method in which the stretching position is held and then relaxed, followed by contraction of the muscle for several counts and immediately stretched again.

STRETCHING, DYNAMIC — Stretching method using controlled swinging of the limbs.

STRETCHING, STATIC — The use of slow, rhythmic movements to desired positions to stretch the muscles. Once the position is reached, the position is to be held between 15 and 30 seconds, then slowly released. The stretching positions should be performed only to the point of stretch.

TORT — Any civil wrong other than a contract. Tort cases arise from any wrong action outside of an agreement.

TRAINING, DURATION OF — The duration of a single training session or a series of training sessions. For instance, a martial arts training session may last for two hours, while running to improve aerobic endurance in martial arts may have a duration of 30 minutes.

TRAINING EFFECT — The effect that training has on one's body so that more training of a higher intensity can be endured. To continue this effect and to improve on it, you need to apply the next load after the student has recovered from the present workout.

TRAINING, FREQUENCY OF — How often the martial arts student trains. It is usually expressed in terms of number of days per week. A minimum requirement to get a "training effect" is to practice three days a week.

TRAINING, INTENSITY OF — How "heavy" a training session is. Depending on the exercise, intensity may be expressed as heart beats per minute (bpm) or as a certain resistance to move, such as in strength training. In martial arts training, heart beats per minute may be used as an indication of intensity, such as when executing a form. Alternatively, one could choose the number of times the students will have to perform certain techniques before a break is allowed.

TRAINING, JUMP — A.k.a., "plyometrics"; a type of power training that typically involves jumping, but really is any sort of activity in which the muscles explode out of a flexed position repetitively. Kicking out of stances is a type of jump training.

TRAINING, MODE OF — The exercise employed to bring about any training effects. For instance, to improve aerobic endurance, running, swimming or bicycling may be used as the mode of training. To improve kicking force, martial arts can be the mode of training. While improvements in strength may be done by using a heavy bag, which is a form of martial arts-specific strength training.

TRAINING, PHASE I — The first year of a student's involvement as a martial artist. The focus at this level is in building the student's enthusiasm for the martial arts, for his school and for earning a black belt. Most of all, you have to motivate the student to want to keep coming back to class. The overall goal is to help the student understand how the benefits of martial arts training can help them achieve their goals and to improve the student's conditioning and coordination.

TRAINING, PHASE II — Phase Two is year two of the student's road to black belt. Now you have a student who is in better shape and you can run a more physically and technically demanding class. Good form is the emphasis at this stage.

TRAINING, PHASE III — Phase Three comprises years three, four and five in a student's training. Begin the process of developing his tenacity, toughness and survival skills. Increase your physical demands, preframed by genuine praise and encouragement. However, you cannot make demands beyond the skills, strategies and tactics you provide to the student.

TRANSFER — The gain or loss in the capability to respond to one task as a result of practice or experience in some other task/skill. Many previously learned skills may have similar component(s) to new skills, and one way to capitalize on the student's previous learning is to point out similarities between the new and old skills. For instance, the body motion of swinging a baseball bat is similar to, and can be drawn upon to learn, the body motion of throwing a reverse punch.

TREAT, AUTHORITY TO — Legal clause in a Release Form giving instructors, staff and responsible adults the power to consent to a child's medical treatment, or even an adult who might be confused after an injury, provided medical professionals don't deny treatment.

WAIVERS; WAIVER, LIABILITY — See RELEASE FORMS.

WARM-UP — The process of increasing blood flow and muscle temperature, increasing respiration and heart rate, and guarding against muscle, tendon and ligament strains. The warm-up should precede the stretching portion of the class.

WARM-UP, GENERAL — Exercises that incorporate large muscles of the upper body such as the back and chest, and the lower body such as hip, hamstring and calf muscles, and require working at a light pace for five to ten minutes.

WARM-UP, SPECIFIC — Exercises involving the same muscles you are planning to train in your martial arts workout.

WARM-UP, TWO TYPES OF — Active and passive. Active warm-ups are accomplished by any physical activity similar to the exercises or activity you will be performing in martial arts, involving the large muscles of the body — mainly, the arms, legs and back. Passive warm-ups can be accomplished with hot baths or showers, steam rooms or saunas. ■